A Year and a Day of
Everyday
Witchcraft

Bobbie Hodges

About the Author

Deborah Blake is the award-winning author of *The Goddess is in the Details, Everyday Witchcraft,* and numerous other books from Llewellyn, along with the popular *Everyday Witch Tarot* kit. She has published articles in Llewellyn annuals, and her ongoing column, "Everyday Witchcraft," is featured in *Witches & Pagans* magazine.

Deborah's also the author of the paranormal romance Baba Yaga series from Berkley Publishing, as well as the Veiled Magic urban fantasies. She can be found online at Facebook, Twitter, and www.deborahblakeauthor.com.

When not writing, Deborah runs the Artisans' Guild, a cooperative shop she founded with a friend in 1999, and also works as a jewelry maker, tarot reader, and energy healer. She lives in a 130-year-old farmhouse in rural upstate New York with various cats who supervise all her activities, magickal and mundane.

A Year and a Day of
Everyday Witchcraft

366 Ways to Witchify Your Life

Deborah Blake

Llewellyn Publications
woodbury, minnesota

FIRST EDITION
First Printing, 2017

Book design by Rebecca Zins
Cover design by Kevin R. Brown
Cover illustration by Jennifer Hewittson

Llewellyn Publications is a registered trademark
of Llewellyn Worldwide Ltd.

Library of Congress Cataloging-in-Publication Data
Names: Blake, Deborah, author.
Title: A year and a day of everyday witchcraft : 366 ways to witchify your
  life / Deborah Blake.
Description: Woodbury : Llewellyn Worldwide, Ltd., 2017. | Includes
  bibliographical references and index.
Identifiers: LCCN 2017035678 (print) | LCCN 2017022832 (ebook) | ISBN
  9780738753966 (ebook) | ISBN 9780738750927 (alk. paper)
Subjects: LCSH: Religious calendars—Wicca.
Classification: LCC BF1572.F37 (print) | LCC BF1572.F37 B53 2017 (ebook) |
  DDC 133.4/3—dc23
LC record available at https://lccn.loc.gov/2017035678

Llewellyn Publications
A Division of Llewellyn Worldwide Ltd.
2143 Wooddale Drive
Woodbury, MN 55125-2989
www.llewellyn.com

Printed in the United States of America

Contents

To Blue Moon Circle, past and present,
and to my readers because y'all rock.
Thanks for asking for this book.

Introduction

Welcome to a year and a day of everyday witchcraft. Why a year and a day instead of 365 days like so many other books? In part because a year and a day is a traditional length of time used in contemporary witchcraft. Sometimes for study, as in those paths that follow a degree system, so that a person would study for a year and day to reach a certain level. Sometimes for a commitment or vow, like a handfasting ritual where the couple chooses to bind themselves for a year and a day, rather than a lifetime.

But there is another reason for the extra day in this book, one which you can choose to use or not, as you desire. I hope that by the time you have finished the rest of the book, you will be inspired to start your next year off in magical style, either with the ritual I've given you or one you write for yourself.

The book is set up to follow an entire year, starting with the first of January, although you can really start with whichever date you happen to pick up the book and circle through from there. And, of course, there is nothing stopping you from simply opening a page at random, if that's the way you roll. There are no rules here, and no one will look over your shoulder. My main intention is to give you simple ways to connect with your witchy self every day—in short, to enable you to witchify your life in small, easy, educational, and (I hope) fun daily bites.

If you choose, however, you can use this book as your own personal "year and a day" journey. Beginners will find the entries helpful as an introduction to a personal magical practice, where more experienced witches and Pagans can use the entries as ways to renew or deepen their existing practice. My readers have been asking me to write a 365-day book and a devotional for some time; this book is a little bit of both—there are suggestions for how you can use that day's snippet (if you want to), and there are also poems and words of witchy wisdom from the authors who inspire me, which I hope will touch you as well.

The book follows the Wheel of the Year and the general seasonal cycle, although depending on where you live, some aspects of it may apply less or more. Feel free to make adjustments to suit your own living situation and style.

The book also touches on various aspects of a modern Pagan practice, including connecting with nature and the Goddess and the God, holiday and lunar observations, easy crafts and recipes, questions to ponder, and, of course, the occasional simple spell, ritual, and affirmation.

Some of these things will appeal to different readers more than others, but it is my hope that you will find most of them helpful, meaningful, and useful. As witches living in the modern world, many of us find it hard to carve out the time to focus on our magical practices as much as we would like. This book is a way to make it easier to witchify your life one day at a time, getting more in touch with your own path, whatever form it might take.

Many blessings on your journey, and thanks for taking me along on the ride.

Deborah Blake

January 1
Intent and Commitment

The first day of the New Year is the perfect time to figure out what you want to focus your time and energy on in the coming months. Many people do that, and most of them, frankly, fail to follow through. As witches, one of the first things we learn is the importance of intent; it powers our magic and is the driving force behind our own personal journeys. This year, rather than making a New Year's resolution, come up with a statement of intent instead.

To arrive at your statement of intent, take a moment to think about what works for you in your life and what doesn't. What do you want to change? But more than that, what is your goal? How do you want to be different at the end of the year? Do you want to be stronger, healthier, wiser, more spiritual, a better parent/child/partner/friend/human being? Write down your intent for the year. Make sure it is a positive statement: "I intend to become a stronger, healthier, happier person" rather than "I will stop being weak and unhappy."

• • •

> **TRY THIS:** *Put that intent out into the universe by making a commitment to yourself and to your deity. Concentrate on your intent, focus all the power of your will on it for that one moment, and then say it out loud.*

January 2
The Focus Board

Human beings tend to be visual creatures. Things we see become imbedded in our brains. That's why one good way to reinforce your commitment to the intention you made on January 1 is to create a focus board.

A focus board is exactly what it says: a board that helps you to focus on a goal or goals. It uses a combination of words and pictures to create a visual reminder of what you are working toward, plus the act of creating the board puts more of your energy into the intention itself. Win-win!

Don't panic if you're not artistic. Use photos, cut pictures out of magazines, print images off the internet, or use clip art from your computer. Get the words or phrases for your focus board in the same places or use markers or crayons to add them directly to the board.

Choose pictures and words that symbolize those things you are working toward. For instance, if you want to bring more love into your life, use pictures of loving couples, a mother and child, a coven dancing together under the full moon—whatever says "love" to you. Then add words such as "togetherness," "love," and "hugs and kisses."

• • •

TRY THIS: *Finish off the board by decorating it any way that adds extra energy and suits your style. Some folks will use glitter and others dried flowers. There is no wrong way. Focus on your intent as you work on your board, and then hang it up somewhere you will see it often.*

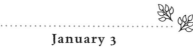

January 3
Holda

Holda—also known as Hulda, Holle, Mother Holle, and Frau Holda (among other names)—is a Teutonic goddess long associated with both winter and witches. As with many other goddesses who were originally seen as beneficial, she was eventually demonized by Christianity into a wild-haired old woman who snatched up misbehaving children. But long before that she was seen as a protector of nature (followed by an entourage of torch-carrying rabbits, no less) and a hearth deity.

Always associated with the weather, it was said that when Holda shook out her feather bed, it caused snow to fall on the earth below. Her festival is celebrated in winter, and she is also associated with the twelve days of Christmas.

• • •

TRY THIS: *Walk outside in the snow, if you have some, or visualize it if you don't. See it as the feathers from a goddess's bed, and thank Holda for watching over all the creatures of nature, including us.*

January 4
Book of Light

It is common for witches to have a Book of Shadows, in which they write down spells, herbal recipes, and anything magical that they use along the way and want to remember. You might or might not want to keep a Book of Shadows for your magical work, but even if such a thing doesn't appeal to you, consider having a Book of Light. (Yes, I just made that up. That doesn't mean it isn't a good idea.)

A Book of Light can be something you create for yourself—it is fun to make your own book and decorate the outside—or use a journal or notebook that catches your eye. If you can, write something in it every day as you walk this witchy journey (but don't worry if you miss a day or two…no one is keeping score). What you write in your Book of Light can be magical or not, spiritual or mundane, as you choose—but it should definitely be positive (hence the name).

• • •

TRY THIS: *Let your Book of Light help you focus on the bright side, even if for just five minutes out of every day. Here are some suggestions to get you started: Write down a poem that inspires you or describe some tiny creature you saw out your window or on a walk. Write about something you did that worked for you, so you won't forget to try it again. Add a picture of a special day or write down an affirmation.*

January 5
A Calendar for the Year

One of the things I do at the beginning of every year is sit down with my calendar and make note of all the important dates. (I usually have a cool Llewellyn calendar just to look at and a cute cat calendar for everyday use; that's the one I mark up.) I write down things like birthdays and anniversaries, but I also take a yellow highlighter and circle all the full moons, and I write the sabbats in with a red pen and circle them too.

This way, when I turn over the page to a new month, I can see right away which nights I want to leave space for spiritual work and when I might want to plan for a special ritual or get together with like-minded friends for something magical.

• • •

TRY THIS: *Make your calendar into a magical tool. You can do what I do and circle/highlight the witchy days or mark them with stickers or symbols or anything else that suits you. If you aren't out of the broom closet, use a small private datebook or small subtle symbols that won't mean anything to anyone but you.*

January 6
Twelfth Night

Twelfth Night is a traditional holiday more often celebrated in Europe than in the United States. It marks the day when the wise men visited the baby Jesus, but it is also the end of the twelve days of Christmas. Some people believe that it is bad luck to leave your holiday decorations up after Twelfth Night. And of course, it is the name of a famous Shakespeare play, *Twelfth Night, or What You Will.*

Its origins go back to an earlier medieval English holiday of the same name that marked the end of a winter holiday season that started on All Hallows' Eve. On Twelfth Night all the rules were turned upside down and the peasants ruled the royalty in a tradition that dates back as far as the Roman Pagan holiday of Saturnalia governed by the Lord of Misrule.

• • •

TRY THIS: *If you were the Lord (or Lady) of Misrule, what would you do with your power? Make a list of twelve things you would change if you were in charge— and then do something to work toward changing a few. As Shakespeare might say, "Do what you will."*

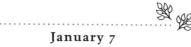

January 7
Janus

Janus is one of the rare Roman gods who has no Greek counterpart. It is believed that the month of January gets its name from him, so it is only fitting that we take a moment to meet him.

Janus is the god of beginnings and endings, passages and transitions, doorways and gates. He is usually depicted as having two faces, one looking toward the past and one toward the future. If you are going through major changes or transitions in your life, he is a good god to call on for help and guidance. He is also associated with births, since that is the ultimate new beginning, as well as marriages, harvests, and even deaths.

• • •

TRY THIS: *As you look forward toward a new*
year, light a candle to this god of new beginnings.
Ask him to guide you and help you let go of anything
that will hold you back as you set off on your path.

January 8
Witchy Words of Wisdom:
Starhawk

Here is an inspirational quote to get your Book of Light off to a good start. This is from Starhawk's book *The Spiral Dance: A Rebirth of the Ancient Religion of the Goddess*, one of the classic books on witchcraft that I recommend to everyone.

> To work magic, I need a basic belief in my ability to do things and cause things to happen. That belief is generated and sustained by my daily actions...to a person who practices honesty and keeps commitments, "As I will, so mote it be" is not just a pretty phrase: it is a statement of fact.

• • •

TRY THIS: *Think about what you believe is necessary for the practice of magic. Do you agree with Starhawk or do you look at things differently? If you haven't thought about it, take a few minutes to do so today.*

January 9

What Do You Want
from the Year to Come?

Most of us are so busy running from place to place in an attempt to keep up with our busy lives that we rarely have a moment to think about anything more crucial than "What am I going to make for dinner?" or "Where did I leave my phone this time?"

But when you walk a spiritual path, whatever form that path takes, it is a good idea to occasionally make the time to ponder what is important to you. Since it is the beginning of the year, now is a good time to look ahead and ask yourself this: What do I want from the year to come?

• • •

TRY THIS: *Sit in a quiet space and visualize how your life will look a year from now. Will it be exactly the same? If so, is that a good thing? If it isn't, what do you want to change? What are your goals for the next twelve months? If you're a list-maker, write down the things you wish to achieve in the coming year and post it where you can see it, so it will remind you of where you are going. If you're not, just close your eyes and see the things you want as clearly as possible. Make them real in your mind. Plan both the magical and mundane actions that can bring them to fruition.*

January 10

Spell to Acknowledge and Release Fear

One of the biggest obstacles in our way as we make our journey through life is the hardest to overcome: our own fear.

Fear is sneaky. It hides in the back of our heads, telling us lies to keep us from moving forward. While there are times when fear can keep us safe, mostly it holds us back, telling us we can't or we're not good enough or that we'll fail if we even try.

Nuts to that.

The thing about the sneaky aspects of ourselves is that they don't do well when we shine a light on them. Once we face them, we often find they're not as scary as we thought. And even if they are, it's okay to ask for help from the God and Goddess or whatever source you draw strength from. Here's a spell to help you acknowledge and release the fear that holds you back, so you can put more of your energy into walking your path in a positive way.

Fear, I see you day to day
Putting obstacles in my way
You seem so dark and solid, true
But I can push and walk right through
You cannot weaken my resolve
For when I look, you will dissolve
Fear's a shadow and faith the light
That gives me strength with which to fight
Fear, you have no power here
Poof, I say! Go disappear!

• • •

TRY THIS: *Say this spell today and aim*
it at all the things that frighten you.

January 11
Snow

We don't usually think of snow as water, but of course it is, just in a frozen state. (As you will be if you go out in it!) If you live in a place that gets snow, you may resent having to wear lots of clothes or slogging through it to travel anywhere or having to shovel. Snow certainly can be treacherous in large amounts.

But snow also serves a purpose. It covers the ground and insulates it against the cold, helping to preserve what lies beneath until spring comes around again. When the weather warms, the snow melts and adds to the groundwater and swells the streams, providing much-needed moisture for growth later on. And, of course, if you happen to like skiing or a good snowball fight, it can even be fun.

Personally, my idea of a winter sport involves sitting on a couch with a cat or two, a good book, and a cup of steaming hot chocolate, but I do appreciate the snow's stark, clean beauty and the silence it brings to the world after a large snowfall.

• • •

TRY THIS: *Take some time to connect with this watery element if it is available to you. Marvel at the individual nature of the snowflakes: amazing crystalline formations, no two alike. Build a snow goddess in your yard. Lie on your back and make snow angels. Go out when the snow is fresh and new and gather some in a jar. After it melts, save it for use in rituals like the gift from the skies it is.*

January 12
Gratitude No. 1

For a lot of us, it becomes a kind of unconscious habit to focus on what we don't have. The things we need and don't have. The things we want and can't get. The bad stuff—be it physical, mental, or emotional. Interestingly, there is scientific proof that being grateful is actually good for you. But even if there wasn't proof, I'm pretty sure the gods don't want to hear us whine all the time (any more than our mothers did).

Many years ago I made it part of my daily practice to end my days by speaking to the gods and saying thank you for the good things in my life. Some days those things are harder to come up with than others, but there is always something: friends, family, cats (thank goodness for cats!), a kind word or a bit of luck, a pretty bird that happened to cross my path just when I needed a lift.

* * *

TRY THIS: *For the rest of the month, come up with just one thing to be grateful for. What is it today?*

January 13
Wolf

The full moon in January is often called the Wolf Moon. In the depths of winter, prey animals grow weak and the wolves go hunting to keep themselves and their pack alive through the long, cold days. Wolves are strong, smart, determined animals, the ancestors from whom the modern dogs who share our homes are descended.

Wolves are group animals who live in packs led by an alpha male, and they rely on each other for survival. They are apex predators—meaning they are at the top of the food chain—but their strength comes from working together, with each member of the pack playing a role. Unfortunately, their numbers are dwindling rapidly due to human encroachment on their territory.

I once took a day trip to a wolf sanctuary. Based on that experience, I can tell you that they are magnificent creatures, even more impressive up close than they appear on TV or in movies. If you ever get a chance to go to someplace like this—not a zoo, but a habitat designed to mimic their life in the wild—I highly recommend it.

• • •

> **TRY THIS:** *Celebrate the wolf today. If you can, contribute in some way to wolf preservation by donating money or signing a petition. Let your own inner wolf out to play and revel in your personal pack, whoever they might be. If the moon is full, go outside and howl at it. Some people see the wolf as their totem animal; this might be a good time to discover if it is yours.*

January 14
Dream Sachets

January is a good month for slowing down and going to bed earlier. The days are short and the nights are long, which makes it the perfect time to explore your dreams.

Dreams can be a significant source of information, both from our own psyche and from the universe. When we sleep, we enter an altered state that allows us to process information differently. Dreams can carry messages to us if we are open enough to receive them.

Some people keep dream diaries, in which they write down whatever they can remember from their dreams when they wake up in the morning. If you're keeping a Book of Light, write your dreams in there too. Then look back on your dreams and see if there was something in them that made more sense later.

Dreams can be a form of divination too. If you have a question or seek guidance on a particular topic, sleep on it in the hope of getting direction or guidance. A dream sachet can help you to enter a state of lucid dreaming, where you can endeavor to guide your journey.

• • •

TRY THIS: *In a small drawstring bag or a cloth sachet,*
place some dried lavender, rose, mugwort, and/or calendula.
Tuck it under your pillow before you go to bed and give
yourself the intention of sleeping well and dreaming
strongly. If there is something in particular you want
an answer to, be sure to visualize it as you fall asleep.

Vesta

Vesta is the Roman goddess of hearth, home, and family. Her Greek counterpart is Hestia. She was symbolized by her sacred fires, which were never allowed to go out, and was considered the protector of both the city of Rome and all the individual homes within it. Her main festival is Vestalia, held in June, but this is one of the days that honor her as well.

The depths of winter are a good time to renew your household protections and give appreciation for the warmth and safety of your home. If you have a fireplace, light a sacred fire and burn a small sacrifice in Vesta's honor, or simply light a candle, thank her for her protection, and ask her to continue to watch over you and your home.

* * *

TRY THIS: *It was traditional to have an altar or niche for the goddess who watched over the house. Today, create one in your own home, whether to Vesta or some other deity.*

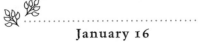

January 16
"Dust of Snow"

This poem seems to me to catch the essence of a winter's day with a particularly witchy spirit.

> The way a crow
> Shook down on me
> The dust of snow
> From a hemlock tree
>
> Has given my heart
> A change of mood
> And saved some part
> Of a day I had rued.

(Robert Frost, 1920)

• • •

TRY THIS: *Find a poem with a witchy feel to you, even if it wasn't meant that way, or write one of your own.*

Basic Kitchen Alchemy

When is cooking more than just cooking? When you stir in a little magic and whip up some kitchen alchemy. Many of the basic ingredients we use to make our meals every day also have magical attributes. What makes the difference between just throwing a few things together in a pot and creating magic? Intent and focus, of course.

Kitchen alchemy is an easy way to integrate magic into your everyday life, even if you are still in the broom closet or don't have time for complicated rituals. Our witchy predecessors used herbs and other supposedly mundane ingredients to witchify their meals. For instance, if you need to do prosperity work, try making a quiche with dill, parsley, basil, and spinach. Need a quick bit of love magic? How about strawberries dipped in chocolate? Just be sure that your intent is clear while you work in the kitchen so that your food is imbued with the magical essence you look to create.

A good resource for magical cooking is *Cunningham's Encyclopedia of Wicca in the Kitchen*.

• • •

TRY THIS: *Figure out what you need a little more of in your life, then whip up some kitchen alchemy with your next meal.*

January 18
Familiars

Historically, witches have been connected with familiars: animals of some sort that are said to aid the witch with magical work, sometimes because they were possessed by a spirit. If my cat Magic is possessed by anything, it is a spirit of mischief. Just sayin'.

What makes an animal a familiar? Some animals seem to be naturally drawn to the use of magic or other paranormal activities. My black cat Magic, for instance, not only shows up for circle every time my coven meets (the other cats couldn't care less), she usually hops up on the table when I am doing tarot readings—even going so far as to sit on the cards, which is probably a little less helpful than she thinks.

Either way, she definitely seems to bring a little something extra to my magical work, and I would call her my familiar—or perhaps I am hers.

You should never adopt a pet only to use that animal as a familiar. But sometimes they show up when you least expect it, so it's a good idea to watch how an animal behaves while you are doing magic.

• • •

> **TRY THIS:** If you live with pets, do a little magic today and keep an eye out to see how they behave. Do they vocalize (yowl or purr or bark) when you cast a circle? Do they seem drawn to the energy or do they run away? Silly as it may seem, ask your animal, "Are you my familiar?" They just might let you know.

The Magical Bath

If you have a tub in your home, you can do some easy magic by taking a magical bath. Add herbs or essential oils to the bathwater for whatever issue you wish to address. Baths are especially good for healing work, but they also have been used traditionally for love magic, prosperity, and, of course, cleansing.

If you use herbs, put them in a small muslin bag so they don't float all over. Add essential oils sparingly along with sea salt, which is both healing and adds a boost of magical cleansing power.

You can take a magical shower if you don't happen to have a bathtub. I keep a spray bottle near my shower that has rosemary, peppermint, grapefruit, and geranium essential oils in it (along with water); spritzing these oils into the water helps to increase my alertness and boost my mood.

If things are particularly rough and you need to wash away the stresses of the world, visualize the water floating away everything negative.

• • •

TRY THIS: *Take a shower or bath. As the water flows over you, say this: "Water, wash away my ills, all my troubles and my pain. Wash me clear, wash me clean, take my troubles down the drain." Really see the nasty stuff going down the drain. If it helps, visualize it as a murky black ick. Then see yourself as clear and shining with a bright light now that all that crap has been washed away.*

January 20
White

Colors are often associated with specific qualities in modern witchcraft. This can be useful when choosing which candle or stone to use or what to wear for a specific ritual.

White is associated with purity, protection, light, truth, and clarity. It is also associated with the Goddess and the moon. Because white is considered to contain all colors, white candles can always be used in place of other colors.

If you want something white to use in a ritual but you can't burn a candle, use a white stone (such as white agate or white moonstone), a shell (such as mother-of-pearl), or a white cloth or ribbon.

When I think of white, I think of the full moon shining round and beautiful up in the sky.

• • •

TRY THIS: *Practice a simple form of stone divination that can be done using two small stones, one white and the other black. Put the two stones in a bag or pass them back and forth behind your back, then ask a question. If you pull the white stone, the answer is yes; the black stone means no.*

January 21
Aquarius

The zodiac sign Aquarius covers those born between January 21 and February 19. (Note that these dates can change slightly depending on which source you use.) Aquarius is an air sign, somewhat ironically symbolized by the water-bearer.

An Aquarius is usually intelligent, intense, energetic, and full of ideas. They are often enthusiastic about humanitarian causes, although they can be somewhat detached from individual people. They are likely to be forceful, faithful, and strong-willed, but these positive traits can also manifest as eccentric or tactless behavior.

The period during which the sun is in Aquarius is a good one for learning new things, working on communication, or becoming involved in projects that benefit others.

• • •

TRY THIS: *Learn something completely different today (yes, you can look it up on the internet) or sign up for volunteer work. Local animal shelters can always use help, or you could read to the elderly in nursing homes. If you want something truly simple, just walk around your neighborhood with an empty plastic bag and pick up stray trash.*

January 22
I Am Wise

Affirmations are simple statements that create and reinforce positive change and growth. They are always said in the present tense, as though the desired outcome has already come to pass. For instance, you wouldn't say "I am getting stronger," you would say "I am strong."

As you look forward to making decisions for the coming year, have faith in your own ability to make good choices. If you feel less than certain about your own inner wisdom, use this affirmation:

I am wise and make good choices.

• • •

TRY THIS: *Keep in mind that affirmations are usually repeated regularly, either at certain times or as needed. Repeat this affirmation as needed today.*

January 23
Feeding the Birds

In the winter months food can be scarce for birds and other wildlife, especially in parts of the country where the winters are long and cold and most growing things die back. Because witches and Pagans are so closely tied to nature, make feeding the birds a simple part of your spiritual practice.

If you have a yard, put up freestanding bird feeders or hang them from trees. Buy suet squares or make your own by buying suet in the meat section of your grocery store, then shaping it into balls that you roll in seeds or nuts and hang outside. Take an apple that is past its prime and push a stick through it, then push the stick into the ground, or simply impale the apple on a nearby branch. For a real treat, roll an apple in peanut butter and then in birdseed. The birds will love you!

TRY THIS: *If you don't have a yard, buy a bird feeder that will stick to the outside of your window and give you a close-up view of your visitors as they feed. (A word of warning: if you have cats, this may drive them completely bonkers.) Or go to a nearby park and feed the birds there. Not only will you be helping Mother Nature's creatures to survive, but watching them may lift your spirits during an otherwise dreary time of year. Even if you don't have a bird feeder, take some time today to put out something for the birds.*

January 24
The Pentacle

For Wiccans, the pentacle is a sacred symbol, with the five points of the star standing for the five elements: earth, air, fire, water, and spirit. The circle surrounding the star may represent unity, the universe, sacred space, or the circle of witches. The pentacle is often drawn in the air during ritual, either with a finger or a tool such as an athame or a wand, usually to invoke or dismiss the quarters. It may also be drawn on the ground with chalk or salt to mark out a magical space. Many witches wear pentacle jewelry as a symbol of their faith.

If you wear a pentacle, what does it symbolize to you? Is it a sacred symbol, much as the cross or the Star of David are to Christians and Jews? Do you wear it so that those who are like-minded will be able to find you in a crowd? For me, the pentacle necklaces I wear (and I have many) serve both those purposes, plus they are part of my dedication to the Goddess.

• • •

TRY THIS: *Draw a five-pointed star on a piece of paper (in your Book of Shadows or Book of Light, if you have one, or just on a blank sheet of paper). Write the words earth, air, fire, water, and spirit at each point, with spirit being the one at the top. Take a moment to meditate on each element and what it means to you. Then draw a circle around the star and feel yourself joined in unity with all the witches who connect with that same symbol.*

Witchy Words of Wisdom:
Melanie Marquis

This quote is from one of my favorite books, Melanie Marquis's *The Witch's Bag of Tricks: Personalize Your Magick & Kickstart Your Craft.* If your witchy practice needs a boost, this is a great book to work with. While this is a very simple-seeming quote, it embraces a very complicated idea in a poetic way.

> Magick is truly the driving and unifying principle under which the recognized forces that govern matter and energy operate. It is the original action, the flowing current stemming from the universal source. It is the source that separates and weaves together the very fabric of existence. Through consciousness, will, and intent, magickal power is activated.

• • •

TRY THIS: *How would you define magic?*
Does this definition resonate with you?

January 26
Ground and Center

There are two primary reasons to ground and center during ritual work. The first is to gather your energy and focus for the ritual ahead. The second is to safely channel away from you any excess energy you might have built up during powerful magical work, so you don't end up bubbling and buzzing all night long after you leave the circle. Grounding and centering are also useful if you are having a bad day or dealing with a crowd of people and need to brace yourself first.

There are many ways to go about grounding and centering, but this is one of my favorites. Close your eyes and take three slow, deep breaths. Visualize your body connecting to the earth below. Then visualize a light coming down from the sky above, bringing with it the energy and clarity of the universe. Feel the energy from the earth and the sky meeting together in your core, and feel your mind quieting.

• • •

> **TRY THIS:** *Visualize yourself as a tree sending roots down into the ground and then reaching up to the sun. See the fire from the center of the earth and the fire from the sun meeting in your center as a glowing ball of light that can fuel your magical work or calm your spirit. Sit for a minute and enjoy the sensation, then remember to integrate grounding and centering into your magical work in the future.*

January 27
Eucalyptus

Since it is winter, you will probably get a cold eventually. If you do, put some eucalyptus essential oil into your bath or a diffuser; it helps clear the head and chase away the germs.

Magically, eucalyptus also has healing properties, as well as being protective. Use the leaves in healing and protection sachets or use the herb in any healing ritual. Tuck a sachet under your pillow if you're feeling ill.

• • •

TRY THIS: *If you're fighting a cold, put a few drops of eucalyptus essential oil in a hot bath and visualize the strong, invigorating scent as a mighty herbal soldier battling the germs and sending them away.*

January 28
Tarot Cards

If you need some help to figure out where you're going, try using some form of divination. Tarot cards are among the most widely used divination tools and come in an incredible variety.

As with all divination tools, some people are better at using the tarot than others, although practice certainly helps. Try a simple one-card "yes or no" question or the relatively easy three-card spread, which gives you past, present, and future. If you have a difficult time getting answers, ask someone else to read the cards for you.

When choosing a deck, find one that resonates with you and spend some time getting to know it. Some people wrap their decks in silk to protect them from negative energy, and store them in special bags or boxes. If nothing else, many decks are stunningly beautiful and fun to experiment with.

· · ·

TRY THIS: *To get an idea of what lies ahead for this year, try the three-card spread, where the first card represents the past; the second, the present; and the third, the future. If you don't like what you see, remember that nothing is written in stone. The cards might be giving you a warning about things you can change or cautioning you about heading down the wrong path. If the reading doesn't make any sense, simply put the cards away and try another day.*

January 29
To Know, To Do, To Will, To Be Silent

These four phrases are considered the essential elements of casting a spell, otherwise known by some as "the Magician's Rules." They may seem simple, but they are the foundation of a powerful magical practice.

To Know—This refers not just to knowing what you want to achieve with the spell, and knowing which tools to use and how to use them, but also to knowing yourself. Why are you doing the spell? What do you truly hope to achieve?

To Do—This means you must put your all into the spell when you do it. You must be completely present and send your energy out into the universe.

To Will—Your will is what powers the spell. It is your determination to succeed, your faith in yourself and in magic as a force for positive change. You have to want it with all your might.

To Be Silent—It is tempting to talk about the cool magical thing you did, to brag about your abilities as a witch and share your experience. The problem is, this can dilute the magic and take some of the energy away from where you want it to be (powering your spell). While your spell is still actively in progress and you are waiting for the results to manifest, it is usually best to keep it to yourself. Do the spell and let it go.

• • •

TRY THIS: *Perform some tiny piece of magic—it doesn't matter what it is. Practice these four elements and see if the magic seems stronger when you keep them in mind.*

January 30
Garnet

Garnet is the January birthstone, but you don't have to have a January birthday to make good use of it. Garnet is a fabulous gemstone for magical work, bringing love, joy, protection, healing, and compassion. Who couldn't use that in the middle of a cold, dark winter? If you don't have a piece of garnet jewelry, get a tumbled stone to put on your altar or find a strand of garnet chips (look online if you aren't lucky enough to have a Pagan or New Age store nearby, or find a place that carries jewelry supplies).

Garnet also makes a great substitute for the more expensive ruby, which it can resemble. It has long been considered a stone for lovers, so perhaps you and your beloved would like to have matching rings or pentacles set with garnet. It is also useful for all kinds of protective magic, including guarding against thieves, negative energy, and nightmares.

• • •

TRY THIS: *Add a few garnet chips to charm bags or sachets for love, healing, or protection.*

January 31
Psychic Development No. 1

For some people, psychic abilities are an innate gift, obvious and easy to use (although not always easy to live with). For others, it takes more practice to develop them, but I believe we all have the potential to do so. Of course, they manifest differently in different folks, so don't worry if you can't read tarot cards or talk to ghosts. (That last one is highly overrated anyway, as far as I'm concerned. *shudder*)

There are plenty of simple ways to practice stretching your psychic muscles. Pick up a pack of Zener cards, which contain twenty-five cards, each of which has one of five symbols. These are used to test ESP by having one person look at a card and another guess which symbol is on it. Don't be discouraged if they don't work for you—I have found that most psychics can read some people better than others. I also have a cool telekinesis exercise kit that is basically a small metal piece balanced on top of a pin. You practice by trying to get it to spin in one direction and then the other. This works with a pendulum too. These kinds of tools can be fun, and they may just help you build those muscles.

• • •

TRY THIS: *When the phone rings, try to guess who it is before you answer. How often are you right?*

February 1
Brigit

Brigit, also called "exalted one" and known as Brigid, Bride, or Brig, is a Celtic triple goddess associated with smithcraft, healing, and creativity (poetry in particular). She was so powerful and well-loved that when the Christians came, they replaced her with a "Saint Brigid" who had many of the same attributes. To this day, many folks in Ireland celebrate her in both forms. She is celebrated at Imbolc on February 2, when she chases away the winter and welcomes the first signs of spring. (Interestingly, St. Brigid's Day also falls on Imbolc.)

Her symbols are an eternal flame or fire, sacred wells and springs, and the cauldron, from which life and creativity flow. Call on her if you need healing or a boost to your creativity.

* * *

TRY THIS: *To honor Brigit, light a candle on Imbolc and do something creative. Don't worry— it doesn't have to be poetry. Draw a picture, sing a song, write a story, knit, or cook; whatever form your creativity takes, dedicate your efforts to Brigit and thank her for the gift of passion and creativity.*

February 2
Imbolc

Imbolc is one of my favorite holidays, even though it celebrates something that is barely true for where I live. In fact, I love it *because* it celebrates something that is barely true for where I live.

The holiday originated as a Celtic celebration of the goddess Brigit, at the time when the first lambs were being born. It signifies the first stirrings of spring and, as such, is a time of hope and renewal. Where I live (in upstate New York) the ground is almost always covered with snow and it's freezing cold at this time of year. Spring seems impossibly far away, which just means we need a holiday filled with hope and renewal more than ever.

Imbolc is a good time to make serious plans for the months ahead. It is too early to plant—that will come with the spring equinox—but now is the perfect time to lay the groundwork for the rest of the year. Some witches do rituals aimed at cleansing and purification, while others do divination (another specialty of Brigit's) as they seek guidance for the path that lies ahead.

• • •

TRY THIS: *Light a bonfire or some candles, write a list of what you plan to put into motion come spring, or do some cleansing and purification magic with sage or salt and water. Remember to be grateful for the slowly returning spring, even if you live in a part of the country where it seems more theoretical than actual on this day.*

February 3
The Cauldron

The cauldron has long been associated with witches, who are often depicted gathered around one to stir up a potion—or some mischief. I suppose cauldrons are occasionally still used for both, but in general the cauldron is more likely to hold a fire or candles during a ritual where a bonfire can't be used.

Originally, the cauldron was nothing more complicated than a kitchen pot (albeit a large and heavy one). Back in the days when cooking was done over an open fire in a hearth, the cauldron served to cook up porridge or stew more often than it did potions.

The cauldron, like its smaller cousin the chalice, represents the Goddess, the feminine, and the womb. They are often made of heavy cast iron and usually either have three legs and stand on their own or a handle for hanging over a fire. If you hold your rituals indoors, a small cauldron is a handy container for candles, although it is best to add a layer of sand (which also gives you something to poke the candles into so they will stand upright if they are not votives or tealights).

* * *

TRY THIS: *The goddess Cerridwen was famous for her cauldron, which could confer wisdom or even life. When you seek knowledge, fill a small cauldron (or bowl) with water and call on Cerridwen to send you a vision in its dark depths.*

February 4
Amethyst

I love amethyst; somehow it just seems extra witchy compared to almost any other stones (except possibly crystal quartz, to which it is related). It's a very goddessy gemstone and is good for almost every type of magic.

Like many other gemstones, it can be found in various forms, including crystals, tumbled stones, chunks, and clusters. It can also range from relatively inexpensive to wildly pricy, but don't feel that you need to invest hundreds of dollars to have one in your collection. In fact, you're better off with a small hunk you resonate with than a gigantic pillar that doesn't move you at all.

Amethyst is associated with love magic and healing, as well as promoting peace and sleep, protection, courage, and increasing psychic ability. Many witches like to keep a small piece of amethyst with whatever tools they use for divination; in fact, I have a small amethyst crystal tucked into the bag that holds my tarot cards. It is generally seen as a spiritual stone and can be worn as jewelry if you need an extra boost.

. . .

TRY THIS: *Find a piece of amethyst and hold it up to the light of the moon to charge it. (If there is no moonlight, simply visualize it or use the sun instead.) Feel the stone vibrate with the energy of love and healing, then hold it next to your heart and take that vibration into yourself.*

February 5
Using Witchcraft to Beat the Winter Blues

I used to spend most of the winter in a state of perpetual depression, longing for the spring to return again; then I became a Pagan and a witch. Once I began to follow the Wheel of the Year, my winter blues vanished. (Mostly.)

One of the most basic aspects of a witchcraft practice is tuning in to the rhythms of the earth and the seasons, and seeing that each one has its own energy and its own benefits. Once I embraced winter's quieter, slower pace—and its more internally focused energy—and stopped fighting it, I suddenly stopped feeling so oppressed by the parts of the season I didn't like.

I still don't love the cold and the snow, but I can appreciate that they serve their purpose in the cycle of life, allowing the earth to rest and regenerate, and allowing us to do the same. Fighting the flow of the natural world is a little like trying to swim against the tide; you might eventually get where you're going, but you're going to expend a lot of extra energy doing so.

* * *

TRY THIS: *If you have a hard time at this time of year, think about whether or not you focus only on the negative aspects of winter and forget about the positive ones. How can you get the most out of what some call "cave time"?*

February 6
Spell for Clarity and Creativity

Sometimes in the dark of winter, it can feel like we are lost in the dark too. Our energy gets lower, and it is hard to come up with a spark of creativity. If that's happening to you, try casting this simple spell for clarity and creativity:

I ask the gods for light in darkness
For clarity of mind and sight
Shine a beacon on my path
And creativity's spark ignite

· · ·

TRY THIS: *Before you say this spell, light a yellow or white candle and close your eyes for a moment, envisioning yourself surrounded by a softly glowing radiance.*

February 7
Pink

Okay, I admit it: I'm not a pink kind of girl. In fact, I'm pretty sure I don't own one pink item of clothing or household decoration, but that doesn't mean I'm anti-pink; quite the contrary. When it comes to magical work, I love this color.

Why? In part because it is the color that represents friendship, love, and serenity, some of my favorite things. Rose quartz, a pink stone, is my go-to for when I need some calming vibes.

Besides, pink is pretty. It reminds me of spring and new beginnings. I love pink flowers, especially if I am creating an altar for Ostara or for any goddess who manifests in maiden form, such as Persephone. When doing magical work for love of any kind (not just romantic), I often use pink rose petals, carnations, or peonies. I am fortunate enough to have delicate, sweet-smelling, old-fashioned pink roses growing in my yard, so when they're in season I'll pick a few and put them on my altar as an offering to the Goddess, just because.

Apparently, I'm not a pink kind of girl, but I'm a pink kind of witch.

• • •

TRY THIS: *Find something pink and make it a part of your witchy practice—reflect on how that color makes you feel.*

February 8

What Does Love Mean to You?

As we approach Valentine's Day, many people start to think about love. If you've got it, you may be trying to come up with ways to show your appreciation for that fact. If you don't, you may be feeling a little blue. Keep in mind that romantic love isn't the only kind of love, and while most of us would like to have a significant other (or others) with whom to share our lives, there are lots of different ways to love and be loved.

I may not be getting flowers and chocolate for Valentine's Day, but my life is overflowing with love. I have the love of family and friends, and that of my wonderful feline companions (who will undoubtedly gift me with something special, like a hairball or a dead mouse). Plus, of course, I have the love of the God and the Goddess, which I carry with me every day. How lucky can one girl get?

* * *

TRY THIS: *Really think about what love means to you. Do you limit yourself by putting narrow parameters on what you count as love? How freely do you love, without expecting anything in return? Are you open to being loved or do you feel unworthy? If you feel unworthy, who made you feel that way, and why do you allow it? We are all worthy of love and capable of both loving and being loved. And I know that the gods love us all unconditionally.*

February 9
Witchy Words of Wisdom:
Dianne Sylvan

One of my go-to Wicca books is a little tome called *The Circle Within: Creating a Wiccan Spiritual Tradition* by Dianne Sylvan. I love this book so much that I recommend it to everyone— and years ago my circle and I all bought copies and studied it together. Sylvan's focus on developing a daily practice helped me to come up with mine. Here are a few words of wisdom to get you started:

> Through daily practice and constant mindfulness of the deep connections between us and all that lives, you can find a way to reach up and take the hand you are offered. By making every act an act of reverence, you can touch something long hidden in yourself. As it stretches sleepy arms and blinks its eyes, you will find the union you so desperately craved.
>
> It is possible. The first step is to come to the understanding—if you haven't already—that there is no distinction between the spiritual and the mundane except the one we draw ourselves.

• • •

TRY THIS: *If you haven't already done so, create your own daily practice. This may help you find a balance between your spiritual and mundane lives.*

February 10
Greeting the Day

One of the most useful things I got out of Dianne Sylvan's book *The Circle Within* was her suggestion to add simple daily spiritual practices to my routine. This seems overwhelming: oh, no, not *one more thing*! But really, it can be as simple as greeting the day when you wake up.

This greeting doesn't have to involve any kind of fancy ritual, and you can do it in your pj's. In fact, I greet the day every morning as soon as I wake up, before I even open my eyes and often with a cat sitting on my head. Like I said, nothing fancy.

I start by greeting the God and the Goddess, asking them to send me the best day possible. (This doesn't guarantee a great day, of course, just the best one that is possible, given all the variables.) I may ask for help or guidance with challenges that I know are waiting for me, and I ask for healing or prosperity or whatever I feel I need the most. Then I ask them to help the world move in a better direction and watch over me and my loved ones.

It doesn't take more than a few minutes, but I do it every morning as a way of connecting myself with the gods and starting my day off on the right foot.

• • •

TRY THIS: *Do some variation of this greeting today, and see what you think.*

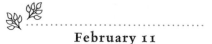

February 11
I Am Worthy of Love

Most of us struggle with the feeling that we aren't worthy of being loved, and that feeling gets in the way of having healthy and successful relationships on many levels. If this sounds like it applies to you, say this simple affirmation:

I am a child of the Goddess, and I am worthy of love.

* * *

> **TRY THIS:** *If feelings of unworthiness are something you struggle with, say these words every day, as often as you need to hear them.*

February 12
Roses

Everyone knows that roses are associated with love. But did you know that in magic they are also associated with healing, psychic powers, and protection?

The healing makes sense: rose hips (the fruit of the rose) are high in vitamin C and have been used for centuries in healing tonics. For magical healing, dry the rose hips (or buy them already dried) and string them into a necklace. You can also make beads from dried rose petals. If you want to use rose petals for a spell or even to sprinkle during a handfasting, consecrate them under a full moon first.

Roses in any form can be used for love spells, of course, or put on the altar in honor of any of the goddesses associated with love or healing. Rose petals can also be put into baths and even eaten (as long as you make sure the roses haven't been sprayed or contaminated in any way). Scott Cunningham has a very cool recipe for rose ice cream in *Cunningham's Encyclopedia of Wicca in the Kitchen*. I want somebody to make that one and tell me how it turns out!

• • •

TRY THIS: *Do a simple spell using roses—or just put one where you can see it and smell it!*

February 13
Chocolate

I'm pretty sure that most people find chocolate to be a magical substance, even if they're not witches. Chocolate can cheer us up when we are down (there's a scientific explanation for that having to do with brain chemistry, but I'm gonna say it's magic anyway). It is often gifted to others as a symbol of love and affection. The good stuff—dark chocolate, without too much sugar in it—is even a health food, believed to protect the heart, which is rather fitting for something so closely associated with love magic.

In witchcraft, chocolate can be used for both love and prosperity work, so it is easy to integrate it into your kitchen witchery. Try making magical hot chocolate to start your day out right, adding an extra sprinkle of cinnamon for health and prosperity.

• • •

TRY THIS: *For a simple love ritual between friends or lovers, bless and consecrate a couple pieces of special chocolate. Truffles, rich and creamy, are especially good for this. Sit with a candle between you—pink for friendship, red for romantic love, or white if that's what you have— and hold one piece of chocolate each on a small plate or bowl. Concentrate your energy and intent on putting all your love for the other person into that piece of chocolate. When you're ready, exchange pieces and let the sweetness dissolve in your mouth as the love flows into your body.*

February 14
Valentine's Day Spell for Love

Valentine's Day can be either romantic or depressing, depending on what kind of shape your love life is in. (See February 13's entry on chocolate for a partial cure.) But you can embrace the energy of the day in positive ways, no matter what your situation. If you have a significant other, do the ritual mentioned on February 13. If not, do a spell to open yourself to love.

Honestly, I'm not a big proponent of love spells. They can involve some very tricky magic and easily backfire if you're not careful. What I recommend is a spell to open yourself to love, and then leave it up to the gods and the universe for exactly how that is going to manifest (and remember that loving yourself definitely counts).

• • •

TRY THIS: *Light a candle—white, pink, or red—and sit in a quiet room. Have some music playing softly. Close your eyes for a few minutes and focus on surrounding your heart with glowing light. See your heart opening up like a blooming flower, ready to receive the gift of love in whatever form is best for you right now. Then say:*

Love is light and light is love
A gift from within and from above
I open myself to love this day
In each and every positive way
So mote it be!

February 15
Venus and Other Love Goddesses

I like to think that all women are goddesses of love, each in her own way. But if you need a little help getting in touch with your inner sexy goddess, call on one of these ladies.

Venus is one of the best known of the Roman goddesses, along with her Greek counterpart, Aphrodite, who actually came first. These lovely ladies, born of the sea and often pictured rising out of the water on a shell, are goddesses of love, sexuality, marriage, and victory in battle. (Go ahead—take a minute to let that one sink in.)

All pantheons seem to have at least one major goddess who takes this role of specializing in love and passion and beauty. The Norse have Freya, goddess of love and sexuality, who rides through the skies in a chariot drawn by cats, wearing a necklace of amber and a feathered cloak. There is also Inanna, Ishtar, and Astarte.

* * *

TRY THIS: *If you haven't already, do a little research on love goddesses and find the one who resonates with you best. Then light a red candle and invite her in for a chat about love or sex or, you know, victory in battle—whatever floats your clamshell.*

February 16
Rose Quartz

It is my humble opinion that, along with such classic stones as amethyst and crystal quartz, every witch should own a piece of rose quartz in one form or another. A form of quartz related to all the others that bear the name, rose quartz is a pale pink stone that practically radiates calm and joy. Who doesn't need more of that in their lives?

In fact, during a difficult time in my life, I went to a local New Age store that carried a large selection of stones and spent over an hour picking up each large chunk and crystal of rose quartz, trying to find the one that resonated the most strongly with me. When I found one that I didn't want to put down again, I knew I'd discovered "my" stone. It pays to be particular about such things. My stone's calming powers helped me get through the ensuing months, and I would often just sit and hold it.

Rose quartz is also associated with love and friendship, and it can be used to open the heart chakra. If you want a necklace to draw love to you, combine rose quartz beads with amethyst.

• • •

TRY THIS: *Walk through a store or gem show and pick up different pieces of rose quartz to see if any of them feel more strongly attuned with your own energy. If you have a piece already, sit quietly with it for a few minutes and let its gentle, calming vibes sink in.*

February 17
Use Coloring Books to Embrace
Your Inner Child

Admit it: you probably loved to color when you were a kid. Maybe you didn't stay inside the lines or you insisted on giving women green hair, but you probably spent long hours happily curled up with a good coloring book and a pile of slightly chewed-looking crayons. I know I did.

What's more, for many years I've had a box of ninety-six crayons with a sharpener built into the back and a few fairly boring coloring books for when there happens to be a child in the house, since it is pretty much a guaranteed form of entertainment, even in this digital age.

Thankfully, for those of us who pine for the old days, the new days are seeing a resurgence of coloring books—this time for adults. It's about time! I now have coloring books that are anything but boring, filled with fantasy images of dragons and fairies and even witches (some of them pictures from my own tarot deck, and if you think that wasn't a thrill…!). I still use crayons on occasion, but since most of these images are much finer, I have indulged in a set or two of colored pencils as well.

I suppose some people think it is a waste of time for grownups to color. Balderdash and hooey! It is relaxing, creative, and—dare I say it—fun.

* * *

TRY THIS: *Put down the remote and pick up a coloring book. Your inner child will thank you.*

February 18
Blessing and Consecrating

One of the easiest ways to put a little extra oomph into your magic is through blessing and consecrating your tools and supplies. I always like to do this with new tools, such as an athame or even a broom, before the first time I use them. Alternatively, if I am going to work a spell, I may bless and consecrate the ingredients as part of the ritual or beforehand if I actually get my act together to think that far ahead.

Blessing and consecrating is essentially a way of saying, "This is a magical item. It has power. I am paying attention to it." You may ask for the blessing of a particular god or goddess, or the elements, or all of the above. If you want to be a little less formal, leave the items out for a night under the full moon.

• • •

TRY THIS: *Create a magical candle for prosperity work. Place the candle on your altar or table and sprinkle it with salt (earth), water (water), waft it with some sage or incense (air), and hold it over a candle (fire). Then say:*

In the name of the God and Goddess
With the power of earth, air, fire, and water
I bless and consecrate this candle for magical use
May it bring prosperity in all positive ways
So mote it be!

February 19
Psychic Development No. 2: Psychometry

Psychometry is the psychic ability to sense feelings or history from inanimate objects. People who are good at this, for instance, might be able to pick up a piece of jewelry and tell you that the woman who wore it was very much in love with the man who gave it to her and quite ill in the last years she wore it.

This is another one of those gifts that comes quite naturally to some people and not to others, but it is a fun way to practice flexing your psychic muscles. If you have a few friends who are willing to try this with you, take turns putting random items (such as keys, a tube of lipstick, a watch—they should be something that is carried or used often, so that the energy of the owner is strongly imbued into the item) into a bowl, and see if you can identify which items belong to which friend.

• • •

TRY THIS: *Go to an antique store and walk around. Touch different items and see if you sense any emotions attached to them or if you are drawn to one item more than another.*

February 20
Pisces

Pisces is the sun sign that rules those born between February 20 and March 20. The symbol for Pisces is the fish, so obviously it is a water sign. And, like water, Pisceans tend to be fluid, hard to pin down, sensitive, and maybe even a little mysterious. Pisces is a sign ruled by emotion, which can be both good and bad. A Pisces can be imaginative and full of big plans but not necessarily practical enough to follow through on them. On the other hand, they can also be compassionate and intuitive.

During this time of the year, even those who are not Pisces may find themselves a bit more emotional than usual, caught up in mid-winter daydreams.

• • •

TRY THIS: *Use this tendency to be more emotional to your advantage by turning your gaze inward to work on those issues you might avoid at other times of the year when there are more distractions. Or turn it outward and use your own compassion to help others.*

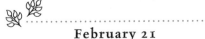

February 21
"How Do I Love Thee?"

This is one of my favorite love poems of all time. It reminds me of the magical quality of love.

How do I love thee? Let me count the ways.
I love thee to the depth and breadth and height
My soul can reach, when feeling out of sight
For the ends of being and ideal grace.
I love thee to the level of every day's
Most quiet need, by sun and candle-light.
I love thee freely, as men strive for right.
I love thee purely, as they turn from praise.
I love thee with the passion put to use
In my old griefs, and with my childhood's faith.
I love thee with a love I seemed to lose
With my lost saints. I love thee with the breath,
Smiles, tears, of all my life; and, if God choose,
I shall but love thee better after death.

(Elizabeth Barrett Browning, 1845)

• • •

TRY THIS: *Find a poem that captures the way you feel about love or write one of your own, if you're so inspired.*

February 22
Magical Names

There is a tradition, of sorts, that says witches should use a magical name. There are a number of reasons for this, some of which may have been based on the not-so good old days when keeping your identity a secret might save your life. Additionally, there can be a benefit to separating your witchy identity from your mundane one; much as donning garb puts you in the mental space to do magical work, so does using your magical name. Also, let's face it—it's kind of cool.

Which isn't to say that you *have* to have one. I practiced for a number of years without having a magical name, and, as far as I can tell, it didn't make any difference to the power of my spells.

Your magical name may come to you out of the blue. You can also ask the gods to tell you what it is, meditate on it, or see if it shows up in a dream or a sign. Certain names seem to be very popular, and you might want to avoid them. There is a joke in Pagan circles that if you go to any large magical gathering and yell the name Raven, a third of the people in the room will turn around, and that's not much of an exaggeration. This is not to say that you can't use a common name if it seems like the right one for you, but it might be worth exploring further to find something unique. Or, you know, simply stick with your mundane name; that's fine too. There's nothing wrong with a witch named Bob.

• • •

TRY THIS: *If you are looking for a witch name,*
sit quietly and just ask the universe what it is.

Knot Magic

Much of the magic our witchy ancestors used was rooted in the basic elements of their daily life—eating, growing food and herbs, and the various crafts they used, such as weaving and spinning and sewing. They might have gathered together under the full moon to dance and pray and cast spells, but most magical work was probably practical daily stuff, such as protection spells spun into a husband's new shirt or healing energy sent into a pot of soup hanging over the fire.

Knot magic is a perfect example of that. All it takes is a piece of string or ribbon. You can easily hide a knot in the design of a rug or piece of clothing, or tie one into a thread and tuck it in a pocket. You could even use a piece of your own hair if it is long enough.

Use knots to hold things, such as spells or wishes. A traditional rhyme often said when doing knot magic is associated with Doreen Valiente, or you can use the one below. Visualize whatever it is you wish to bind within your knots, and then say these words as you tie nine knots into whatever you are using:

> I *tie the knot and set it right*
> I *tie it true and tie it right*
> I *tie the knot and count to nine*
> And *now the thing* I *want is mine*

TRY THIS: *Tie a knot into a string and make a wish.*

February 24
Indoor Pagan Gatherings

There are two basic types of large public Pagan gatherings: indoor and outdoor. They have a lot in common, obviously, but they also can have very different vibes.

One of my favorite indoor Pagan conventions falls around this time of year and is held in San Jose, California. PantheaCon is a huge gathering of witches and Pagans of every ilk. There are plenty of other indoor gatherings held both in the United States and elsewhere, especially in England. You can often find popular authors, workshops on various topics, rituals, demonstrations, live music, and vendors who will tempt you with their magical wares.

Although larger crowds can be very overwhelming to those of us who are sensitive, there are some real benefits to attending a Pagan convention. For one thing, it is truly amazing to stand in a room and realize that you are—for once—surrounded by people who believe more or less what you believe. For some of us, that will never happen in any other place. You also get exposed to lots of different flavors of witchy and Pagan practices, which can be both enlightening and inspiring.

• • •

TRY THIS: *Find out more about indoor Pagan gatherings and their dates and locations. Even if you have to travel to get there, consider going to one at least once in your lifetime.*

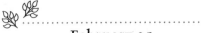

February 25
Books, Books, and More Books

I admit it—I'm a book junkie. I blame my mother. (No, really. She was a librarian.) Books are in every room of my house. But the cupboards downstairs hold the real treasure: shelf after shelf of nonfiction, including a lot of books on witchcraft, Paganism, mythology, fairy tales, and, of course, cats, both magical and otherwise.

If I have a question, I sometimes turn to the internet for a fast answer, but I don't find that nearly as satisfying as pulling out tomes by some of my favorite authors and searching through them for what I need, usually stumbling across all sorts of cool other stuff in the process.

I believe that continuing to learn and increase my knowledge of the Craft and spiritual matters in general is part of becoming the best witch that I can be, and I think that every witch should own at least a few books. Books about magic and spell casting. Books about gods and goddesses. Books about crystals and herbs and tarot. Find your own favorites and start your own witchcraft library. But do own books, even if it is only a few treasured ones you read and reread. It's no accident that one of the witch's most treasured possessions is their Book of Shadows. Books and witches go together.

• • •

TRY THIS: *Step back from the internet and sit down with a good book. Start your own collection, even if it is only a few books to begin with.*

······························

February 26
Thor

Those of us who go to the movies probably have a mental image of Thor as a gorgeous blond guy with lots of muscles and a big hammer—and I'm not saying that's a bad thing. But the Thor from mythology doesn't bear a lot of resemblance to the one from the comic books.

For one thing, in the Norse mythology from which he sprang, Thor is depicted as having red hair and a red beard, although he does have huge muscles and a magical hammer named Mjolnir (Destroyer), which could crush mountains, cause the thunder to sound, and was responsible for breaking the ice of winter each year.

The day Thursday comes from his name: Thor's day. And his hammer, in the form of a T-shaped symbol, is still worn by those who follow the Norse traditions. If you feel a need for a powerful ally or additional strength, invoke Thor. Do so on a Thursday if you can, and be sure to ask politely. He is the god of thunder, after all.

• • •

TRY THIS: *On the next Thursday, put out an offering to Thor such as a cup of ale or mead and say hello.*

February 27
Breathing

In general, as a society, we breathe all wrong. I know, you wouldn't think there was a right way and a wrong way, but there is, and we're doing it wrong. Don't believe me? Stop reading for a minute and concentrate on your breathing. Is it slow and deep, going down into your diaphragm or is it rapid and shallow? Uh-huh. Me too.

Some of this has to do with how busy and rushed and tense we all are. Some of it is a lack of mindfulness. We just don't pay any attention to our breathing and, unfortunately, we pay for that with increased anxiety and other physical and mental issues. And, of course, that makes it more difficult to be spiritual. It's no accident that much of yoga practice focuses on the breath.

• • •

TRY THIS: *Pay attention to your breathing when you do magical work. Once you cast your circle, take your place in front of your altar or go outside to stand under the moon and take a few moments to simply breathe. Consciously slow down and breathe more deeply. Feel the movement of the air in your lungs. Allow anything negative to be floated out when you exhale, and breathe in positive energy when you inhale. See if this makes a difference in the power of your magic. And when you feel particularly anxious or stressed, remember this feeling of calmness and power and take a few deep breaths.*

February 28
Healing Bath Salts

I live in an old farmhouse with a giant cast-iron clawfoot tub in the bathroom. That means that in the middle of the cold winter, I can indulge in a hot bath. This is nice all by itself, but it is also the perfect opportunity for some simple magic.

Healing bath salts are easy to make and don't have to be either complicated or expensive, so you can see why they're one of my favorite everyday magical treats.

Start off with some kind of bath salt. Sea salt is probably the most widely used, but if you feel achy, use Epsom salts instead. Or mix them both, which is what I like to do. Then add either essential oils or dried herbs or a magical healing oil that is consecrated and ready to go.

Oils and herbs that are particularly good for healing use (both magically and otherwise) include calendula, lavender, lemon balm, and rosemary. If you feel ill, peppermint or eucalyptus are also nice. A few rose petals can be spiritually therapeutic as well, although rose essential oil can be quite pricy.

* * *

TRY THIS: *Mix some salts and oils/herbs together and sprinkle them into your bath's hot water, visualizing them forming a magical healing pool in which you can soak away your troubles. Swirl them in clockwise and say:*

Salt and herbs that sooth and heal
Help improve the way I feel.

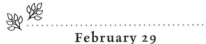

February 29
Leap Day

Once every four years we get an extra day in February. There are technical reasons for this, having to do with catching up with the leftover hours that don't quite come out evenly in our regular calendar. Mostly, I just find it both intriguing and a tiny bit disconcerting to suddenly have an extra day show up.

There are a few interesting traditions and superstitions associated with the day. It was supposed to be the one time when a woman could propose to a man instead of waiting around for him to get to it. (I think we might have outgrown that one, but hey, feel free to use it as an excuse, ladies.) At one point in Scotland there was a law that punished a man who turned down a proposal made on this day. That must have made for some amusing moments.

Even if you aren't in the mood to propose to someone, do something fun today. Take a leap—do something you never do. Indulge yourself in a triple-scoop banana split or eat extra bacon. Hell, put the bacon on top of your banana split; I won't judge you.

The point is, do something you would only do once every four years. Take a day trip to someplace special. Hide out and do nothing at all. Get together with friends and have a leap year day party.

· · ·

TRY THIS: *Do something, anything—because in this crazy busy world, an extra day is a gift. Make the most of it.*

March 1
The Altar

Back in ancient times, many homes had altars or niches dedicated to the household gods. People would burn candles or incense and leave offerings there or ask their particular deity for a boon. I think altars serve an important purpose for witches, one that goes well beyond a place to rest our athames. They are spots dedicated to magical and spiritual work, for one thing. If you stand in front of your altar, you are already halfway into the right mindset for the work you are going to do. They also are a good visual reminder to actually do the work. If you're like me, your witchy life sometimes gets a little lost in the day-to-day rush. Having an altar staring you in the face reminds you, "Hey, it has been a while since I did something spiritual."

Not everyone has the freedom to have an altar out in the open, but an altar doesn't have to be obvious to serve its purpose. Can't have a statue of the Goddess and the God? Use an abalone shell and a cool stick. Can't have quarter candles? Use a feather to represent air, a chunk of rock for earth, a shell or a bowl of water for water, and something red for fire. People will just think you like nature, and they wouldn't be wrong.

* * *

TRY THIS: *Create an altar, or if you already have one, stand in front of it and make an offering to your personal household gods or just say hello.*

March 2
The Wiccan Rede

"An it harm none, do as ye will."

Eight simple words by which I try to live my life, although it isn't as easy as it seems. Even before I came to the Craft, I did my best not to harm anyone else. I've always been a big believer in "do unto others as you would have them do unto you" because it made sense to me that you wouldn't want to do something to someone else that you wouldn't want done to you.

But you can't always predict how your words or actions will affect others, can you? And sometimes you have to make difficult choices and put yourself and your own needs first. How do we as witches make our way through the world and still live by the Wiccan Rede? (Not that everyone does, and that's okay too.)

I don't have the answer to that question because it is something we have to figure out for ourselves, but I do think it is a question worth pondering.

• • •

TRY THIS: *Take a few minutes to think about the eight words that make up the Wiccan Rede. Do you try to live by them, even if you don't consider yourself a Wiccan? What does "harm none" mean to you? (To me, it also includes not harming myself, so I think that bowl of potato chips might have been a no-no.) Step back and assess your recent behavior. Are you living up to your own ideals for how you wish to treat others or yourself? If not, what are you going to do to change that?*

March 3
Fire Element Meditation

Fire is probably the element our ancestors appreciated the most in the middle of the winter. It gives much-needed warmth, yes, but it also brings light to the darkness and creates a place to gather together. In our modern world, we tend to take fire for granted. Use this meditation to deepen your connection with this element, no matter what the weather is like.

If you can, sit in front of some form of fire: a fireplace, a bonfire, or a candle in a cast-iron cauldron or fire-safe holder. If you can't have an open flame, visualize it. Your surroundings should be dark and quiet so that the fire takes center stage.

Stare at the flames and think about what it might have been like for long-ago humans to learn how to use it—to cook, to heat their caves, and eventually to make tools. Then think about how rich and varied all of fire's forms are: the bonfire, the volcano, the candle, the sun. Close your eyes and feel the warmth of the sun on your face. Smell the scents of food cooked over a grill and the smoke from a campfire. Hear the bonfire's flames crackle and snap.

• • •

TRY THIS: *As you meditate, think of all the ways that the fire element brings its power to your life and take them into yourself with gratitude.*

March 4
Bloodstone

The official birthstone of those born in March is the aquamarine, but it can be an expensive stone, so the less pricy alternative is bloodstone, which I prefer. A deep green chalcedony with occasional spots of red, I find bloodstone to be a much more interesting stone and occasionally make jewelry with it, in part because I like the fact that it has a long historical association with magic.

It was called bloodstone because it was believed that the stone could stop bleeding, and it eventually became associated with healing of every kind. Like other green stones, it is good for prosperity work (I don't know about you, but having a little money in my pocket tends to make me feel better too).

Here's one of my favorite bits of trivia about bloodstone, from Scott Cunningham's *Cunningham's Encyclopedia of Crystal, Gem, and Metal Magic* (my go-to book for magical work with stones):

> In the thirteenth century, bloodstones were engraved with the figure of a bat. These talismans were worn by magicians to increase the effectiveness of spells and magical rites.

Now I want to find a bloodstone engraved with a bat; don't you?

• • •

TRY THIS: *If you have a piece of bloodstone, spend a few minutes sitting with it to get a feel for its special energy. Consider whether you prefer bloodstone or aquamarine and why.*

March 5
Witchy Words of Wisdom:
Tess Whitehurst

Tess Whitehurst is one of my favorite modern witchcraft authors. She has a practical, down-to-earth style that suits my own magical approach. She has written several books, but my favorite is *Magical Housekeeping: Simple Charms and Practical Tips for Creating a Harmonious Home*. This might be because I am a Taurus, and therefore I am all about my home and my roots or it might just be because it is a darn good book. She starts right out in chapter 1 talking about clutter clearing and how our homes reflect ourselves.

> Everything is connected. When we look at our homes with this in mind, we see that they are like extensions or reflections of our bodies, lives, and emotional landscapes. This is an illustration of Hermes Trismegistus's famous magical precept, "As above, so below." Above, the seen and externally manifested world (our homes), and below, the unseen and internally manifested world (or thoughts, feelings, and experiences), are not only mirrors of each other, but they are also one and the same.

• • •

TRY THIS: *Think about this quote and then look around your own home. Ask yourself if your home is a mirror of yourself. If so, do you like what you see?*

March 6
Gratitude No. 2

Here's your challenge: find three things to be grateful for today and each day for the rest of the month. Write them down in a journal, Book of Shadows, or Book of Light, or post them on the refrigerator to help you remember the good things when you are having a tough day.

I'll help you out; here are my three for today:

God and Goddess, I thank you for my friends, my family, and my cats.

• • •

TRY THIS: *Now it's your turn. What are three things you are grateful for?*

March 7
The Base Chakra

Every once in a while when someone says, "Hi, how are you today?" I want to respond, "Actually, my base chakra is a little out of whack," just to see the look on their face.

You've probably heard of chakras, even if you aren't clear on what they are. Based on a Sanskrit word for "wheels," the seven chakras are spinning energy centers found at various places on the body. Each one is associated with a different color and effect on your body.

The base chakra (or root chakra) has to do with being grounded and stable. It is what roots you to the earth, and when it is out of balance, you can feel insecure or off balance without realizing why. In theory, a truly healthy person has all their chakras spinning freely and the energy flowing easily between the base chakra and the crown chakra, but sometimes they get blocked or stuck.

• • •

TRY THIS: *Check in with your base chakra. Visualize a red glowing light at the bottom of your torso. See if you can sense if it is spinning freely or is stagnant and sluggish. Mentally spin it in one direction and then another. If it still seems a bit stuck, visualize energy from the universe coming in to give it a boost. You can also burn a red candle or even wear red underwear on days when you need an extra bit of grounding or stability.*

March 8
Osiris

Spring is all about rebirth, and there is no better god to represent that than the Egyptian god of the underworld, Osiris. Osiris is the son of the earth (Geb) and the sky (Nut) and is married to Isis, who was also his sister. (Things worked a little differently in ancient Egypt; don't judge.) Osiris is associated with the seasonal flooding of the river Nile, which is necessary for the life and prosperity of those who live near it.

Osiris's story of death and resurrection is both brutal and full of hope. He was torn apart by his brother Set, who scattered the parts of his body. Isis found the pieces and put them back together, bringing Osiris back to life temporarily using a spell she learned from her father. She kept him alive long enough to conceive a son, Horus.

Magic and rebirth—how witchy can you get?

• • •

TRY THIS: *Read up on Egyptian mythology, which is very different from the Roman, Greek, and Celtic mythology most of us are familiar with. See if any of their gods appeal to you. Or light a candle on your altar for Osiris, and thank him for the rebirth of spring.*

March 9
"Flower God, God of the Spring"

This poem exactly captures the way I feel about spring!

> Flower god, god of the spring, beautiful, bountiful,
> Cold-dyed shield in the sky, lover of versicles,
> Here I wander in April
> Cold, grey-headed; and still to my
> Heart, Spring comes with a bound, Spring the deliverer,
> Spring, song-leader in woods, chorally resonant;
> Spring, flower-planter in meadows,
> Child-conductor in willowy
> Fields deep dotted with bloom, daisies and crocuses:
> Here that child from his heart drinks of eternity:
> O child, happy are children!
> She still smiles on their innocence,
> She, dear mother in God, fostering violets,
> Fills earth full of her scents, voices and violins:
> Thus one cunning in music
> Wakes old chords in the memory:
> Thus fair earth in the Spring leads her performances.
> One more touch of the bow, smell of the virginal
> Green—one more, and my bosom
> Feels new life with an ecstasy.

(Robert Louis Stevenson, 1883)

• • •

> **TRY THIS:** *Write down how spring makes you
> feel. Don't worry, it doesn't have to be poetry.*

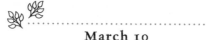

March 10
Charm Bag for Protection

Charm bags are one of the most basic and easy-to-create forms of magic. You can make them for pretty much anything: love, healing, peace, whatever you need. I have a protection charm bag hanging by my front door, for instance. I consider it a bit of added magical insurance against Bad Stuff.

The ingredients are simple (and you can change them up as you prefer). I use dried herbs (rosemary, basil, and sage), a clove of garlic, and a tumbled agate. You could substitute any stone that has protective properties, such as black onyx, red jasper, turquoise, or malachite. It is also traditional to add a couple of straight pins. Use either a premade bag of some natural material such as cotton, silk, or leather, or make your own by taking a small piece of cloth and sewing three sides together with an opening at the top.

• • •

TRY THIS: *Gather everything I mentioned here and put all your ingredients inside a bag or cloth, then tie the top with a piece of red or black yarn (string will do). Consecrate the bag on your altar or under the full moon, and/or use the spell for protection that follows on March 11.*

March 11
Spell for Protection

I don't know about you, but I find the world to be kind of a scary place. Between natural disasters, scary people, illness, and all the other things that can go wrong, I am happy to have magic to create a few extra tools to help keep me and mine safe.

Here is a simple protection spell. As you say the spell, visualize yourself or whomever or whatever you are trying to protect surrounded by a powerful white light.

> Protect me with this magic's charms
> Safe from all that hurts or harms
> Protection all around me be
> From hurt or harm keep me free

TRY THIS: Use this spell in conjunction with a charm bag or a protection talisman (say the spell as you consecrate the item) or write the spell on a piece of paper and stick it in your car, your wallet, or somewhere in your home.

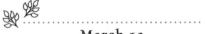

March 12
I Am Strong and Capable

It can be easy to feel overwhelmed and over-matched by the challenges we all face. Say this affirmation when you feel like you just aren't up to the tasks that face you.

I am strong and capable. I can do anything I put my mind to.

• • •

TRY THIS: *Close your eyes. Concentrate on your breathing. Now say this affirmation and really believe in yourself.*

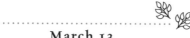

March 13
Lucky Thirteen

Do you suffer from triskaidekaphobia? No, that's not a nasty skin disease. In fact, there is an actual word for the fear of the number thirteen. (I'll just give you a minute to wrap your brain around that.) I guess that means it is pretty widespread.

There are several theories on how the number thirteen came to be viewed as unlucky, including a Norse legend about twelve gods who gathered at a feast that was going well until the trickster Loki joined them, and the Christian story of the Last Supper, where Jesus ate a meal with his twelve disciples. To this day, some people refuse to have thirteen people at dinner.

Plus, of course, there is the idea that there should be thirteen witches in a coven. For some reason, people find that alarming too. Go figure. I guess that's one of the reasons I think of thirteen as lucky instead of unlucky. Friday the thirteenth is one of my favorite days. I'm contrary that way.

• • •

TRY THIS: *Think about it: are you afraid of the number thirteen or would you happily sit down and share a dinner with twelve other witches?*

March 14
Rabbit and Hare

Rabbits and their longer-eared cousins the hares have traditionally been associated with witchcraft, especially in the spring. One of my favorite sights as I look out my window is a couple of rabbits sitting under the birdfeeder or chasing each other around the yard. They never fail to make me smile with their comical antics.

The hare, in particular, is considered one of the Goddess's creatures and a lunar animal. Rabbits and hares are often symbols used at the spring equinox (Ostara), and Christians adopted them when they co-opted the holiday and turned it into Easter. (What, you thought it made sense for a Christian holiday to use a fertility symbol?) In the Chinese zodiac, those born under the sign of the rabbit are said to be friendly, sensitive, and compassionate.

• • •

TRY THIS: *Some people carry a rabbit's foot for luck, but that hardly seems lucky for the poor rabbit! Instead, put a statue or a picture of a rabbit or a hare on your spring altar to bring in abundance, fertility, and luck.*

March 15
Fishtanks

I have a small garden pond where a number of goldfish reside. Before I got a heated gizmo that kept the pond from freezing over in the winter, I would bring the fish in every year in the fall and let them hang out in a twenty-gallon tank until things warmed up enough in the spring for them to return to their outside home. (I'm pretty sure the cats thought it was kitty television, as they would sit and gaze at the tank for hours.)

Fishtanks are an easy and fun way to connect with the element of water. They are a miniature ecosystem that has to be maintained in balance, much like the waters outside. If they get too hot or too dirty, everything in them dies. But with a little effort they can be a source of beauty. Watching fish is very calming, and the sound of the filter bubbling away can create a soothing background noise.

Fish can range from my own inexpensive and relatively uncomplicated goldfish to exotic saltwater fish in bright colors and fanciful shapes. Fishtanks are great for kids, too, and can introduce them to the responsibility of caring for another creature, as well as allowing them to see the natural world in miniature. In truth, fishtanks are a great way to connect with the element of water whether you are young or simply young at heart.

· · ·

TRY THIS: *To start small, get one of the kinds of fish that can live in a simple fishbowl.*

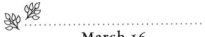

March 16

Spring Cleaning Your Magical Tools

We often think about spring cleaning in terms of our homes, but spring is also the perfect time to freshen up your magical tools. Over time and with use anything can pick up bits of sludge or negativity, especially if you do magical work with others.

There are some simple ways to clean and clear magical tools, and which ones you use will depend to some extent on the tool and your circumstances. Soaking a drum in salt and water, for instance, is not a great idea. Some tools may require actual cleaning to shine them up or to remove dust or dirt. But in general, spring cleaning your tools is more about clearing their energy.

Leaving a tool out for a night under the full moon is one way to do that. Or put the tool inside on a windowsill or table where the moonlight will fall. Salt and water are also good, either separately or together. For tools that won't be harmed by getting wet, wash them clean under running water or leave them to soak in a bowl with some sea salt added to it. For items that shouldn't get wet, sprinkle them with salt and a tiny flick of water from the ends of your fingers. Tools can also be cleansed with the smoke from a sage smudge stick.

• • •

TRY THIS: *Take the time either today or soon to do a bit of spring cleaning on your magical tools, then see how they feel the next time you use them. Can you tell the difference? I'll bet you can.*

March 17
Sage Smudge Sticks

Whether you're using it to cleanse your tools or your aura, sage is one of the best herbs for clearing and cleansing. I consider my sage smudge sticks to be one of my most useful magical implements.

The use of sage smudge sticks for cleansing was adopted from Native American practices. Magically, it was more traditional to use the herb for wisdom (hence the name sage), longevity, protection, and wish-making.

I add the dried herb to my protection mixes, but mostly I use it to cleanse myself or my home (or occasionally one of my energy healing clients who has come in with icky energy). My coven, Blue Moon Circle, always starts our rituals by passing a sage smudge stick from person to person. It helps us to wash away all the mundane cares of the day we might have brought with us into circle, and the sharp scent reminds us that we are in sacred space, ready to do our magical work.

• • •

TRY THIS: *Get a sage smudge stick if you don't already have one. Smudge yourself and any problem areas of your home and see if you can tell the difference in the energy.*

March 18
The Broom

Brooms and witches have been associated for centuries. I suppose I'm associated with brooms too, since I wrote *The Witch's Broom*, an entire book about them. I discovered some fascinating facts about them in the process.

You probably knew that the original witch's broom was called a besom and was made from twigs tied to a stick, rather than the broomcorn of our modern version. Can you imagine sweeping up dirt with a bundle of twigs? Oh boy.

Or, rather, oh girl. One of the things I discovered was that brooms may have been associated with witches back in the day because they are common household tools used primarily by women. Another thing I hadn't realized was that the broom is the only tool that is both masculine and feminine. The long handle is the masculine part, and the brush is feminine. How cool is that?

One of my favorite things about the broom is that you can use it for practical jobs while practicing a little bit of magic at the same time. If you bless and consecrate your household broom for magical cleansing, or spritz it with a little cleansing oil, or even just dip it in a mixture of salt and water, you can energetically clean your house at the same time you sweep up dirt. Now that's what I call multitasking.

* * *

TRY THIS: *While you sweep your home, visualize the broom sweeping away negative energy at the same time.*

March 19
Friendship

If your witchcraft practice and Pagan beliefs are an important part of your life, it makes things much easier if your friends accept that you are a witch. Even better, of course, is having witchy friends with whom you can share your beliefs, whether or not you actually practice together.

Some of us are lucky enough to have those friends nearby, but for others, their witchy connections are mostly folks they have met online or at conventions. Sadly, I often get letters from witches who have no one to share their spiritual life with, and they end up feeling isolated and alone. Many of them have to stay in the broom closet because of where they live or because the religious beliefs of family and friends aren't flexible enough to see witchcraft as a positive spiritual path.

I am extremely fortunate in that a number of my friends are also witches or, at the very least, Pagan-friendly. Don't forget that friendship is a two-way street. If you want people to accept your beliefs, you have to be willing to accept theirs, even if they don't match up with yours.

• • •

TRY THIS: *If you don't have friends who share or at least accept your beliefs, reach out to folks online or look for local gatherings that might attract the witchy sort.*

March 20
Eggs

Which came first, the chicken or the egg? When you're talking about spiritual matters, it was probably the egg. Often symbolizing the universe (since there is a tiny universe contained within them) or the earth (which is also spherical), eggs can come in tiny sizes, like that of the vervain hummingbird, or huge, like those an ostrich lays.

Eggs are most commonly used magically as a fertility symbol. This makes perfect sense, since actual living beings come out of them. Even human beings come from eggs in the beginning. At Ostara we decorate them—and, of course, eat them—in celebration of the fertility of spring.

In many cultures eggs also have been associated with healing and protection. Think about how strong an eggshell can be, despite its seeming fragility. In the good old days most people raised chickens and collected the eggs every day. What we get from the grocery store these days are eggs that have been mass produced, often from chickens fed and treated badly.

If you want to really experience an egg, buy them fresh at a farmers' market or from a local farmer. If you can't do that, get organic, free-range eggs. You'll be amazed at the flavor and the beautiful orange yolk, like a sunrise, in the middle. (They're more nutritious too.)

• • •

TRY THIS: *Buy fresh eggs and see if you can taste the difference from ones bought at a regular grocery store.*

March 21
Spring Equinox

Hooray! Spring is here! Okay, in some parts of the country, including where I live in upstate New York, spring is sometimes more theoretical than actual, but we can celebrate it nonetheless. It's a time for hope and new beginnings and increasing energy.

One of the things I love about this holiday is that the spring equinox is one of only two days of the year (the other being the fall equinox) when the day and the night are equal. Maybe it is because I am always striving to find balance in my own life, but to me there is something particularly magical about knowing that the darkness and the light are, for this one day, in perfect balance with each other.

After today the light will continue to increase, which is something to celebrate in and of itself, but for now let's enjoy this rare moment of balance.

. . .

TRY THIS: *If you need a little more balance in your life, light a white candle and a black candle and say this simple spell:*

On this day of balance true
Make me balanced through and through

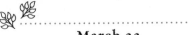

March 22
Aries

Aries is the sun sign that rules those born between March 21 and April 20. Those born under this fire sign tend to be energetic, adventurous, and filled with passion and creativity. Their passions may run away with them, though, so they aren't always the most practical of people—great for starting new ventures, for example, but not always patient enough to follow through.

• • •

TRY THIS: *During the time that Aries rules, let your passions rise to the surface. Is there something you've wanted to try but haven't quite gotten around to? Let the Aries energy empower you. Have an adventure, fall in love, start something new. Just make sure that you are willing to finish what you started.*

March 23
The Green Man

These days, the Green Man is such a common symbol, most people don't even associate it with the Paganism from which he came. I suppose that's understandable because his image can be found on ancient churches across Europe. (That's what happens when you co-opt a preexisting religion and its people.)

The Green Man is most often depicted as a head with leaves coming out of his mouth, eyes, and ears. I have a cool ceramic one, made by a local potter, hanging on my wall. It is a container with an open spot for planting small herbs or flowers or leaving offerings.

Some think that the Green Man is based on Sylvanus, the god of the woods. To me, he symbolizes the essence of nature itself, always growing from any nook and cranny available. For those not out of the broom closet yet, the Green Man is a symbol you can display without worry, since many non-witchy folks have them too.

• • •

> **TRY THIS:** *Now that the spring leaves are appearing, make your own Green Man. Using stiff paper (or even a paper plate if you are doing this with children), cut out the shape of a face, with eyes, a nose, and a mouth, and glue on as many leaves as you can fit. It's more about the feel of the thing than how it looks, so don't worry if it's not perfect. Have fun and celebrate the greening of the land.*

March 24
Feng Shui

By now, most people have heard of feng shui even if they're not quite sure what it is, how to use it, or if it is just so much New Age nonsense.

It is the opposite of New Age. Old age, in fact, if by that you mean an ancient system of harmonizing with your surrounding environment created by the Chinese many thousands of years ago. At its most basic, it says that there is a right place for everything, and when all is placed as it should be, life will go more smoothly and you will feel better.

For a fabulous source to help you achieve better feng shui in your home and in your magical work, check out Tess Whitehurst's *Magical Housekeeping: Simple Charms and Practical Tips for Creating a Harmonious Home*. You can start with a few basics, such as getting rid of clutter (anything that doesn't have an actual right place) and making sure that your front door, which is the entrance to your space, is as attractive and welcoming as you can make it.

• • •

TRY THIS: *Start decluttering today by throwing out or giving away ten things you don't use or don't need. Don't you feel lighter already?*

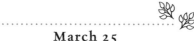

March 25
What Seeds Will I Plant?

As the spring unfolds around us and the earth begins to blossom, it is the perfect time to figure out what seeds you want to plant in the coming season and what you want to blossom in your life over the course of the rest of the year.

I always like to establish some kind of long-term goal at this point in the year and use the energy of spring to help me get off and running. Today, think about what seeds you want to plant. What do you want more of in your life? What do you want to bring in that isn't there now, and how can you nurture whatever new start you make?

* * *

TRY THIS: *Sit down with a piece of paper or your Book of Light (or Shadows). Make a list of the things you'd like to have blossom and grow in your life. Study it, maybe cross off a couple of things if they aren't really important, and put stars by the ones that mean the most. Then pick one and start working on it.*

March 26
Deviled Eggs

How do you make the perfect spring food even better? By adding fresh herbs, one of the symbols of the season. Start with free-range eggs and add the herbs of your choice.

You will need:

1 dozen eggs, hard-boiled and peeled

½ cup mayonnaise

1 tablespoon Dijon or horseradish mustard

Salt and pepper to taste

A dash or two of hot sauce (optional)

Herbs: chopped fresh dill, parsley, chives, and/or basil

Cut eggs in half the long way and remove the yolks. Mix yolks with all other ingredients (if you prefer, save the herbs to sprinkle on top instead). Put a heaping spoonful of yolk mixture inside the egg white shell and sprinkle with bits of chopped herb.

• • •

TRY THIS: *If you have kids or kitchen-inclined friends, create this recipe together.*

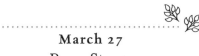

March 27
Rune Stones

Most witches have their favorite form of divination. For those who find the tarot confusing and overly complicated, or who just want another option, the rune stones are a popular second choice. A set of twenty-four pieces, usually made of either stone or wood, rune stones come to us from the Norse traditions. In later years a blank stone was added, but a lot of folks don't use it.

Runes usually look like a round or rectangular lozenge with a carved letter from the runic alphabet on one side. I have three sets: one that I made myself with my first coven out of clay, one made from colorful fused glass by a crafty member of Blue Moon Circle, and a clay store-bought set. Most people keep theirs in a drawstring pouch of some kind.

Like the tarot, the simplest way to use rune stones is to either pull one for a basic answer, such as "What should I expect from my day?" or do a three-stone reading for past, present, and future.

My original high priestess set us an interesting task: pull one rune stone a day (in the morning) for a month. We wrote down what the stone was and our interpretation, and then whether the day that followed in any way reflected the stone we had pulled. The results were surprisingly spot-on.

* * *

TRY THIS: *Pull a rune stone for yourself*
every day. Keep track of the results for a week or
a month, and see if they worked for you.

March 28
Witchy Words of Wisdom:
Scott Cunningham

Scott Cunningham is one of the acknowledged leaders of the modern Wiccan movement. He wrote more than thirty books before his death in 1993, including many that are considered classics in the field. Entire generations have grown up using his books on herbs, gemstones, and household magic, and his book *Wicca: A Guide for the Solitary Practitioner* is many witches' first introduction to the practice of magic.

I have a number of his books in my own library, but one of my favorites is *Cunningham's Encyclopedia of Wicca in the Kitchen*. Here's what he has to say about food:

> Food is magic. Its power over us is undeniable. From the sweet, rich lure of a freshly baked brownie to an exquisite steamed artichoke, food continues to seduce us.
>
> Food is life. We can't continue to live without its magic. Food, however, also harbors energies. When we eat, our bodies absorb those energies, just as they absorb vitamins, minerals, amino acids, carbohydrates, and other nutrients. Though we may not be aware of any effect other than a sated appetite, the food has subtly changed us...Eating is merging with the earth. It is a life-affirming act. Ritually preparing and eating specific foods is an effective method of enhancing and improving our lives.

· · ·

TRY THIS: *The next time you eat, think about this quote and feel the food doing its magical work inside you.*

March 29

Spell for Banishing Negativity

As we move into the fresh new energy of spring, it is the perfect time to let go of all the gloom that we may have been dragging around through the cold, dark months. If you feel as though the shadows linger around you, try doing this simple spell to banish negativity.

Light a white candle and sit in a quiet, peaceful space. Visualize yourself surrounded by a bright, shining light that is so powerful it pushes the darkness away. When the light has filled the space around you, say in a strong, decisive voice:

> *Negativity, I banish thee*
> *The light has won; it sets me free*
> *Shadows hang around no more*
> *I kick your asses out the door!*

* * *

TRY THIS: *After you say this spell, in your mind's eye slam a door shut, with the negativity on the other side. Feel free to cackle maniacally.*

March 30
Smoky Quartz

If you need some help banishing negativity, work with smoky quartz. Like all other members of the quartz family, it is magically powerful. I might even like it more than the supercharged clear crystal quartz (although I love that one too).

Smoky quartz is a great mental health stone. Not only does it help to rid you of negativity, it elevates your mood and helps in dealing with depression. It is also a great grounding stone. You can do magical work with a nice hunk of smoky quartz, but if you have serious issues, wear it as a necklace or place a piece in your pocket to help you through the day.

• • •

TRY THIS: *Get a piece of smoky quartz (or jewelry made with it) and carry or wear it when you are feeling down.*

March 31

Luna and the Feast of the Moon

On this date way back in the day, the Romans celebrated the feast of the moon in honor of the goddess Luna. As you might have guessed by her name, Luna is the goddess of the moon, symbolized by the crescent moon and the chariot. Her Greek counterpart is called Selena.

As witches, the moon is a large part of our spiritual practices, so hold your own festival in honor of Luna today. Have a feast and raise your glass to the lady of the moon. And if you can, go outside and look at her, appreciating her beauty no matter where she is in the ever-changing cycle from dark to full and back again. Hail Luna, goddess of the moon!

• • •

TRY THIS: *On the next full moon, call Luna by name when you invoke her. See if it feels right to you or if you feel like you get a response back.*

April 1
April Fools' Day

Despite its silly reputation, this day has fascinating roots. Some think it dates back to fifteenth-century France, when someone had the bright idea to change the date of the New Year holiday (celebrated from March 25 until the first of April) to January 1. Those who celebrated on the old date were referred to as April Fools. No matter where it started, April Fools' Day is now celebrated in much of Europe, the United States, and as far away as India.

Maybe this has something to do with the way that many cultures look at the fool, who was often seen as someone blessed by the gods. The figure of the fool is linked to the jester, both of whom often entertained in the courts of kings, bringing much-needed humor in the days before sitcoms.

The Fool is the first card in the tarot deck for a reason: all journeys start with a first step and a leap of faith. If you have a deck, pull out the Fool card (or print one out from the internet). Look at that silly person, ready to step off a cliff as if he doesn't have a care in the world, everything he owns in a bag over his shoulder and his adoring dog following behind. Don't you wish you could be that carefree?

• • •

TRY THIS: *Take time today to meditate on the Fool.
Is there something you have wanted to do but have held
back because of fear or because it just isn't practical? Maybe
it is time to be an April Fool and take a leap of faith.*

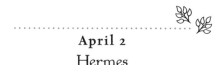

April 2
Hermes

If you spend a lot of time sending text messages and emails, you should probably thank Hermes. Hermes is one of the Greek gods, the son of Zeus, and he acts as a messenger for the gods as well as being the link between the gods and mortals. A trickster god (not unlike the Norse Loki), he is also the protector of thieves, athletes, and travelers. It sounds like he would be right at home in the modern world, doesn't it?

Of course, he also has a more serious side. Because he can move easily between the various worlds, he guides the souls of the dead to the underworld, so he is considered a god of transitions. He is often pictured with winged sandals, cap, and staff.

• • •

TRY THIS: *If you are in the midst of a major transition, call on Hermes. Ask for his guidance when you get that nagging feeling that the universe is trying to send you a message, but you just can't figure out what it is. Write him a note or place a feather on your altar and call his name. My guess is that he can hear you.*

April 3
Spell for Communication

Good communication is at the basis of all relationships, whether they are with a significant other, family, friends, or work. But communication is hard. Even when you try your best, you often don't communicate clearly (even when you think you do) or you let emotions get in the way. If I had a nickel for every time I thought I'd been absolutely clear about something, and yet the person I was talking to misunderstood or took it the wrong way, I'd be a wealthy woman and wouldn't have to write all these books.

Here is a simple spell to help communication go a little more smoothly.

> *Hermes, help my tongue speak clearly*
> *Let words flow well and as I mean them*
> *Let my heart be open and my mind be wise*
> *For good communication now and always*
> *So mote it be!*

> **TRY THIS:** Use this spell anytime you have an important conversation coming up or feel as though you have communication difficulties with someone.

April 4
"My April Lady"

Where I live, April can be a very changeable month. I love the way this poem captures its ups and downs.

When down the stair at morning
The sunbeams round her float,
Sweet rivulets of laughter
Are bubbling in her throat;
The gladness of her greeting
Is gold without alloy;
And in the morning sunlight
I think her name is Joy.

When in the evening twilight
The quiet book-room lies,
We read the sad old ballads,
While from her hidden eyes
The tears are falling, falling,
That give her heart relief;
And in the evening twilight,
I think her name is Grief.

My little April lady,
Of sunshine and of showers,
She weaves the old spring magic,
And breaks my heart in flowers!

But when her moods are ended,
She nestles like a dove;
Then, by the pain and rapture,
I know her name is Love.

(Henry Van Dyke, 1911)

TRY THIS: As the month of April unfolds, watch her
different moods and see how those moods affect your own.

April 5
Kwan Yin

Kwan Yin is a Buddhist goddess of compassion and mercy, widely revered in China and elsewhere. Her name means something like "she who hears," meaning that she hears the cries and prayers of all human beings. She is usually depicted as being gracious and beautiful, with a serene and kind expression.

Many Pagans like to have a statue of Kwan Yin even if they have no other Buddhist leanings. After all, who doesn't need a little more compassion?

She is also a good reminder for us to be compassionate toward each other.

• • •

TRY THIS: *For the next few days, make an effort to channel the goddess and be just a little kinder to the people around you. Who knows—you may find it so addictive, you'll want to do it all the time.*

April 6
Saying Thank You

We're going to change things up a little bit here. If you've followed along from the beginning, you know that periodically I have had a day dedicated to gratitude.

Yes, I still want you to focus on gratitude—it's a good thing and makes your heart expand while at the same time changing your focus from the negative to the positive. But for April I am going to give you a different challenge.

Today, and for the rest of this month, find four people to say thank you to. These people can be anyone from a random person who opens a door for you to the cashier at the supermarket. Or go out of your way to say thank you to someone who you may have needed to show gratitude to for a while: your mother, a friend who goes above and beyond, a colleague who makes work more enjoyable.

And one of those people can be you. Did *you* do a good job getting through the day? It's okay to thank yourself.

• • •

TRY THIS: *Say thank you to four people. How does it feel? How good would it feel if people thanked you a little more often for the effort you make? Who knows—if you start putting that out there, maybe it will find its way back around to you.*

April 7
The Wand

The wand is one of the witch's basic tools. Sadly, in real life, they don't work magic the way Harry Potter's wand does (although wouldn't it be cool if they did?). What they are used for, mostly, is to point and direct energy—for instance, while casting a circle or calling the quarters.

The great thing about wands is that you don't have to spend a lot of money on some fancy store-bought one, although of course you can if you want. At its heart, a wand is, after all, a stick. A nice stick, but still a stick. Go for a walk in the woods or maybe a nearby park and find just the right piece of wood. It should be straight and about as long as the space between your hand and your elbow, although I don't think anyone is going to show up at your house and measure to make sure you got it right.

If you want something with a little more pizzazz, carve or wood-burn runes or other symbols into it to make it your own, or add feathers or gemstones. Personally, I'm partial to a simple piece of wood that calls to the heart and says, "Use me for magic!"

• • •

TRY THIS: *Make yourself a wand. It can be simple or fancy, but make sure it reflects your own witchy nature.*

April 8
Rain

April showers bring May flowers, at least in most parts of the country (sorry, California). Sometimes when it is raining for days, it can feel dreary and you might get tired of the gray skies and constant wetness. But spring rain not only brings life-giving moisture to the ground and nourishes the growing things, it can also give you a great way to connect with the element of water.

The next time it rains, go outside and stand in it. No, really. You're not the Wicked Witch of the West; you won't melt. Go out and feel the raindrops on your skin, and send out appreciation for all the rain does for the land. Take in that nourishing energy of water and let it wash you clean of stress and negativity. If you can, do this in bare feet. And if you find a mud puddle, by all means JUMP!

• • •

TRY THIS: *Is it raining today? If so, go outside and enjoy it. If you are in an area where it hardly ever rains, either run through a sprinkler or stand in the shower and pretend you are in the midst of a lovely spring rainstorm.*

April 9
What Do I Want the Rain to Wash Away?

If you're going to stand out in the rain (and of course you are), give some thought to what you would like the spring rain to wash away. What are you holding on to that drags you down? Are you carrying around negative energy—yours or someone else's—that it is time to let go of? Maybe it is just time to wash the slate clean for a fresh start.

• • •

TRY THIS: *Make a list of what you want to wash out of your life. Then pick one thing and get started.*

April 10
The Second Chakra

The second chakra, also known as the sacral chakra, is located at the pelvis and is usually pictured as being orange in color. This energy center is key for sexuality and hormonal balance, which affects the entire body. No matter what stage of life you are at, this chakra can be thrown off by trauma or illness.

Some people are uncomfortable with their own sexuality, and that can throw this chakra out of whack too. If you have issues in this area, sit in a quiet space and visualize a bright orange light. Get it to spin in a clockwise direction. If it seems stuck or stagnant, send love and acceptance to that area of your body and see if that helps.

• • •

TRY THIS: *Place an orange stone on top of your sacral chakra—a light carnelian works well for this, or amber, which is very healing. Close your eyes and visualize the energy of the stone glowing brightly, and see that glow spread through the chakra, healing and reinvigorating it.*

April 11
Fortuna

On this day the Romans held a festival in honor of Fortuna, the goddess of luck. Who couldn't use a little more of that?

The truth is, while most of life's successes are based on your own hard work, there is often a bit of luck involved: being at the right place at the right time, meeting the person who can connect you to the job or lover or opportunity that is just right for you.

Mind you, Fortuna is the goddess of luck, both good and bad. So if you send out a prayer to her or light a candle in her honor, be sure to specify which kind you want!

TRY THIS: *During this festival it was common to ask Fortuna to tell you what fate had in store, so do a tarot reading, pull a few rune stones, or simply ask for guidance. If you want, say this simple spell and then either use your divination tools or sit quietly and see if something comes to you.*

Fortuna great, Fortuna wise
Tell me what before me lies.

April 12
Tree Identification

I have a confession to make. (Hangs head.) I am not very good at identifying trees. I mean, I'm fine with the obvious ones, like pines or willows, but after that I'm kind of lost. I find this a bit embarrassing, considering that not only do I live in an area full of beautiful trees, but also I'm a nature-loving witch, for goodness' sake.

My plan is to buy a tree and shrub identification book and start walking around with it. If you're not great with this type of knowledge, try doing this too. After all, if we're going to be tree-hugging Pagans, we should probably know which trees we're hugging.

In my yard I have lots of pines (of various types…don't ask me which is which), a couple of very tall oaks, a few spindly willows, apple trees, a cherry tree, a flowering crabapple that gets beautiful blossoms in the spring, and a whole bunch of shrubs, including elderberry, forsythia, lilac, and hydrangea.

• • •

TRY THIS: *What trees grow in your yard or on your street, in your neighborhood, or in the nearest park? If you don't know, work on finding out.*

April 13
Totem Animals

Totem animals are not pets, but rather symbols by which we connect to the world of nature and mysticism. You can't just pick one because you think it is cool; if anything, a totem animal picks you. (For a very long time, my totem animal was a flock of sheep. Seriously. Other people get hawks or wolves; I got a flock of sheep.)

Sometimes it becomes clear that something is your totem animal because it shows up constantly or at times to signify important shifts and changes. You need to pay attention, though, or you might miss these signs.

If you don't already know your totem animal, find it through shamanic journeying or meditating on the question. Go to a place where you can connect to nature—the woods, for example, or someplace else quiet and private. Sit under a tree or lie on the ground. Ask the gods to send you your totem animal. You might get a vision of a particular animal or open your eyes and see something that contains a clue. If you're lucky, you might even see the animal itself, depending on where you are.

• • •

TRY THIS: *If you don't get an answer right away, look around and find a bit of nature to take home with you—a stone, a feather, a leaf. Put it under your pillow and perhaps your totem animal will come to you in your dreams.*

April 14
Peppermint

I love the smell of peppermint. I like a hot cup of peppermint tea on a cold winter's day or when my stomach is feeling a bit off. The Farmers' Museum in Cooperstown, New York, has the best old-fashioned peppermint candy sticks on the planet. I also love peppermint's practical usefulness. I add a few drops of peppermint essential oil to a spray that keeps away ants and other bugs, and I put it in a diffuser to ease a stuffy head.

Magically, peppermint is just as useful. Its classic applications are for healing and purification, but it is also one of my favorite herbs for prosperity work. Scott Cunningham suggests tucking a few leaves into your wallet or purse. I always add some essential oil of peppermint to my magical prosperity oils and dab a drop or two on a candle while saying a spell for abundance.

Peppermint, like all mints, is easy to grow—to the point of being invasive in a garden, if you're not careful.

• • •

TRY THIS: *Plant a few seeds and start your own peppermint patch (inside on a windowsill, if necessary). After all, who couldn't use a little more healing, purification, and prosperity? (Plus, you can make tea.)*

April 15
Spell for Prosperity

Prosperity is more than just having money (although goodness knows that's nice too). Sometimes prosperity comes to us in the form of unexpected gifts or opportunities, so when you do prosperity work, make sure you leave the universe an opening to help you out in ways you might not have thought of. If you need something specific (like a new job or the money to get your car fixed), ask for that—just be prepared for help to come in unexpected forms.

Here is a simple prosperity spell. When I need to add an extra boost to my prosperity work, I usually light a green candle that I've inscribed with runes and symbols connected to prosperity and abundance. Remember to focus your intent for positive sources of prosperity, with harm to none.

> *Green and gold, abundance flow*
> *In all positive ways you will*
> *Bring prosperity to my life*
> *My pockets and my wallet fill*
> *Fortune's favor, gifts galore*
> *Enough for life's necessity*
> *I ask this with an open heart*
> *As I will, so mote it be!*

• • •

TRY THIS: *Prosperity is also a state of mind.*
How much do you need to be happy?

April 16

I Deserve Prosperity and Abundance

Sometimes you can get bogged down with a feeling that you are never going to have enough money. You try and try, work hard, and it just doesn't seem to happen. I don't know about you, but I hate that feeling. I have found that focusing on the feeling of lack tends to perpetuate the cycle. After all, if you are constantly thinking—or worse, saying out loud—"I never have enough money," think what you are putting out into the universe. Instead, state this positive affirmation:

I deserve prosperity and abundance, and the universe provides it to me.

• • •

TRY THIS: *Recognize the prosperity and abundance you currently have in your life.*

April 17
Planting Seeds

This is the time of year that we start planting seeds, both in our gardens and in our spiritual lives. Planting seeds is in some ways an act of faith—you put this tiny thing into the dirt and hope that something will bloom from it. Starting new endeavors in our lives is much the same. We water them with our efforts and our dreams and wait to see if they grow to fruition.

Today, plant the seeds for something. They can be actual seeds (if you don't have a garden, use a small pot on a windowsill) or the first steps toward achieving a goal in your life. Tap in to the abundant spring energy for growth and take advantage of this time to draw some of that energy into whatever you do. I hope your seeds grow well.

* * *

TRY THIS: *To make the most of the energy that comes from starting new seeds, plant a couple of seeds—maybe for herbs you can use in your magical work—and tuck a piece of paper into the soil as you do so. On the paper, write down something that you would like to grow and increase in your life.*

Witchy Words of Wisdom:
Ellen Dugan

Ellen Dugan is known as "the Garden Witch" for good reason. Both a witch and a Master Gardener, she melds the two to help us find our way back to our green witchcraft roots. In her book *Garden Witchery: Magick from the Ground Up*, she sums up the reason I like to grow some of my own magical ingredients when I can:

> There is nothing quite like making—or growing, for that matter—a magickal tool yourself. As you know, a self-created magickal tool or object becomes twice as powerful from absorbing the energy you expend in the making of the item. So the same can be said for cultivating your own magickal flowers and herbs. As you sow, raise, and then harvest your herbs and plants, your energy has seeped into the plant every time you touched it. Now all that energy is waiting to be programmed or released.

• • •

TRY THIS: *If you can, grow some magical herbs,*
even if you only have a windowsill to put them on.
As you plant them and they grow, focus on your
intent to use them for magical work. When you
finally use them, see if you can feel a difference.

April 19
Money-Drawing Coin

In prosperity magic, one of the easiest projects is to create a money-drawing coin. I like to use a fancy coin for this—something like a Susan B. Anthony dollar or a half-dollar—but you can use a simple quarter if you like. Dab the coin with prosperity oil or oils if you have them (such as basil, cinnamon, clove, ginger, patchouli, peppermint, or sandalwood) or sprinkle the coin with a couple of the dried herbs. Consecrate it on your altar and ask the gods and the elements to bless the coin to draw prosperity in only positive ways.

Then tuck it in your wallet or purse, or place it on your altar. (I confess, when I really need it to work, I tuck mine in my bra!) If I'm doing prosperity magic later, I often place the coin under my candleholder for an extra boost.

• • •

TRY THIS: *Make a money-drawing coin and then do a prosperity spell to make it even more powerful.*

April 20
The Pendulum

A pendulum is one of the simplest tools for divination, although its use is limited primarily to questions that can be answered with a yes or a no. I have a number of truly beautiful ones, including one with a star-shaped carved quartz crystal and one with a lovely translucent amethyst pointed drop. But I've also seen perfectly useful pendulums made out of nothing more complicated or expensive than strong thread and a paperclip. You can also use a stone with a natural hole in it or anything else that can be made to dangle from a string or thin chain.

It is easy to use a pendulum, but before you get started, figure out exactly how that particular pendulum will respond. Usually it will either swing clockwise/counterclockwise or sway from left to right/backwards and forwards. To figure out how yours answers, ask a question you know the answer to, like "Is my name _____?" and see which direction it moves in. Then test it with another question for which you know the answer will be no. Once you have that settled, you are ready to ask your questions.

· · ·

TRY THIS: *Remember to clear your mind as much as you can before you start, and ask questions that have a yes or a no answer. Sometimes the pendulum won't move, and that usually means that the answer can't be known at that time or that you're asking the wrong question.*

April 21
Taurus

Those born between April 21 and May 21 are considered to be under the sun sign of Taurus. An earth sign, Taureans tend to be dependable, patient, practical, warm-hearted, and determined—also (ahem) a tad bit stubborn and inflexible. Yes, I'm a Taurus. And if I'm being honest, most of those descriptions fit me pretty well. I am definitely practical and loyal, but may be too rooted since it can be hard to get me to leave my house.

On the other hand, in theory, those born under the Taurus sun sign are often focused on possessions and can be obsessive about owning and collecting stuff, which doesn't fit me at all. I guess this just goes to prove that while being born under a particular sign may give a person certain innate tendencies, everyone is still an individual and there is no such thing as "one sign fits all." Have you found that your sign describes you pretty accurately or not?

· · ·

TRY THIS: *This is a good time for you to indulge your earthy side. Plant something or tend to your home, but watch out for any stubborn inclinations!*

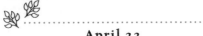

April 22
Earth Day

If you want to get technical, every day is Earth Day if you are a witch or a Pagan. But since the whole Unites States celebrates Earth Day now, it is a great excuse to make an extra effort to do something for Mother Earth.

What you do is up to you, but it should be practical and useful. Try taking a walk and picking up litter on your road or in a nearby park. (Some communities have cleanup days on Earth Day, especially by rivers and in parks, so check around to see if there is a group effort you can join in on.) Plant a tree or a shrub; if you don't have a yard to put one in, either plant one elsewhere or contribute to one of the foundations that will plant them for you. Sign petitions that encourage politicians to vote for earth-friendly measures. There are a million different ways to celebrate the planet we call home; you just have to choose the one that suits you best.

• • •

TRY THIS: *Make sure you get outside too.*
Put your bare feet on the ground and say,
"Thank you for being my mother."

April 23
Willows

When I was a kid, we had a huge weeping willow tree in the backyard whose branches swept so low to the ground that it made the perfect hiding place for a shy girl, her cat, and her book. Even then I knew that willows were magical.

A willow's supple and pliable branches can be easily woven into baskets, furniture, or fences, and they often have been used to bind a witch's broom or be made into wands. Willow's other magical uses include protection, love magic, and healing (not surprising, considering that white willow bark is the origin of salicin, from which aspirin was eventually synthesized, and has long been used medicinally).

The willow tree likes to keep its feet wet and is often found along rivers or in marshy ground. Because of its ghostly white bark, the willow has been associated with the Goddess, the moon, and also death and grief. (Is that why they call it a weeping willow, I wonder?) Personally, I have always found them ethereally beautiful and somehow mysterious. Plus, they're great to sit under with a good book, witchy or otherwise.

• • •

TRY THIS: *Find a willow tree and make friends with it. Bring it small gifts, such as pretty rocks, to put at its roots.*

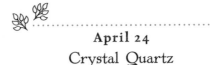

April 24
Crystal Quartz

Clear crystal quartz may be the most commonly used magical stone of them all. Certainly it is associated with many aspects of witchcraft, including the Goddess, the moon, the sun, and the element of spirit.

A simple quartz crystal can be used for virtually any magical task, especially those involving healing, protection, or psychic abilities. It is considered to amplify any spell or magical working. Quartz crystals are often used to top wands or staffs, or they are hung from silver chains to make pendulums. I almost always have a fairly large quartz crystal out on my full moon altar, and I often use them in my energy healing work because of their ability to clear away negativity.

Quartz actually comes in many different colors, including rose quartz (pink) and smoky quartz (gray), as well as stones like amethyst, which is also a form of quartz. But if you can only have one magical stone, my suggestion is that you get a nice piece of crystal quartz.

...

TRY THIS: *Find a piece of quartz or pick out one you already own. Cleanse it under the light of a full moon and use it anytime your magic needs a boost.*

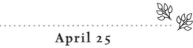

April 25
Spring Breezes

What could be more wonderful than to push open the window after a long, stuffy winter and feel the spring breezes wafting inside, blowing away the energetic cobwebs of a long, cold season? Even if you are fortunate enough to live someplace where you can actually open your windows in December without creating a snowdrift in the middle of your living room, there is nothing as fresh and cleansing as a sweet spring breeze, carrying with it the scent of new growth and possibilities.

Use the spring breezes for more than airing out your home, though. Try connecting with the element of air by focusing your awareness on the breeze.

• • •

TRY THIS: If you can, go outside and feel the winds on your skin. Let them play with your hair and tickle your tongue. Breathe them in (perhaps not too deeply if you're like me and have spring allergies). Do the spring breezes smell different from those of summer or fall? Do they feel different? You don't have to do anything special, just be with the breeze and say thank you to the air for cleansing you of any murky energy leftover from the darker months of winter.

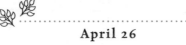

April 26
Sleep

"To sleep, perchance to dream," said Shakespeare in *Hamlet*. In *Macbeth* he said, "Sleep that knits up the ravell'd sleave of care." Smart guy, Shakespeare; he knew that without enough sleep, we would have no chance to process our day through dreaming, nor the opportunity to let our bodies and minds recuperate from the stresses we've put them through.

So what does sleep have to do with being a witch, you might ask? (Go ahead. I know you want to.) The answer is, more than you might think.

Here's the thing—it's hard to be focused on your spiritual life when you are so exhausted from your mundane one that you can hardly find the energy to brush your teeth. Nonetheless, do some kind of nighttime ritual, be it talking to the gods, looking at the moon, or, yes, dreaming.

And yet for many of us, that's the way we live. Yes, me too. I stay up too late trying to get things done and wake up too early because I don't sleep well (and also because of hungry cats).

· · ·

TRY THIS: *Commit to getting more sleep. If you have a hard time falling asleep, try a couple drops of lavender essential oil on a sachet by your pillow or in a pre-bedtime bath. Get off the computer and turn of the TV earlier in the evening, and try a calming meditation instead. Wander outside and see what the moon is doing. Talk to the Goddess about your day. Then go to sleep, perchance to dream.*

April 27
The Internet

The internet is a mixed blessing for witches. On the one hand, it gives us access to tons of information on all things witchy, as well as a way to reach out to others who believe as we do. On the other hand, much of that information is crap, and some people are either unkind, misleading, or out to take your money. Plus, of course, there is the issue we face in all facets of our lives, which is that the internet can be so distracting that it steals time away from other, more important things, like your spiritual practice.

Here are a few suggestions for making your witchy internet use as positive a factor as possible. First: don't believe everything you read online. Double-check anything that seems dubious to you. Beware of absolutes, like the folks who say, "All witches must…" or "You're not a real witch unless you…" There is no one right way, and anyone who tells you so is missing the point of this spiritual path.

Keep away from trolls and nasty people. Most folks who are online are perfectly lovely. There's no reason to put up with the ones who spew negativity. And, occasionally, *turn it off.*

* * *

TRY THIS: *Take a day a week to stay off of the internet. (You can check your email if you need to.) I try to keep my internet use to a minimum on the weekends, and it is amazing how much more I get done. Try it today and see if it works that way for you too.*

April 28
Birthdays

How does that Beatles song go? "They say it's your birthday! Well, it's my birthday too, yeah!" Actually, it *is* my birthday today. No, really, no need to get me presents. Well, if you insist.

This seemed like a good day to talk about birthdays in general, but with a witchy twist, of course. People often have mixed feelings about birthdays. On the one hand, they're a cause for celebration—*yay!* On the other hand, they mean you're another year older—*boo!* Luckily, Pagans don't look at aging exactly the same way most other folks do. Not that we're all jumping up and down, saying, "Oh yippee, I'm getting older," but we also don't automatically think age is a bad thing. Traditionally, witches and Pagans tend to see getting older simply as part of the cycle of life and an opportunity to gather wisdom and perhaps even share it with others.

Besides, there's always cake, right?

· · ·

TRY THIS: *Is this the way you look at having another birthday? If not, maybe it is time to ponder a change in attitude. Getting older isn't a bad thing. It means you've survived another year. Good for you. Hopefully, you are stronger and wiser because of it. Celebrate the birth of you. After all, there is only one of you, and that is something worth celebrating.*

April 29
Flora

Around this time of year, the Romans held a holiday called Floralia in celebration of Flora, the goddess of flowers. A spring goddess, Flora is also associated with sex and love.

Today, make some time to connect with Flora. Put some flowers in your hair (or at least on your altar, if you have one) and dance in your bare feet. Plant some flower seeds in her name, burn a flower-scented incense like rose or lavender, or put on a perfume that makes you feel sexy. Take time to smell the roses—or the carnations or whichever ones are your favorite.

Go for a walk. See if there are flowers growing wild near where you live or if your neighbors have a pretty flower garden you've never noticed before.

• • •

TRY THIS: *Give flowers to someone you love or gift them to yourself. And by all means, if you are lucky enough to have a partner to celebrate the day with, have some erotic fun. I assure you, Flora is one goddess who would definitely approve.*

April 30
Edible Flowers

Most of us think of flowers as strictly decorative, but, surprisingly, some of them are edible as well. The blossoms from chives and garlic, marigolds, roses, and carnations are all edible, and stuffed squash blossoms are a fall treat. Be sure to do your research before eating any flowers since not all of them are tasty and safe.

If you serve flowers as part of a meal, make sure to get them from a place where you know they have not been treated with pesticides (so don't pick them from the side of a road, and you probably won't be able to use a florist either, alas). These days, you can sometimes find edible flowers in the fresh herb section of your grocery store!

You don't need many flowers to add a bit of spice and beauty to a spring dish, and they are particularly suitable for the Beltane feast table or to decorate the edges of a wedding cake.

• • •

TRY THIS: *Make a salad and sprinkle a few edible flowers on top, just to see what you think. Or make a fancy meal for someone you love and top a cheesecake or some other dessert with a few rose petals.*

May 1
Beltane

For me, Beltane always conjures up the image of brightly clad Pagans laughing as they dance around the Maypole. Of course, when my own (fairly small) group celebrates, we usually settle for hanging ribbons on a bush and making wishes on them. But every once in a while we make the trek to join a larger group just for the fun of taking part in a more raucous, joy-filled event.

Mind you, Beltane—or May Day—doesn't have to be over-the-top. In fact, one of the women in my group is uncomfortable with the bawdier, overtly sexual/sensual aspects of the holiday that sometimes manifest in larger celebrations, which is why we often stay home.

It's true that the origins of May Day go back to rural agricultural days when it was primarily a fertility festival, in which the fields were blessed in the hope of abundance in the days to come. In some places this really did mean a symbolic, er, spilling of the seed. But you can make your own Beltane as sedate or sexy as you like (and please don't let anyone pressure you into something you're not comfortable with). I like to think of it as a holiday that celebrates love in all its forms and abundance in the many aspects it can manifest in our lives.

· · ·

TRY THIS: *Find a tree you can hang ribbons from and dance around it. If you can't do that, use a houseplant!*

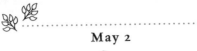

May 2
Sex

Let's face it: a lot of religions have hang-ups about sex and many rules to go with those hang-ups—a bunch of "thou shalt nots," if you will. Luckily for us, most witches and Pagans have a much more relaxed attitude toward sex, sexual orientation, gender identity, and the rest.

This is probably one of the reasons why modern witchcraft tends to attract people who aren't welcomed or accepted in other religions. Casual sex isn't considered a sin as long as all parties involved are willing and capable of giving consent. In fact, "sin" doesn't come into it at all. Really, as with other aspects of life, the only real rule is "an it harm none, do as ye will."

There are plenty of witchy types who are part of the lesbian, gay, bisexual, transgender (LGBT) community or are in non-traditional relationships of one sort or another or don't identify with the basic "male or female" genders that tend to be the norm in our society. I like to think of witches and Pagans as accepting of all the variations of sex and sexuality that the Goddess has created. Love is love is love. (And sex is sex is sex. Hurrah for that!)

• • •

TRY THIS: No, I'm not going to give you specific suggestions for those kinds of activities, although you're welcome to come up with your own. But do take a minute to consider your attitudes about the topic and whether or not you are as open and accepting as you would like to be.

May 3

Welcoming New Babies

First comes love, then comes marriage (or not), and then comes baby in the baby carriage—or so the old rhyme goes, more or less. If you are fortunate enough to have a new baby to welcome to this turn around the wheel—whether yours or someone else's—take a witchy approach to that too.

A Wiccaning is one way to celebrate the birth of a child. Unlike a Christening, which dedicates the child to the church, a Wiccaning is simply a coming together of family and community to bless and greet the infant. It is often led by a high priest or priestess who introduces the child and the parent or parents. The attendees may then take turns presenting the child with gifts. Much like the fairies in the old tales, at one I attended, people gifted the child with good wishes for health, wisdom, talent, etc. It was lovely and moving and filled with great energy, which is a wonderful way to start out a new life.

• • •

TRY THIS: *If you know someone in your witchy community who is having a baby or if you are having one, consider having a Wiccaning as a way of adding a little bit of magic to the new baby's life.*

May 4

What Forms of Love Are in My Life?

On Beltane I wrote about how I felt that the holiday celebrated love in all its forms, not just sexual or romantic love (although I'm a fan of those as well, of course). There is the love for family, the love of a parent for a child, love of friends and companion animals, platonic love, as well as love of community and country. Plus, of course, the love of deity, spirit, nature…

• • •

TRY THIS: *Reflect on all the forms of love in your life. How many ways does it show up in your life, and what do you do to nurture and encourage it? Even if you can't always have love in all the specific forms you desire, there are always ways to give and receive love. What can you do to increase the amount of love in your life?*

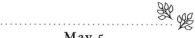

May 5

Saying Thank You at the End of the Day

It is easy to lose track of the good stuff in our lives when we are overwhelmed by bad news, never-ending to-do lists, and cats throwing up hairballs right where you're going to walk. (What? That's just me?)

To make sure I am paying attention to all the positives and not just the negatives—and also to show the gods my appreciation for the gifts they send me, because nobody likes an ingrate—I always say thank you at the end of the day.

This isn't a complicated ritual, although you could certainly light a candle and stand in front of your altar if you are so moved. In fact, I do it in bed, right after I turn out the light. I like ending my day with gratitude, but if you'd rather do this at dinner or at some other time of the day, you certainly could.

I say, "God and Goddess, I greet you at the end of another day and thank you for the many blessings in my life." Then I list whatever I'm grateful for that day, which always includes friends, family, cats, and good food to eat. I finish with, "Watch over me and those that I love."

See? Simple. Feel free to change it to whatever suits you or even to just sit in silence and feel gratitude, so long as you are paying attention to the good stuff.

• • •

TRY THIS: *Say thank you at the end of the day in whichever ritual or form suits you best. Try it for a week and see if this is something you want to add to your daily routine.*

May 6
Agate

Agate is a common stone that can be found in many variations, including blue lace agate, crazy lace agate (I love that name, don't you?), and black, white, red, green, and moss agates. It is often seen as either a tumbled rock or in the form of showier agate slices, which often have tiny crystalline formations on the inside. Unlike some of its fancier cousins, agate is generally inexpensive and therefore within the reach of most witches, no matter their budget.

Magically, its uses are generally for protection, strength, courage, gardening/fertility, and love, although specific forms of agate have their own associations. Blue lace agate, for instance, is associated with peace and calm. I like tree agate, which is white with green markings that look like tree branches or some other growing thing. As you might guess from its "growth" look, it can be used for prosperity, or you can bury a chunk in the garden for increased crops. Plus, of course, it makes a very pretty necklace.

Agate slices are often dyed to make them more dramatic looking (which isn't exactly natural, but I love the way they look, with their bands of different colors). I have a great night-light I picked up at PantheaCon one year that is made from an agate slice. So, crafty witches, think about what cool things you could make using agate.

• • •

TRY THIS: *Find a way to use agate
in a craft project or spell.*

May 7
Witchy Words of Wisdom:
Denise Dumars

The book you hold right now was partially inspired by *Be Blessed: Daily Devotions for Busy Wiccans and Pagans*, written by Denise Dumars.

While *Be Blessed* is not a 365-day book, it is intended to help you live your best witchy life every day, just like this book. I love Dumars's straight-talking, down-to-earth approach. Here's what she had to say about talking to deity:

> The simplest way to approach a deity is to say, "Lady (or Lord), please hear me. I've been having a tough time lately." Then go on with your story. Our gods understand that we sometimes need to get things off our chests, and when there is no one else to talk to, the gods are always there to listen. That in itself should give one a feeling of enormous relief and an island of peace in the eye of the hurricane.

· · ·

TRY THIS: *Do you talk to deity? Take a moment today to light a candle (or at least sit in a quiet room) and talk to the god or goddess of your choice. See if you hear them answer. I suspect you'll feel better just for saying whatever it is you have to say.*

May 8
The Athame

My first witchy tool was an athame. It wasn't fancy or expensive, but, I must confess, using it made me really feel like a witch.

An athame, or witch's knife, is traditionally double-bladed and has a black handle, although I have seen them made of bone, light-colored wood, and even stone. Although it is a knife, an athame is never used for cutting; in fact, it is like an extension of the hand, directing energy or pointing during ritual. A witch's athame is intensely personal and should never be touched without permission.

Some people like to carve runes or other mystical symbols into the handle or sheath, or dangle feathers, charms, or other magical items from it. There are lots of superstitions associated with athames and other witchy tools. When I first started practicing the Craft, I was told that I shouldn't buy my own tools, the athame especially. Instead, they should be gifted by another witch. But I have bought most of mine, and, as far as I can tell, it hasn't hurt anything. On the other hand, I have given away athames when I felt they were no longer the right fit for me and wanted to replace them with something else.

. . .

TRY THIS: *Find yourself the perfect athame or reconsecrate and dedicate the one you have already.*

May 9

Spell for Peace and Calm

Everyone who has no need for more calm and peace, raise your hand. Yeah, that's what I thought. Don't worry—mine isn't raised either. In fact, "find more peace and calm" is on the top of my to-do list. Too bad the list itself is such a source for stress!

Here is a simple spell for peace and calm to do today and any day you need it.

> *I open myself to the energy of the universe*
> *Constantly spinning yet never frantic*
> *And take that peace and calm into myself*
> *With every breath, with every movement*
> *I may be spinning, but still I am calm*
> *And at peace with myself and the universe*

> **TRY THIS:** *If you have the time and space, light a*
> *white candle, say this spell, and sit quietly for a while.*
> *But even if you only have five minutes, you can take a*
> *few deep breaths and say this spell/prayer as you hide*
> *in the bathroom while your kids, your significant other,*
> *and your dog wait impatiently for you to fix dinner.*

May 10
Dreamcatchers

Dreamcatchers originated with the Native American Ojibwe people, although they were later adopted by other tribes and, of course, now by many folks, both Pagan and otherwise. Said to be a gift of the Spider Woman, dreamcatchers are usually a circle traditionally made from willow branches, with a web of string or leather in the middle that has been decorated with beads, feathers, or other sacred items.

Dreamcatchers are intended to catch nightmares. I have a lovely large handcrafted one hanging near my bed. Unlike some of the garish mass-produced ones, this one is made of woven grapevine with brown feathers that dangle underneath, autumn-colored ribbons, some carved wooden beads, and bits of dried moss and leaves. It is truly a work of art. While the woman who made it isn't Native American, she imbues her craft with a great appreciation for its origins, and I think that makes all the difference in its energy.

Dreamcatchers are actually quite easy to make, and my first coven created our own as one of our craft projects. They were simple—just leather thong wrapped around a circular form, with a pentacle woven across the circle in twine and a few pieces of leather hanging down.

• • •

TRY THIS: *Make a dreamcatcher for yourself
using natural materials, and remember to
thank the Spider Woman for her gift.*

May 11
Bast

One of the most common goddess statues found in witchy and Pagan homes is that of an upright cat representing the Egyptian goddess Bast. I have one myself, sitting on my desk. I don't follow the Egyptian pantheon per se, but who doesn't like a goddess of protection and—you guessed it—cats?

Bast is the daughter of Ra, the sun god; maybe that's why cats like to lie in the sun. Her main festivals are celebrated during April and May. These festivals feature music, dancing, and wine…throw in a few cats and you have my kind of party! People bring offerings to lay on the altar in her name.

• • •

TRY THIS: *Why not have your own Bast celebration, either by yourself or with friends? Do the wine and dancing part, of course, but also gather together offerings of cat food, litter, old towels, or anything else that might be useful to taking care of a cat. After the celebration, donate the items to a local animal shelter. And if you happen to have a feline or two in your own home, be sure to include them in the party by giving them treats and extra attention. I'm sure Bast would approve.*

May 12
Cats

If you have read any of my other books (or seen my tarot deck, followed me on Facebook, or read my blog), I'm sure it will not come as any surprise to you that I am a cat person. My black cat, Magic the Cat Queen of the Universe, even co-wrote some of my previous books. Yes, she is the boss of me.

Cats are amazing creatures—agile, independent, smart, and beautiful. They can be as loyal as a dog (although they might be subtler about it) and make deep connections to their person/ people, or they might ignore you unless it is dinnertime. You never know with a cat.

Witches and cats have been associated for centuries. I'm not sure anyone knows why, but certainly cats seem to lend them- selves to the practice of witchcraft in a way that few dogs do, although some witches have canine familiars. Cats can seem mysterious and otherworldly, and if you've ever been on the receiving end of a narrow-eyed cat stare, you too were probably convinced that they knew something they weren't telling.

But cats have a magic that goes far beyond anything to do with spellcraft. A purring cat can ease a troubled spirit and cheer up the saddest heart. Watching kittens play is one of the most joy-filled, amusing activities there is. You don't have to have a cat just because you are a witch, but I highly recommend it.

• • •

TRY THIS: *Spend some time with a cat today. Can you sense a magic about them?*

May 13
I Am at Peace

Most of us live hectic, stress-filled lives, despite all our intentions to cut back and chill out. If we're lucky, we get to occasionally go on vacation, but even those are rarely as peaceful as we'd like them to be.

For the in-between times, when you feel stressed and can't have an actual break, take a few deep breaths and say this affirmation slowly and calmly:

> I *am calm and at peace.* I *am rooted in the ground,*
> *and the gods smile down upon me from the sky.*
> I *am serene like the moon.* I *am at peace.*

• • •

TRY THIS: *Outside of meditation, my most peaceful moments are usually those spent out in nature or curled up in bed with a purring cat. Where can you go today for a moment's peace?*

May 14
Water Element Meditation

Water is all around us, but we rarely think about it unless there is too little or too much of it. This meditation is intended to raise our awareness of our connection to the element of water.

Do this sitting by some form of water—a lake, stream, or indoor fountain—or by an open window if it is raining. If you don't have any of those handy, just close your eyes and use your imagination.

Think about all the different forms that water can take, from the tiniest creek to the deep, vast ocean. Ponds and lakes, all home to myriad creatures. Hear the sounds of water: the soothing pitter-pat of a gentle rain, the fury of a sudden summer storm, the rhythmic music of waves against the shore. Feel the water on your face as you ran outside in the rain as a child and the joy of jumping in puddles. Remember how good it feels to take a shower or soak in a tub. Think about how water sustains our bodies and how good it tastes when you are thirsty.

Concentrate for a moment on how all water is connected. A drop of rain may have originated an ocean away, seeped down into the water table, and ended up in your garden or your glass. The human body is made up of mostly water, and as all water is connected, so are we all connected.

• • •

TRY THIS: *Take a moment to feel the connection to the element of water and to all those who carry it within them. We are the element of water made manifest.*

May 15
Frog and Toad

I have frogs that live in the small pond in my garden, and I often go out on a summer's day and talk to them. They can be quite good conversationalists, although mostly they simply sit and stare at me, as if wondering what on earth I am doing babbling at them when they are trying to concentrate on important matters like catching bugs. (And no, I have never tried to kiss one. If there is an unfortunate prince out there, he will have to stay in his current form.)

Frogs and toads have long been associated with witches. There were many superstitions involving their use as witches' familiars, and more than one poor woman was accused of witchcraft just because she happened to have a toad in her garden. They were also thought to be useful for various spells and folk cures, none of which ended well for the toads and frogs, as you might imagine.

If you ever caught tadpoles as a child or lived someplace where you could watch the lifecycle of a frog, you can understand why they symbolize transformation and change, as they move from a tiny wiggling thing to something caught halfway between fishtail and legs to a hopping creature free to move from water to land and back again.

· · ·

TRY THIS: *If you have toads or frogs where you live,*
go out and make friends with one or at least have a chat.
Otherwise, watch a video online and see how many
variations there are of these magical amphibians.

May 16
The Threefold Law

The threefold law, also known as the law of returns, is a pretty simple concept. Basically, it says that whatever you put out into the universe will come back to you, possibly multiplied three times. This idea didn't originate with Wiccans; you've heard of karma, right?

I believe in this rule, for the most part. I've seen it work. Put out something good and often you will reap good in return. Put out crap and it will come back to bite you. Of course, you can look around and see people who seem to get away with doing horrible things, and other folks who do nothing but good deeds and yet have nothing but suffering.

I can't explain that, but despite these exceptions, I have found that it is still a good practice to go through life putting out what you want to get back. And when it comes to magic, this goes double. Think of it this way: any witch who believes in it would never cast a spell that would cause harm to another because if you inflicted warts on someone, you'd probably end up with a bad rash.

Not everyone believes in the law of returns. Some witches think that they can do whatever they want and there will be no karmic payback. I won't argue, but I'm still not going to wish warts on anyone, just in case.

* * *

TRY THIS: *Think about whether you have done anything recently you wouldn't want coming back to you, threefold or otherwise.*

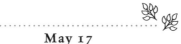

May 17
Volunteer Work

It is relatively easy to connect with the elements of earth, air, fire, and water. They are all around us in many forms. The fifth element, that of spirit, may present a greater challenge, but we're witches; we can do it.

One way you can connect with spirit is by doing things for others. You can help others in whichever way your own spirit moves you, large and small, but I highly recommend doing some form of volunteer work. It is good for others, good for the soul, and a great way to make that elusive connection to spirit.

There are plenty of different ways to volunteer. Most towns have soup kitchens of some sort. Animal shelters almost always need volunteers to clean cages, walk dogs, and socialize the animals so they will be more adoptable. Nursing homes and hospitals sometimes utilize volunteers to read to the ill and elderly. Small things help, too, if you can't commit to something on a regular basis. Join in a cleanup day for your local river or highway. Donate blood. Help an elderly neighbor by mowing their lawn or shoveling the walk. The idea is to turn your focus away from yourself and do something good for someone else (or nature, or whatever). Volunteer work can help with depression and isolation too.

• • •

TRY THIS: *Do some form of volunteer work*
and see if it doesn't make your heart open as
you connect to the element of spirit.

May 18
"Fog"

This has always been one of my favorite poems, maybe because it seems to capture the essence of fog in so few words. (Of course, it probably doesn't hurt that it mentions cats.)

> The fog comes
> on little cat feet.
>
> It sits looking
> over harbor and city
> on silent haunches
> and then moves on.

(Carl Sandburg, 1916)

TRY THIS: *This poem has such vivid imagery. Sit quietly for a minute and reflect on how you see fog.*

May 19
Chanting

I love chanting. The power that comes from a group of witches all raising their voices together in song and sound can be truly amazing.

Chanting is used in almost all religions in one form or another. Have you ever heard Gregorian chants? The sound is beautiful and very moving, even if Christianity isn't your thing. Tibetan Buddhist monks have a different form of chanting that will make the hair on your arms stand up. I especially love it when witches and Pagans chant.

There are many great examples of witchy chants online; I highly recommend listening to some if you can't hear them in person. If you belong to a group and haven't done any chanting because you were afraid it was too complicated or people don't think their voices are good enough, keep in mind that chanting isn't about perfection. It is about raising energy in circle, singing the praises of the God and the Goddess, and sending your vibrations out into the universe.

• • •

TRY THIS: *You don't need to be with others to chant. It is perfectly possible to chant all by yourself. Do it in the shower or in your car or standing in front of your altar. Try some simple ones, like "Water am I, fire am I, earth and air and spirit am I," to start out with. Find examples on YouTube if you don't have any favorite chants already.*

May 20
Gardening

Gardening as a child was the start of my connection with nature and part of what led me to the Pagan path I walk today. I love having my fingers in the dirt, planting tiny seeds and nurturing them until they grow fruit that eventually turns around and nurtures me. Being in the garden is a lot of hard work, but it is also a kind of therapy, helping me to decompress after a long day. It reminds me of what is real and where our food actually comes from and how close to the earth our ancestors were and how they depended on a successful crop to keep from starving. When I clip a bit of aromatic herb, I feel connected to all the witches who went before me and used that same herb for cooking and creating magic.

. . .

TRY THIS: *If you don't have a place to grow your own healthy veggies or beautiful flowers, find out if there is a community garden you can have a plot in. Or do as my friend Ellen does and occasionally help out someone you know who has a garden—they'll probably repay your labor with whatever is ripe at the time. You can also have a couple of herbs growing on a windowsill or under grow lights. The important thing is to occasionally get your fingers into the dirt and make that connection to the earth that is mother to us all.*

May 21
Witches on TV

My first exposure to witches on television came from watching *Bewitched* as a child. I must have practiced twitching my nose in the mirror for hours, trying to duplicate Samantha Stephens's magical powers (with no success, alas). Although I confess, I was perhaps a tad more impressed with her mother, Endora, who tended to be a bit more dramatic with her witchcraft.

Later I watched *Charmed*, in which three sisters with magical powers fought the forces of evil. While not much more realistic than *Bewitched*, at least *Charmed* tried to give some accurate bits and pieces about modern witchcraft. The character of Willow on the show *Buffy the Vampire Slayer* also had her moments.

Witches on TV are entertaining, and they have had both a positive and negative effect on how non-witches perceive the real thing. In some ways television brings awareness of witches to the general public. Certainly *Bewitched* and *Charmed* made witches seem pretty cool, but they also don't have much to do with the reality of modern witchcraft.

• • •

TRY THIS: *Who are your favorite TV witches? Did they influence your practice of the Craft? Go back and watch an episode of an early witchy show and see if your perception of it has changed now that you are a witch.*

May 22
Gemini

Gemini is the sun sign for those who were born between May 22 and June 21. It is an air sign represented by the twins, which signifies an association with the mind and thought. Gemini people tend to be good communicators and adjust well to changes, although they also can be flighty or superficial, easily distracted by the next thing that catches their interest. They are often creative, intelligent, and drawn to the arts in some way. Maybe it is the twin thing, but those involved with Gemini will sometimes feel like they are dealing with two different people, depending on the day.

• • •

TRY THIS: *The sun in Gemini period is a good time to work on anything that requires communication or mental focus. Dig deep and come up with your best new ideas, but make sure you don't get sidetracked by the next shiny thing that comes along.*

May 23
Yellow

Yellow is a bright and cheery color, and nothing perks me up after a long winter like the vivid yellow flowers of spring and early summer. Magically, yellow is associated with spring, the element of air, and therefore the intellect. Of course, it also symbolizes the sun, as anyone who has ever wielded a crayon will know.

Burn a yellow candle when doing magical work for depression, to lift your spirits, or for anything intellectual, such as doing well on a test or increasing the kind of creativity that goes with, say, writing. (Runs off to light a candle.) If you feel down, wear something yellow or buy yourself a bunch of yellow flowers and place them in a vase where you will see them often. I guarantee that they will cheer you up.

I have mostly cream-colored walls (what can I say—I'm boring, and I like cream because I find it soothing) but my mudroom, where people come into my home, is painted a bright and cheery yellow. It not only makes an uplifting first impression, but it also gives me a tiny subconscious boost of energy every morning when I leave the house to face the world.

• • •

TRY THIS: *Do you have anything yellow in your house? If so, sit in front of it (or hold it) and concentrate on how the color makes you feel.*

May 24
Spinach and Strawberry Salad with Fresh Herbs

At this point in the year, only the earliest fruits and veggies are up in the garden. Most of what we've planted is still putting down roots and gathering the energy of the sun before producing anything we can actually eat, but luckily, two of my favorite foods are often available: spinach and strawberries.

These are two things I always grow in my garden, in part because I love them and in part because they are among the produce that tests highest for pesticide use. The slightly bitter taste of the spinach goes surprisingly well with the sweetness of the strawberries, and the bright red berries are a vivid and cheerful contrast against the dark green leaves. To bring in even more spring energy, I like to toss in some fresh herbs.

As always, change things up to suit your tastes, but this is what I use: fresh spinach (if you're buying it from the store, you can easily find organic baby spinach in the salad section), torn into smallish pieces; strawberries (about a fifth of how much spinach you use), sliced; fresh herbs—my favorites for this dish are parsley, chives, and dill; crumbled blue cheese (if you don't like blue cheese, try substituting shredded parmesan); sunflower seeds. Top with a simple vinaigrette.

• • •

TRY THIS: *For a really pretty salad, pile the spinach on the bottom, dot with strawberries, and then sprinkle with the rest of the ingredients. It's like spring on a plate!*

May 25
A Simple Spell with Air

As witches, we are always trying to find ways to connect with the elements. Here's one you might not have thought about that you do all day long: breathing.

Think about it. With every breath, we take the element of air into ourselves, where it literally becomes a part of us, keeping us alive and giving us the energy to move our bodies forward. When we exhale, a tiny bit of our own essence is carried outward into the world through the power of air. How cool is that? And who knew breathing could be so magical?

Why not use that basic act to create a simple spell while connecting with the element of air at the same time?

• • •

TRY THIS: *Sit for a moment and breathe. As you inhale, say a simple spell. It can be one or two lines, such as, "With air divine, prosperity (or health or balance or peace) is mine." As you exhale, visualize your will sending that spell out into the universe. Repeat for a few minutes.*

May 26
"Part Two: Nature"

Emily Dickinson is one of my favorite poets. I love the way she describes Nature as if she were an actual mother. No wonder we call her "Mother Nature."

> Nature, the gentlest mother,
> Impatient of no child,
> The feeblest or the waywardest, —
> Her admonition mild
>
> In forest and the hill
> By traveller is heard,
> Restraining rampant squirrel
> Or too impetuous bird.
>
> How fair her conversation,
> A summer afternoon, —
> Her household, her assembly;
> And when the sun goes down
>
> Her voice among the aisles
> Incites the timid prayer
> Of the minutest cricket,
> The most unworthy flower.
>
> When all the children sleep
> She turns as long away
> As will suffice to light her lamps;
> Then, bending from the sky,

With infinite affection
And infiniter care,
Her golden finger on her lip,
Wills silence everywhere.

(Emily Dickinson, 1896)

. . .

TRY THIS: *Sit quietly and think of Nature as Mother. Can you feel her strength, protection, and love?*

May 27
Raising Pagan Children

A number of my witchy and Pagan friends have raised their children in the Craft, and all of those kids—without exception—have turned out to be pretty amazing.

But it is not an easy thing, even in this day and age, to raise Pagan children. They are almost always forced to keep their religion a secret and not talk about it at school. All the parents I know try to walk a fine line between teaching their children about nature and magic and their Pagan values while still allowing the youngsters to make their own choices about what path they will eventually follow.

As a community we need to support each other, especially those who are raising the next generation of witches. Some rituals are kid-friendly and some aren't, though, so be sure to check before you attend one with which you are unfamiliar.

My coven was very kid-friendly when our members had small children, and in the early days there were often times when nursing babies were passed around the circle so that mom could participate freely. Not all those in the group were raising their kids as Pagans, but those who were usually brought them to sabbats, which were very much a family affair, while we reserved the full moons for more serious, adults-only practice.

• • •

TRY THIS: *If you have children, share something witchy with them today in a way they can understand.*

May 28
Calendula

Calendula is one of my favorite herbs. You might have it in your garden and not even know it since it is commonly known as marigold. The sunny bright yellow and orange flowers grow easily from seed and will often come back year after year without any additional effort on your behalf. Even without their magical or medicinal properties, they are well worth having in your yard just because they are so pretty.

Herbs often have folk names, and my favorite for this plant is "summer's bride." Calendula is truly a summer flower, associated with the sun and fire, and is best gathered right around noon. Magically, it is used in love magic, for general happiness, and to increase psychic abilities. I also like to add it to any herb mix for increased energy and vitality. Medicinally, it is often used in skin ointments because of its soothing nature—ironically opposite to the heat it brings to magical work.

• • •

TRY THIS: *Calendula is an edible flower and makes a vivid and cheerful garnish on any plate. If you're making a dish for the one you love, sprinkle a couple of petals on top just for that added boost of happiness. Place some on your altar as a cheerful offering to the gods.*

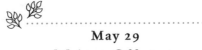

May 29
Making Offerings

Making offerings is a tradition that goes back thousands of years and was a part of many different religions. Those faiths that favored household gods, such as the Romans, and those who set up altars for their ancestors, like Shinto, often made it a regular practice to place offerings on their altars. These might include incense, food, flowers, or candles.

Larger celebrations were known for more showy offerings, such as an entire bull. My guess is that you're not going to try that one at home. But it is a nice idea to place offerings on the altar for the God and the Goddess, especially at the sabbats. Blue Moon Circle often uses fresh flowers or symbols of whichever holiday it is—bread at Lammas, for instance, or chocolate eggs in colorful foil wrappings at Ostara. And yes, in this case it is okay to eat the offerings later.

When one of my cats dies, I usually set up an altar in their honor for a month or two. If you want to do that when you lose someone close to you, it is a nice gesture to place an offering there periodically. Offerings are a kind of gift, so whether you give them to the gods or to the spirits of your beloved dead, it is a way of saying "thank you" and "I'm thinking of you." There is no rule about what to use; simply follow your heart.

* * *

TRY THIS: *Place an offering on your altar or outside under a tree.*

May 30
Memorial Day

Memorial Day is a US federal holiday dedicated to honoring those who died while serving in the military. The roots of the holiday go back as far as the Civil War. People decorate the graves of fallen soldiers, often with flowers or flags. In some areas of the country, families use this day to clear off and clean a family member's grave site and then picnic together afterward.

What does this day have to do with witches and Pagans? Just ask Roberta Stewart, the widow of Sgt. Patrick Stewart, who died in Afghanistan during Desert Storm. In the early 2000s she fought for years (with the help of notable Pagans such as Selena Fox of Circle Sanctuary) for the right to have a pentacle carved on her husband's tombstone—a right which they eventually won for other Pagans as well.

Pagans in the military have a tough time since many of them feel the need to keep their beliefs secret, despite the official acceptance of Wiccan and Paganism as official religions. It is not unusual for witches and Pagans serving in the military to feel isolated, although organizations such as Circle Sanctuary practice active outreach and support, sending books and other supplies to our service people.

* * *

TRY THIS: *On Memorial Day as you remember our honored dead, also do what you can to support those still alive and away from home. Contribute to one of these organizations or find a more personal way to reach out, such as sending a card.*

May 31
Prayer for the Dead

Here is a simple prayer for the dead:

Goddess
Watch over those we have lost
Let them know that they are still in our hearts
And in our minds
That they are not forgotten
That they are loved
That they live on
With every breath we take
And every heartbeat
Always and forever
Loved

· · ·

TRY THIS: *Say this prayer on Memorial Day or any other time you feel the need to remember someone you have lost.*

June 1
Writing Spells

Many people don't feel comfortable writing their own spells. There's nothing wrong with that, and there are plenty of books out there filled with ones you can use. But sometimes there is an issue that needs your own special touch or you may not be in a position to track down just the right one in a book or online, so it is a good idea to know the basics of how to construct your own.

First of all, understand that there is no One Right Way. In truth, as long as you speak from the heart and be honest with yourself and the gods, you will be fine. At its most basic, a spell or ritual is a way to reach out to deity/the universe and ask for help, and everyone is capable of doing that.

Here are the basics: Figure out your goal for the spell. Try to find a way to word your spell that is specific but also leaves the gods leeway to give you what you need in ways that you may not have thought of. Follow up on your spell with action. The gods help those who help themselves.

Don't worry too much about whether or not you are using the proper form or if your spell rhymes. Some of mine do, and some don't. I assure you, the gods don't care about that stuff. Just use the words that feel right to you, and you'll be just fine.

• • •

TRY THIS: *Write a spell today—any spell;*
it doesn't matter what for. Consider it practice.
You might be better at it than you think.

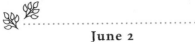

June 2
Juno

As we move into the month of June, known for its weddings, what better goddess to look at than Juno, the Roman goddess of marriage, after whom the month is named? Juno is the queen of the gods, married to Jupiter; their Greek counterparts were Hera and Zeus. She is also known for her protection of women and children, and a festival was held in her honor around this date.

Juno is symbolized by peacocks and their feathers, by extravagant garments (befitting a queen), and by the moon, silver, and figs. If you plan to be married soon and want to ask for her blessing, offer up some fresh figs on the night of the full moon. If you are a woman in need of strength or protection, ask for her help and try to channel some of her indomitable energy. Hang a peacock feather over your altar in her honor if you want her to watch over your married life.

. . .

TRY THIS: *Set up an altar to Juno for the month of June.*

June 3
"A Fairy Song"

I confess, I am a big Shakespeare fan. I don't know if that's because I majored in Theater and was an English teacher or if those things happened in part because I loved Shakespeare. All I know is that I started reading him before I was in high school, and I am still enamored of his writing. In a month when we celebrate the Fair Folk, we have to include a poem by the man who wrote A *Midsummer Night's Dream*.

> Over hill, over dale,
> Thorough bush, thorough brier,
> Over park, over pale,
> Thorough flood, thorough fire,
> I do wander everywhere,
> Swifter than the moon's sphere;
> And I serve the fairy queen,
> To dew her orbs upon the green,
> The cowslips tall her pensioners be:
> In their gold coats spots you see;
> Those be rubies, fairy favours,
> In those freckles live their savours:
> I must go seek some dewdrops here
> And hang a pearl in every cowslip's ear.

(William Shakespeare, 1595)

* * *

TRY THIS: *Go outside and recite this poem for the fairies. See if you can sense a response.*

June 4
Pearls and Mother-of-Pearl

Speaking of pearls, the pearl is the June birthstone. Yes, I know pearls aren't actually stones. Don't blame me; I don't make this stuff up.

Pearls are associated with the moon, no doubt because of their appearance, which can resemble a miniature full moon. They also are used in magic for love, protection, and luck. Don't worry if you can't afford an expensive pearl necklace, since the less expensive freshwater pearls and mother-of-pearl (which I love for its shimmer) have the same basic magical attributes.

In *Cunningham's Encyclopedia of Crystal, Gem & Metal Magic* Scott Cunningham wrote that he didn't like to use pearls because they only could be harvested by killing the oysters that contain them. I'm not sure I find that to be an issue for me (I'll eat an oyster if it is cooked right), but I can see his point about not wanting to do magic with something that came from that kind of source. What do you think?

• • •

TRY THIS: *If you have a pearl necklace or earrings, consecrate them for magical work and wear them on the full moon or when you need to do magic for one of the things they're good for.*

June 5
Handfastings

There is nothing more uplifting than watching two people who love each other join themselves together in a sacred union—unless it is actually taking part in such a ritual. I have been fortunate enough to do that a number of times, officiating at the weddings or handfastings of a number of couples, including one of the members of Blue Moon Circle.

Handfastings are a Pagan wedding ceremony, and they can vary from the extremely simple (a couple and a few of their friends, with very little ritual) to something as ornate as any mundane wedding. They often include specifically Pagan touches such as jumping the broom, binding the wrists together (the "hand fastening" the name comes from), and lighting a unity candle. Sometimes they are also legal weddings and sometimes they aren't.

Some handfastings are made for "as long as we both shall live," just like a more traditional wedding, while others are for "a year and a day." Either way they are a celebration of love, and it doesn't get better than that.

• • •

TRY THIS: If you are planning to get married or know someone who is, see if there are Pagan touches that can be integrated into the ceremony. Over the years the church has adopted many ritual actions, so odds are that no one will even notice.

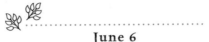

June 6
The Chalice

My circle is blessed to have a special chalice handcrafted by one of the members, who is a potter. She brought it to us before it was fired, and we all helped to draw symbols on the clay. It holds a place of honor on my altar, and we use it for all our rituals.

You don't necessarily need to go to these lengths with your own chalice, but you probably want to pick out something special. After all, the chalice is not only a cup to hold the wine or whatever you use during the cakes and ale part of ritual, it represents the Goddess herself (in the same way the athame represents the God).

One of the most touching and powerful moments I have seen in Wiccan rituals is the symbolic joining of God and Goddess using a chalice and an athame. The high priest (or equivalent) holds the athame over the chalice, held by the high priestess, and they say the following:

HPS: As the chalice is to the female, so the athame is to the male.

HP: Let it be known that no man is greater than a woman...

HPS: Nor woman greater than a man.

HPS: For what one lacks, the other can give.

HP (LOWERING THE ATHAME INTO THE CHALICE) RECITES WITH THE HPS: And when they are joined it is magic in truth—for there is no greater magic in the world than love.

. . .

TRY THIS: *Create your own special chalice by making one yourself, drawing on a glass goblet with special pens, or commissioning one from a local artist.*

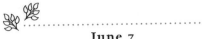

June 7
Unconventional Gifts

If you attend a handfasting (or any other celebration featuring primarily witches and Pagan folk), it is likely to be a somewhat unconventional gathering. So consider giving an unconventional gift.

Obviously, you want the gift to suit the occasion and the recipient, but this is a great opportunity to think outside the box. If the occasion is a handfasting, perhaps the gift is a new broom or a basket full of magical supplies that the couple can use together. Maybe matching chalices and a bottle of locally produced mead? For a new couple with a house or a new baby, gift a tree or bush that will grow along with the one to whom it is given.

Gifts that symbolize nature in some way (beeswax candles, seeds, handcrafted items) or witchy-themed goodies can be as fun to receive as they are to give. If you are giving to a couple who are both Pagans, items for the home or altar are always welcome.

If the recipient is a foodie and a witch, what about a gift basket full of ingredients for a magical dish? For the crafty witch, gather all the components necessary to create a magical craft project. The point is, you don't have to settle for something mundane.

• • •

TRY THIS: *For your next special occasion, come up with a gift that is as special and delightful as the person it is for. Find some way to make it magical!*

June 8
Gratitude No. 3:
A List of Six Things

Here we are, almost halfway through the year already. How the heck did that happen? Has it been a good year so far? Are you achieving what you'd hoped to or do you struggle to make a dent in your list of goals?

Either way, it is always a good idea to pause and count your blessings, no matter how many challenges you face. Since we're in the sixth month, your exercise in gratitude is to come up with six things you are grateful for this year.

Here's my list so far: family, friends, cats, a job I love (most days), the ability to be creative, and the strength to keep moving forward.

See, that wasn't so hard, was it? Now, what are *you* grateful for?

• • •

TRY THIS: *If you really want to challenge yourself, make a new list every day this month, and don't duplicate—find six additional things to add every day. You might be surprised to discover just how much there is to be grateful for in your life.*

June 9
Strawberry Celebration

I love to celebrate special occasions with special food, but I don't always have time to create an elaborate dish. If you're going to have a party, a post-ritual feast, or you need to bring something to contribute to a handfasting, an easy summer dessert that everyone loves is this variation on strawberry shortcake.

All you need are some fresh strawberries (organic is best), an angel food cake (or any other kind of cake you feel like making), and some homemade whipped cream. Make the whipped cream (seriously, this is so easy: all you need is some whipping cream and an electric beater, and you beat the cream until it is frothy). Add a bit of sugar or chocolate if you like, or add a drop of peppermint oil if you want to give it a touch of prosperity magic.

Slice the cake in half the long way, so you have a bottom half and a top half. Fill the middle with the strawberries and whipped cream, then top with more of both.

• • •

TRY THIS: *For a special touch, add mint leaves or edible flowers or a sprinkle of shaved chocolate.*

June 10
Air Element Meditation

The element of air is all around us, but because it is invisible it is easy to ignore. Yet it is absolutely vital (try breathing without it) and can be as powerful as a hurricane. Here is a simple meditation to help you connect with the element.

Sit where it is quiet. If possible, do this meditation outside or near an open window where you can feel the breeze. If you want, light a yellow candle or burn some sweet-smelling incense.

Close your eyes. Feel the air on your skin. Its presence is subtle, but it is always there. Take a deep breath. Feel the air entering your body, bringing with it oxygen to energize you and keep you alive. Blow it back out slowly, feeling the air you create with your breath.

Think of the forms that air can take: a gentle breeze, a gusty wind that cools you down when it is hot, the power of tornados and hurricanes that can topple buildings and pull down trees. Think about the mutability of air and how unpredictable it can be. Ponder the way air carries smells with it—good smells, like cooking or freshly mown grass; less appetizing smells, like skunk or garbage—and yet, it also takes air to carry those smells away again.

Air is the quietest element, as subtle as a feather, but without it none of the other elements matter.

* * *

TRY THIS: *Take a moment to breathe in and out, making the air a part of your own body, and thank it for always being there for you.*

June 11
Bees

We have a bee crisis. Huge populations of bees are dying off, almost certainly because of humans using pesticides.

If a pesky bee and its friends have ever bothered you at a picnic, you may not think this crisis is a big deal—you might even be grateful. But bees are truly magical creatures, and they provide a vital service in the chain of life. Bees are pollinators. When they collect nectar (the basis of honey) from plants, they also incidentally transfer pollen (a fine powder that male plants make) to female flowers, which allows those plants to reproduce. Without bees, we will not only lose the beautiful flowers they buzz around, we could lose most of our food. Yikes.

Bees and the honey they make have always been used in magical work. They symbolize prosperity, fertility, sexuality, healing, love, happiness, energy, wisdom, and purification. Honey not only tastes sweet, but it can be used to heal wounds and, of course, mead can be made from it. That's a lot of miracles from one little bee!

· · ·

TRY THIS: *The next time you see a bee hovering around your picnic, set aside a bit of something for it and say thank you. Plant flowers and herbs they like to attract them to your house.*

June 12
The Drum

You may not think of drums as a magical tool, but shamans and other spirit workers have used them since the dawn of humanity. They mimic the sound of the human heartbeat and promote a light trance state during ritual. They also bring people together.

Blue Moon Circle sometimes does drumming in ritual—often enough that I have an entire collection of drums, all handmade by local craftspeople. We drum to build energy into a spell and then send it out into the universe. I've also taken part in some large drum circles, and they can be quite remarkable.

Don't worry about being "good" at it or whether or not you can keep the rhythm. For this kind of drumming, those things just don't matter. And you don't have to be part of a group to drum either.

• • •

TRY THIS: *Take a drum outside under the full moon and let your heart beat in time with the Goddess's. Inside works, too, if you can't go out.*

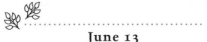

June 13
Gerald Gardner

Today is the birthday of Gerald Gardner, arguably the father of modern witchcraft. While there is much debate about the validity of some of his claims, there is no question that Gardner was pivotal in the creation of what we now call Wicca. In 1951 England finally repealed their laws against witchcraft. Gardner formed his own coven, followed by the publication of his book *Witchcraft Today*, in 1954.

Gardner knew and was influenced by such famous figures as Margaret Murray (author of *The Witch-Cult in Western Europe*) and Aleister Crowley. He was the founder of Gardnerian witchcraft, which formed the basis of much of the organized Wiccan covens that followed soon after.

Things have changed a lot since Gardner's days. Many of us have chosen paths that are very different from the hierarchical mystical system he used (although some still use it and variations on it). But whatever path we walk, those first stones were laid by him, so it is with great respect and appreciation that we celebrate his birthday today.

· · ·

TRY THIS: *Light a candle on your altar and wish Gerald Gardner a happy birthday. If you're not familiar with him or his work, go read up about him.*

June 14
Fairies

These days when we talk about fairies, people are likely to envision cute little winged creatures flitting about and sipping nectar from flowers. Um, no. Not really.

This version of the Fair Folk, or fae, is a relatively new development, and it bears very little relationship to the legends that came out of the Old World. There, fairies could range from the mildly mischievous (who could be placated with gifts and offerings) to the downright dangerous (who stole human children and left changelings in their places). They were powerful and arrogant and nothing to be trifled with. Many stories told of people who visited the fairy world and came back forever changed…if they came back at all.

The other way of looking at fairies is as elemental beings, entities made of and part of the natural world. Mostly unseen, they may be all around us, especially in wooded places. It is said that Midsummer, when the veil between the worlds is thin, is the day when the fairies are most likely to be present.

· · ·

TRY THIS: *On Midsummer put out little gifts of flowers or shiny stones and share your cakes and ale—just in case.*

June 15
Fairy Tea Party

If you have kids—or friends who are young at heart—this is the perfect time of year to have a fairy tea party. (Or, if you are all adults, a fairy wine party. I won't judge.)

The gathering is meant to be for lighthearted fun, but it is also a way to express your appreciation for the fairy folk. You have to dress up, of course. If you have kids, craft some simple fairy wings out of inexpensive materials such as coat hangers, stockings or tissue paper, ribbons, and glitter. Everyone should wear something floaty and colorful. If you really want to get into the spirit of things, a little temporary hair color (or a few ribbons) can make things even more festive. Weave some flower crowns. Shiny jewelry would be lovely too.

If at all possible, hold your tea party someplace where it feels like the fairies might like to come—a garden or backyard, or a forest or a park. But if all you have available is your living room, it is okay to pretend.

. . .

TRY THIS: *Set out a tea party feast of tiny sandwiches and yummy cookies. Be sure to have a few flowers for your table or picnic cloth. If you have small plates and cups, use those. For a grown-up version, get fancy with goblets and the good china (or the really good paper plates). Set aside some of your goodies for the fairies since you are having this party in their honor.*

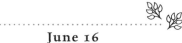

June 16

Camping

You might not think of camping as a particularly witchy activity, but what could be more Pagan than getting back to nature?

My family went camping most summers when I was a kid. We often went to Cape Cod, which meant we not only got to camp out, we got to spend time at the ocean too. Heaven!

Of course, camping itself wasn't always heaven. It usually rained, and cooking over an open fire could be a challenge, and there were bugs. But crisp, damp mornings still bring back memories of the times I spent sleeping under the stars, waking up to find the dew still wet on the outside of the tent, smelling the wood smoke, and telling tales around the fire.

If you have children, I highly recommend taking them camping. Leave the electronic gizmos at home (or at least in the car) and spend time together rediscovering nature. Go for walks in the woods and see who can spot the most birds, or go to the ocean and play in the waves. If you don't have children, well, go camping anyway. If you're not feeling up to roughing it, rent a cabin or stay in a campsite that has actual flush toilets.

But when you're sitting around the campfire, looking up at the stars, you'll realize why sometimes it is a good idea to get out of the house and back to nature.

• • •

TRY THIS: *You don't have to take a major trip to go camping. Find someplace nearby or use your own backyard. Don't forget to roast marshmallows.*

June 17
Witchy Words of Wisdom:
Starhawk

Today is the birthday of Miriam Simos, more commonly known as Starhawk. She is one of the true mothers of modern witchcraft, and her book *The Spiral Dance* has shaped the lives and paths of uncounted witches. Here is what she has to say about the essence of magic.

> Magic, the art of sensing and shaping the subtle, unseen forces that flow through the world, of awakening deeper levels of consciousness beyond the rational, is an element common to all traditions of witchcraft. Craft rituals are magical rites: they stimulate an awareness of the hidden side of reality and awaken long-forgotten powers of the human mind.

Happy birthday, Starhawk!

• • •

TRY THIS: *If you haven't read her book yet, search out a copy today!*

June 18
Sacred Springs and Wells

If you travel through Europe, you will discover that almost every country has certain places that are considered to be sacred or particularly blessed. Many of these locations are springs and wells (and occasionally other forms of water) that are said to be imbued with special healing powers or other magical attributes.

Someday I would love to make a pilgrimage to these places, which can be far off the beaten path or right in the middle of a town. I can't think of any better way to connect with the element of water than through a sacred spring or well.

If, however, you are unable to take such a trip, create your own sacred water at home.

• • •

TRY THIS: *Start with water as pure as you can get it—from a spring or well near you, if you have one, or a fast-running stream or creek, or collect some rainwater. Put it in a clear container or an open bowl and leave it out under the full moon for three nights. (A windowsill will do if you can't leave it outside.) Each night ask the Goddess to bless the water, and when you're done, put it into a special container so you can use it later in rituals.*

June 19
Apollo

For being one of the Greek gods, Apollo is incredibly well-rounded. He isn't just the god of one thing, like, say, the under-world. Oh, no. This guy gets around. In a chariot, for instance, which he uses to pull the sun across the sky. Apollo is a sun god and a god of light, but he is also a god of music (he played a harp-like instrument called the lyre), poetry, archery, and healing. He is associated with truth and prophecy and was the patron god of the Delphic Oracle, where people went to ask questions of his priestess, Pythia.

Call on Apollo if you need help with healing or if you plan to do some form of divination, like reading the tarot cards or runes. If you do invoke him, make sure to do so during the day, preferably under the sun, since it is then that he is at the height of his powers.

• • •

TRY THIS: *Create an altar in Apollo's honor or simply sit outside under the noonday sun and bask in his glory.*

June 20
Spell for Healing

We can all use a little healing from time to time, whether physical, emotional, or spiritual. Here is a simple spell to use any time you feel the need:

> Gods of healing, passion, and fire
> Hear my plea, grant my desire
> Heal my body, my soul, and my heart
> And on this day let healing start

• • •

TRY THIS: *Make an offering to Apollo or some other healing god, and/or light a blue candle before reciting this spell. When calling on Apollo, do the spell at noon or when the sun is shining, if you can.*

June 21
Summer Solstice

I love the summer solstice so much, I wrote a whole book about it. But seriously, what's not to like? Midsummer is a holiday that celebrates all that is glorious about the summer. It is the longest day of the year, and the land is filled with energy and vitality. As witches, we can tap in to that energy and use it to fuel our own plans and desires. If you planted seeds (metaphorical or otherwise) in the spring, they should be coming to fruition by now. And if they need a little push, this is the perfect time to embrace the exuberant growth around us.

The summer solstice is also associated with fairies (you remember Shakespeare's play A *Midsummer Night's Dream*, right?), so put out some gifts for them or honor them in your ritual. I always like to celebrate this holiday with a mixture of serious magic and playful enjoyment. After all, it's summer, and the warmth and light will be gone before you know it. You definitely want to be outside if you can.

* * *

TRY THIS: *Have a feast or a picnic, drink some mead or fresh fruit juice, and dance in the noontime sun. Midsummer is a perfect time to celebrate with your Pagan-friendly but non-witchy friends, since the Summer Solstice is a universal concept.*

June 22
Cancer

Cancer, the sign of the crab, is the sun sign that rules from June 22 to July 22. As you might guess from the crab, Cancer is a water sign, and, like water, Cancers can be both dynamic and changeable.

Like other water signs, Cancers are often emotional, intuitive, and sensitive. They may seem to have a hard shell on the outside, but underneath they are probably more vulnerable than they would like to appear. When they're upset they tend to retreat into a safe home environment.

• • •

TRY THIS: *During this period, whether or not you're a Cancer, focus on your own home and watch out for out-of-control emotions that might color your perceptions.*

June 23
I Am Deserving of Healing

Many of us struggle with issues of self-worth, and this can negatively affect our healing work, both magical and mundane. It is a sad truth that if we don't feel worthy of being healed and feeling better, no matter what we try, it may not be as effective as it should be. It is as though a part of us fights to remain sick or in pain because we don't think we deserve to be okay.

Here is a simple affirmation to help you replace some of those negative feelings with more positive ones:

> I am a child of the Goddess, and I am deserving of being healed.

. . .

TRY THIS: *Repeat this a few times a day if you struggle with any form of health problem. If you're really struggling, say it while standing in front of a mirror, tell it to yourself firmly, and really mean it. You can say "the universe" if you don't follow the Goddess.*

June 24
Is My Life in Full Bloom?

As we revel in the summer sunlight, plants in bloom surround us. Showy roses, delicate daisies, beans climbing trellises in the garden…everything is growing and hitting its peak.

At this time of year, any plans you made should be showing their own fruit. When the earth's energy is at its height, we should all be at our own energetic best.

Are you?

Ask yourself if your life is unfolding the way you want it to and if your time and energy are going toward growing those things that are truly important to you. If so, pat yourself on the back, and don't forget to leave some time for relaxing. But if not, ask yourself what you can change to make your life come into full bloom.

· · ·

> **TRY THIS:** *Check back in on any goals you wrote down at the beginning of the year. Are those still the things you want? If not, it is okay to move on to other ones. If you haven't made as much progress as you'd like—life does tend to get in the way of such things—do some magic to work on whatever it is you need. It is okay to ask for help—from the gods or your friends—or break down your goals into smaller, more easily attainable pieces if you find them overwhelming. Remember that as a witch, you have all kinds of tools at your disposal!*

June 25
Blowing Bubbles

You might not think about blowing bubbles in conjunction with sacred ritual, but I'm going to change your mind on that. I first did this years ago when one of the women in Blue Moon Circle had two young children who came to ritual most of the time. The kids did a fabulous job of participating, and I tried to make it easier by incorporating elements that the kids would enjoy. Of course, these also had to be things that the adult members of the group would enjoy as well, and that made sense with the ritual itself.

One summer solstice I got the idea of using bubbles. Rather than wrestle with large, messy containers where the wands always fell inside, one of the craftier ladies in the group came across a pack of small bubble vials that were intended for use at weddings.

As an element of both air and water combined, we used the bubbles to carry our wishes out into the universe and up to the gods. It worked so well, we kept using it on occasion for outside rituals, long after the kids stopped coming. The bubbles add a fun and playful note, which is particularly appropriate at summer solstice but works at other times of year as well. Reverence and mirth, after all—and, apparently, bubbles.

• • •

TRY THIS: *Find some way to integrate blowing bubbles into your next spell or ritual, or just blow some bubbles today to send your wishes out into the world.*

June 26
Viking Boats

Don't worry, I'm not suggesting that you build a boat—at least, not a full-sized one. (You don't have to wear the Viking helmet either, unless you really want to.)

But in some cultures it was traditional to celebrate the Midsummer holiday by making small boats. These boats were then filled with offerings and floated away on a body of water. It is easy enough to create a simple boat made out of paper (try following the instructions at wikihow.com/Make-a-Paper-Boat). Before you fold up the paper, write wishes or things you want to let go of on it. To make it more waterproof, so it will float longer, use waxed paper found at art stores or color the outside completely with a crayon (maybe creating a lovely piece of art while you do it).

You can also make boats from Popsicle sticks or large leaves.

• • •

TRY THIS: If you have a river, lake, or ocean where you can send your boat sailing away, put a few lightweight offerings inside, such as flowers, and have it carry your wishes away. If you have things you want to get rid of (and it is safe to do so), put the boat on the water and set fire to it, Viking style.

June 27
Witchy Words of Wisdom: Scott Cunningham

Today is the birthday of Scott Cunningham, arguably one of the most influential Wiccans of our time. Many of us started our journeys by reading his book *Wicca: A Guide for the Solitary Practitioner*, and it is still one of the books I recommend often to those just beginning to walk the magical path. So let's celebrate Cunningham's birthday with one of my favorite quotes from that book:

> Wicca is a religion that utilizes magic. This is one of its most appealing and unique features. Religious magic? This isn't as strange as it might seem. Catholic priests use "magic" to transform a piece of bread into the body of a long-deceased "savior." Prayer—a common tool to many religions—is simply a form of concentration and communication with Deity. If the concentration is extended, energies are sent out with the thoughts that may in time make the prayer come true. Prayer is a form of religious magic.
>
> Magic is the practice of moving natural (although little-understood) energies to effect needed change. In Wicca, magic is used as a tool to sanctify ritual areas, to improve ourselves and the world in which we live.

• • •

TRY THIS: *Reread your favorite passages from* Wicca: A Guide for the Solitary Practitioner *or find another Scott Cunningham book to add to your witchy collection.*

June 28
Maladaptive Inertia

We all know what inertia is. Basically, it is a law of physics that says that a body at rest is most likely to stay at rest or to continue in a straight line unless acted on by an outside force. Let's face it: we all have moments of inertia. You know, those mornings when you keep hitting the snooze button, or the evenings when you watch one more hour of television instead of doing the dishes.

But you've probably never heard the term "maladaptive inertia." That's because I made it up. (Snicker.) I sometimes tell people I have a serious case of maladaptive inertia, by which I mean the kind of inertia that really works against my own benefit.

We all fight the inclination to sit still when we should be moving, or avoid making the big shifts that would create positive changes in the direction of our lives. But I call it "maladaptive" for a reason. Occasionally indulging in an extra couple of pages of reading isn't a bad thing, but consistent lack of forward movement can be incredibly destructive. If you struggle with maladaptive inertia, it is time to fight back. Get up and move. Because a body in motion is more likely to stay in motion, and that will get a lot more done!

• • •

TRY THIS: *Get up and do something constructive, even if you don't feel like it. Then reward yourself with some small treat. If you're really stuck, do some magical work for energy or productivity.*

June 29
Ginger

Ginger is a "hot" herb and is therefore associated with the element of fire. It is used to "fire up" or energize magical work of all kinds, although it is specifically associated with love and prosperity spells and those done for success and power. I include it in healing work as well, since the herb itself has such great healing properties.

You can grow your own ginger by planting a section in a pot. Most of us probably won't bother with that, so buy it as a whole root, in a powdered form, or as an essential oil. Less commonly you can find ginger incense, but make sure it contains actual ginger and not just the artificial scent.

Ginger lends itself well to kitchen witchery, since it is so easy to cook with. And you can make either ginger tea or ginger soda (using the fresh root or ginger syrup) to use as the "ale" part of your cakes and ale in ritual. One of our Blue Moon Circle members regularly makes miniature ginger cookies for our cakes and stamps a pentacle sign into them before she bakes them. It might or might not boost the magic we've just done, but they sure taste delicious!

· · ·

TRY THIS: *Do some magic with ginger today.*
Integrate it into some kitchen alchemy or eat or
drink it to connect with its heat and energy.

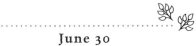

June 30
Red

Red is the color associated with the element of fire and with passion and energy and sex. Did I mention it is one of my favorite colors?

Magically, it is used for all these things, as well as protective magic. One of my preferred stones to use for protection work is red jasper, and I put a tumbled piece in some of the protection charm bags I make. Red is often used in love magic as well, especially when it is directed at the sexual, passionate kind of love, as opposed to the softer, romantic type, where pink is often used instead. Of course, if you want both, you can use candles of both colors and perhaps a rose of each hue.

On the days I feel like I need a boost of energy, I often wear a red shirt and some carnelian jewelry to go with it. (If things are really urgent, I might put on some red underwear as well. Underwear is a great way to sneak the color you need into your day.)

In some covens witches would wear cords of various colors. When Blue Moon Circle did a ritual years ago to formalize our commitment to each other, we each braided sections of red yarn and then tied them together to symbolize our unity. That red cord is tucked away in a special glass box in my magical cupboard, and the energy in it still resonates today.

• • •

TRY THIS: *Find something red and sit with it for a few minutes. Meditate on its color and see how it makes you feel. What does red symbolize for you?*

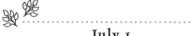

July 1
Herbs

You might not think of herbs as a tool, but I consider them to be one of the most powerful implements in my witchy toolbox. I use herbs all the time: in kitchen alchemy, charm bags, magical baths, teas, oils, and room sprays. In fact, if you think about it, herbs may be one of the most versatile of all the tools we witches use.

They come in so many different and useful forms, too. Fresh herbs, of course, and dried; tinctures, incense, essential oils. Herbs are added to food and drunk as teas. You can find lots of great books on the witchy use of herbs. They were even mentioned in Shakespeare. You remember that wonderful scene with the three witches, in which they recited an incantation that included eye of newt and adder's tongue? Those were folk names for herbs. Adder's tongue was a common name for the dogtooth violet, and eye of newt was probably daylily.

Witchcraft recipes are often full of exotic herbs, almost as rare as eye of newt. You don't need to use those when there are so many fabulous herbs that have multiple uses—medicinal, culinary, and magical—and can be found as close as the nearest field or your neighborhood grocery store.

• • •

TRY THIS: *Some of my favorites include rosemary, sage, peppermint, lemon balm, lavender, and dill. Think about your favorite herbs and how you use them. What other ways could you integrate herbs into your magic? Try one today.*

July 2
"It Is the Hour"

I love this poem's perfect description of the moment of twilight, when everything is magical.

It is the hour when from the boughs
The nightingale's high note is heard;
It is the hour—when lover's vows
Seem sweet in every whisper'd word;
And gentle winds and waters near,
Make music to the lonely ear.
Each flower the dews have lightly wet,
And in the sky the stars are met,
And on the wave is deeper blue,
And on the leaf a browner hue,
And in the Heaven that clear obscure
So softly dark, and darkly pure,
That follows the decline of day
As twilight melts beneath the moon away.

(Lord Byron, 1815)

TRY THIS: *Tonight, if you can, steal away at twilight and read this one aloud.*

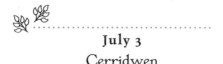

July 3
Cerridwen

One of the more powerful of the Celtic goddesses, Cerridwen is a crone goddess, keeper of the cauldron of knowledge and inspiration. She is also associated with prophecy, the moon, motherhood, and the underworld, as well as the herbs that go into her potions. Her magic cauldron symbolizes rebirth and transformation, which makes her a good goddess to call on when your life is in need of drastic change.

Cerridwen has three children, including the famous poet Taliesin, considered to be the greatest of all Welsh poets. Little wonder she is the patron goddess of all those involved in the creative arts, especially writers and poets.

• • •

TRY THIS: *If you have a miniature cauldron on your altar, as I do, call on Cerridwen when you use it in magic for change, wisdom, or a creative boost. Don't be surprised if you don't get exactly what you expected.*

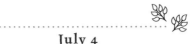

July 4
Independence Day

Independence Day is a holiday observed in the United States on the Fourth of July. It celebrates the early Americans declaring their independence from England, who once ruled over what started out as their colonies. To me, it symbolizes not so much that particular occasion but any and all battles for freedom.

There are a lot of different ways of being under the power of someone or something. Poverty makes us feel helpless and hopeless. The dynamics in some relationships place one person at the mercy of another. Jobs we hate can drain our energy. Drugs and alcohol and our own fears can enslave us and keep us from moving forward in positive ways.

The colonists, when they rose up against what they perceived to be the oppressive tyrannies of King George, did not do so on their own. They banded together and fought hard, making incredible sacrifices for what they believed in.

On this Independence Day, give some thought to your own life. Are you as independent as you want to be or is there something or someone (including yourself) standing in the way of you achieving your own freedom? Who can you work with to become independent of whatever is holding you back?

• • •

TRY THIS: *Think about this question:*
Are you free? And if you're not, what can you do
to declare your own day of independence?

July 5
I Am Strong and Self-Reliant

Here is a simple affirmation to help you become your best, strongest, most independent self.

I am strong and self-reliant. Nothing and no one can stand in the way of my achieving my dreams.

* * *

TRY THIS: *Repeat this affirmation as needed, especially in situations where you need to be strong and you can feel yourself wavering.*

July 6
Witchy Words of Wisdom:
Ann Moura

There are many different approaches to witchcraft, and some of those paths have acknowledged experts whose names are practically synonymous with that particular path. When it comes to green witchcraft, which focuses primarily on our connection to the earth and growing things, that name is Ann Moura. Her book *Green Witchcraft: Folk Magic, Fairy Lore & Herb Craft* is considered a classic in the field. It was originally published in 1996, and the copy I own was from the fifteenth printing, back in 2005. I strongly recommend you read the whole book, but in the meanwhile, here is just a little taste of her wisdom:

> The Green element of the Craft is basically an herbal one, and herbs are used both for medicinal and magical purposes…The very contact with Mother Earth and green growing things is a source of renewal of energy and power for any witch.
>
> The central Green element of all Craft expression is the Goddess as undying, threefold, and associated with the earth, the moon, and the living (sacred) waters, and the God as undying, threefold, and associated with the earth, the sun, and the sky. As God of grain and solar phases, he is also the willing sacrifice who "dies" and is "reborn" in the Goddess in the yearly cycle of the seasons.

• • •

TRY THIS: *With summer and its abundance all around us, think about ways to incorporate plants, herbs, and other natural elements into your witchy practice.*

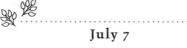

July 7
Oceans

I really love the ocean. Just being by the shore makes me happy. My home is nowhere near one, so I have to satisfy my craving with the occasional trip. When I visit my parents in San Diego, I always spend some time at the ocean, even if it is in February. I know they think I'm crazy when I wade into the water when it is only sixty degrees, but I'm not going to be near the ocean without sticking my feet in it. There may also be some childlike jumping up and down for joy.

What is it about the ocean that pulls at us so? Maybe it is that the saltwater in the seas calls to the water in our own body, which contains salt in the amount (a little under 1 percent) that it is believed was in the ocean at the time humans evolved. Maybe it is the way it ebbs and flows like so much else in our lives, always changing and sometimes bringing us treasures when we least expect it. Mostly, I think there is just something primal about our connection to the ocean—something unexplainable and yet deeply rooted in many of us that calls us back to the sea from time to time. This is the power of the element of water. It calls to our souls in the voices of the whales and the dolphins, bidding us to come home.

• • •

TRY THIS: *If you can, stick your feet in the ocean. If you can't, connect the best you can by watching a video of it or looking at a photo or listening to whale song.*

July 8
Vacation

Vacations are important to the spirit, I think. We all need to take a break from our lives sometimes and decompress—hit pause, as it were. Like many of you, it is hard for me to find the time, money, and energy to go away on vacation. There is always something that seems more important, but taking a break *is* important. If you don't feed your spirit, eventually all that running, running, running will cause you to run out of steam.

Vacation means different things to different people. If you have children, you may want to take them to someplace like Disney World, but also consider spending a vacation somewhere quieter, where you can really connect as a family. Some of my best memories as a child are from family vacations where we sat around a campfire telling stories and roasting marshmallows for s'mores.

If you are part of a couple, you may want to go someplace romantic where you can focus on the love and passion you feel for each other without the distractions of everyday life. You may want to take an adventure and travel to a place you have never been before. If you really need a break, consider going to a yoga retreat or some other spiritual destination.

> **TRY THIS:** *Even if you can't afford to go away, set aside a couple of days for a "staycation." Stay in the comfort of your own home but take it easy, have fun, and relax, and maybe even do a ritual or two.*

July 9
Sacred Sites

For witches and Pagans, one way to make a vacation extra special is to journey to a sacred site. There are many spiritual destinations around the world—Stonehenge in England, Machu Picchu in Peru, and the Great Pyramids in Egypt—and plenty of other places in the UK and Europe that provide a focal point for a once-in-a-lifetime vacation.

If you can't manage that, though, you might be surprised to find that there is likely some kind of sacred site closer to home. Here in the United States we have our own "Stonehenge," in Salem, New Hampshire. If you're heading to the western states, visit the Bighorn Medicine Wheel in Lovell, Wyoming, or Sedona, Arizona. Both are known for their amazing spiritual energy. There is also the Serpent Mound in Peebles, Ohio, where an ancient serpent effigy marks the direction of sunset on the summer solstice.

Of course, what constitutes a sacred site may mean different things to different people. Just getting back to nature—whether it is a visit to the ocean or a few days spent deep in the woods— can be a sacred journey if that is the way you view it.

• • •

TRY THIS: *Make a pilgrimage to a sacred site near you. If you can't go now, start researching possibilities.*

July 10
The Sun

One of the simplest ways to connect with the element of fire may be right outside your door. After all, the sun is actually a big ball of fire, the essence of the element. (Be careful how you worship it, though, since you can easily get burned.)

The sun supports all life on the planet, just as earth does. Without it, there would be no food. It also cheers us up, gives us warmth and light, and provides much-needed vitamin D that we absorb through our skin like the gift that it is.

More than that, though, the energy of the sun, viewed magically, is a source for power and inspiration. We observe its waxing and waning much as we do the moon (for instance, at the solstices and equinoxes), and there are many gods associated specifically with the sun.

• • •

TRY THIS: *For a simple exercise to connect with the element of fire, go outside on a sunny day. Stand with your eyes closed and feel the warmth on your skin. See the light through your closed lids. Let the warmth and light enfold you like a hug, and send your gratitude out into the sun above. Find a sun god you connect with and open yourself up to his presence.*

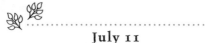

July 11

Where Would You Go if
You Could Go Anywhere?

Where *would* you go if you could go anywhere?

Some people have destinations they dream about for years: Greece or Scotland or Hawaii. If you have someplace you long to go, what are you doing to work toward getting there? If not, maybe it is time to start dreaming

• • •

TRY THIS: *Find more information or even inspiration*
on places to go by browsing the travel shelves of the library
or a bookstore or looking online. Be open to the possibilities.
Perhaps do some dreamwork to see what shows up.

July 12
Fireflies

If you want to see something truly magical, find a place where the fireflies gather and spend a few minutes there at dusk on a summer's night. Suddenly, at twilight, the sky will fill with the glow of dozens of tiny lights flickering on and off. These are the beetles known as fireflies. Science says something called "bioluminescence" causes their glow, but if you have seen them, I think you'll agree that it is truly magical.

Many years ago, a boyfriend took me to a secret place he had never shown anyone else. We drove to the end of a quiet dirt road, where we walked to a small break in the shrubbery that opened into a large, otherwise enclosed field. And inside that field was a sight I have never forgotten: hundreds and hundreds of fireflies dancing their mating dance under the moonlit sky, completely oblivious to the presence of two insignificant humans.

I sincerely hope that someday you too get to see something that utterly enchanting. But even a couple of fireflies are enough to remind us that life is amazing, mysterious, and filled with magic that has nothing to do with rituals or spells and everything to do with nature.

• • •

TRY THIS: *Find a place where the fireflies gather. If you live in the city, try the parks, or if there is no place close, watch a video. Connect with firefly energy, so brief and intense.*

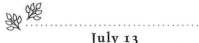

July 13
Spell for Joy and Happiness

Life can be tough. We all know it. Sometimes, no matter how hard you work and no matter how many good things you put out into the universe, it seems as though the darkness outweighs the light. Sometimes you just need a little joy and happiness to give you a boost and help you keep going.

Whether that joy and happiness is lasting (which I sincerely hope) or merely a break in the clouds, here is a spell to ask the gods to send it to you:

> *God and goddess, powers that be*
> *Send joy and gladness here to me*
> *Send me light to break the gloom*
> *Send enough joy to fill a room*
> *Send me happiness to fill my day*
> *Ease my burdens in every way*
> *A minute or hour will do for a start*
> *So send joy and happiness to my heart*

> • • •
> **TRY THIS:** *Don't forget to open yourself to joy and happiness once you have done the spell.*

July 14
Lemon Balm

Lemon balm is one of my favorite herbs. A member of the mint family, it will take over your garden if you're not careful, but it smells so heavenly, you might not even care. Its traits are right there in its name: it smells like lemon, and the word "balm" means to soothe or comfort (often in ointment form). Medicinally, lemon balm is used as a calming tea, for insomnia, and in the treatment of cold sores, among other things.

Magically, as you might expect, lemon balm is used in healing spells and tinctures, but it is also associated with prosperity and success (like many other plants in the mint family) as well as love.

I like to grow my own since it is so easy to do, and I hang it to dry in the kitchen, where it gives off a fabulous lemony-herby smell. Once it has dried, I simply pop it into plastic baggies to keep it fresh, and then I use the dried herb in bath sachets, for tea, or for any calming magic I do later on.

* * *

TRY THIS: *Use lemon balm in a spell or toss some in a healing bath or charm bag.*

July 15
Butterfly Gardens

Near where I live there is a butterfly conservatory. Inside an unimposing building are three thousand square feet of tropical paradise, filled with birds, reptiles, and, yes, butterflies of every size, shape, and color. It is pretty darned cool. But you don't have to come to my neighborhood to see butterflies. All you have to do is provide them with an environment they like, and the butterflies will come to you.

Butterflies like a sunny, sheltered spot with a source of water. They are also attracted to specific plants, many of which are quite pretty in their own right. Check online to see which plants attract the butterflies in your area, then plant a garden with plenty of sources for nectar and food for the caterpillar that is the larval form of the insect.

I like to think of a butterfly garden as a way of serving nature that, in turn, rewards us with beauty and charm. Planting a butterfly garden is a great way to introduce kids to working with the natural world too, so if you have children and a yard, consider making this a project you work on together. Think of how excited they will be when the first butterflies arrive! (I'll bet you will be too.)

• • •

TRY THIS: *If you have space, plant some flowers to attract butterflies (a balcony pot or window box will do). If not, find a place to visit them.*

July 16
The Third Chakra

The third chakra, or solar plexus chakra, is located in the area right above your belly button. It is considered to be the center of the body, the place from which energy is generated. In fact, there have been times when I gave or received energy healing that I felt a ball of heat in that exact spot.

The third chakra is usually visualized as yellow in color. If it is out of balance, that can show up in a lack of energy flow or in issues with the stomach, liver, pancreas, adrenals, or other nearby organs. This chakra is also associated with self-esteem and self-confidence.

• • •

TRY THIS: *One way to test if this chakra is blocked is to try to move energy up from your feet to your head or down in the other direction. If the energy seems to get stuck along the way, then visualize your third chakra as a yellow glow growing brighter and then spinning clockwise with a stronger and stronger movement. If that seems to work, try moving the energy again.*

July 17
"Back Yard"

I love the way this poem captures a summer night.

> Shine on, O moon of summer.
> Shine to the leaves of grass, catalpa and oak,
> All silver under your rain to-night.
>
> An Italian boy is sending songs to you to-night
>   from an accordion.
> A Polish boy is out with his best girl; they marry
>   next month; to-night they are throwing you kisses.
>
> An old man next door is dreaming over a sheen
> that sits in a cherry tree in his back yard.
>
> The clocks say I must go—I stay here sitting on the
>   back porch drinking
>   white thoughts you rain down.
>
> Shine on, O moon,
> Shake out more and more silver changes.

(Carl Sandburg, 1916)

• • •

TRY THIS: *Do you have a favorite poet who captures the essence of the things that matter to you? Even if you think you don't like poetry, it might be worth checking out a few. Modern poets like Maya Angelou might appeal if you don't like the classics.*

July 18
Renaissance Faires

I love Renaissance Faires. To me, they are one of the most magical places on earth. (Sorry, Disney.) Most Renaissance Faires (or Ren Faires, as they are known to frequent attendees) feature people dressed up in colorful costumes, unusual entertainment, food, handcrafted goods for sale, and sometimes even jousting—actual men (and sometimes women) riding horses and fighting, just like knights in shining armor! What's not to like?

There was a time when my group, Blue Moon Circle, went to Ren Faires almost every summer. We'd pack up the kids and husbands and spend a three-day weekend camping out together. Not only was it a blast, but it also helped to bring us closer together.

Renaissance Faires are great places to go as a family because they are more interactive than your average amusement park, and while they aren't strictly accurate renditions of, well, anything, they provide a good opportunity to talk about history and how people lived in the past. Also, did I mention the knights in shining armor? But you don't have to have kids to enjoy this brief respite from modern reality. Just being young at heart will do quite well.

. . .

TRY THIS: *Visit a Ren Faire if you can. Find information and photos online and see if it looks like your kind of thing. If you can't get to one, dress up with some friends and have a Ren Faire day in your backyard.*

July 19
Ruby

The official birthstone of people born in the month of July is the ruby, a beautiful deep red precious stone. Magically, this stone is associated with fire, wealth, protection, and joy. (Heck, if I had some rubies, I'd have joy too.) Because it is a precious stone, ruby can be quite pricy, so if you aren't worried about the birthstone aspect, you can substitute garnet, another stone with much the same coloring. Garnet is primarily a protective stone, although it is also used for healing, love, and joy.

Traditionally, rubies were considered to be the perfect offering to Buddha and Krishna, but I think the Goddess would be perfectly happy with a nice piece of tumbled garnet or a garnet chip bracelet.

Do you have a favorite stone, birthstone or otherwise? If so, consider putting a piece on your altar.

• • •

TRY THIS: *If you have a piece of ruby or garnet, sit with it for a while and get in touch with its energy. If there is a Pagan or New Age shop nearby, you may be able to find some tumbled garnet or an inexpensive piece of jewelry set with garnet.*

July 20
Rock Meditation

For a simple way to connect with the element of earth, do a rock meditation. This doesn't mean you have to go out and sit on a large rock (although if you happen to have one handy, go for it). Find a rock that fits nicely in your hand and just feels right—it can be a special quartz crystal point or just a stone you found on the ground that calls to you in some way.

Sit in a comfortable position and hold the rock between your palms. Close your eyes and feel the energy of the rock. Does it feel warm or cool? Does it seem to grow heavier as you hold it? Think about the earth beneath you and feel its solid dependability holding you up. It is always there, even when you aren't aware of it. Realize that the rock in your hands is a piece of that larger earth, connected to it even now that it is no longer in the ground. Who knows how old it is or how far it has traveled from its original place? Yet it is still from the earth and of the earth, and as you hold it, so are you.

• • •

TRY THIS: *Right before you meditate, light a green or brown candle (the colors of earth) and put on some quiet background music.*

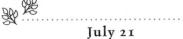

July 21
Blue

I think it is interesting that blue is used to mean sad (as in "I'm feeling blue") but is also associated with happiness ("nothing but blue skies," "the bluebird of happiness"). Not surprisingly, blue is the color associated with emotions and with the element of water, both of which are quite changeable. It is also often considered to represent the direction west, where water is usually found in Wiccan-type magical work.

One of the most restful colors, blue is a good color to have in your bedroom or use in working magic for sleep, calm, or healing. It also comes in an amazing array of hues, from baby blue (not my favorite—except, you know, on babies) to vivid royal blue to the deep navy blue of the dusk on a summer's night. I love the blues of the ocean and the sky. Since I can use all the calming vibes I can get, I have a handmade cover on my bed with primarily blue shades, with a fabulous wall hanging above it that was done by the same artist and features a goddess figure dressed in matching blues, holding a black cat in one hand and a flame in the other.

• • •

TRY THIS: *Do you think of blue as a happy color, a sad one, or a calming one—or maybe all three? Light a blue candle or put on a blue shirt today and see how it makes you feel.*

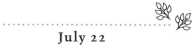

July 22
Picking Berries

One of the great pleasures of the summer months is eating fresh berries. The berries you buy in the grocery store have often traveled many thousands of miles (sometimes from other countries) and are likely to have been sprayed with pesticides, unless you buy organic. They rarely taste anything like what a real berry is supposed to taste like.

But if you're lucky, in the summer you can find a place nearby to pick them yourself fresh off the bush. If you're anything like me, half of what you pick probably won't even make it into your basket and will instead go straight into your mouth while still warm from the sun.

I grow a few berries in my yard and garden. I have a bed of strawberries, red raspberry bushes, and a few blueberry bushes, although mostly the birds and critters get those before I do. I love stepping right outside my door and picking a handful of berries to eat with my breakfast.

If you can't grow berries yourself (there are miniature blueberry or strawberry plants you can put in a small space), find a "you pick it" berry farm within driving distance. It is well worth making an excursion to such a place if you end up with lots of yummy berries at the end of the day to eat or cook with.

• • •

TRY THIS: *If you can't pick your own berries, find a farmers' market or a shop that carries local produce.*

July 23
Leo

Leo, the lion, rules those born between July 23 and August 21. As one might expect from the symbol, Leos tend to be powerful and charismatic, affectionate friends and lovers, and natural leaders. A fire sign, they often have boundless enthusiasm and can be very creative. The downside of all this is that they can sometimes come across as bossy or overwhelming. It's hard to be king.

• • •

TRY THIS: *During this period of the year, use the abundant Leo energy to boost your own leadership skills, become more assertive and affectionate, and throw yourself into some project you've been waiting to have enough energy to tackle. If you feel the impulse to let out a little roar on occasion, I promise I won't judge.*

July 24
Summer Blessings

Summers are all too brief and it sometimes seems as though they are over almost as soon as they've begun. We rarely manage to accomplish the things we want to do during these few warm months. Still, I hope you are having fun, spending some time outside and enjoying a few special occasions with friends and family. (If you're not, maybe you should consider doing so!)

Today, take a moment to count your summer blessings. Don't worry about what you haven't done yet; just list what you're grateful for. In case you need some inspiration, here's my list:

Warm weather (especially appreciated if you live through the long, cold upstate New York winters), fresh fruits and vegetables from the garden, listening to the rain through the open windows, having rituals outside, beautiful flowers, longer days with more light, and time spent with friends.

• • •

TRY THIS: *Make as long a list as you can, then add a few items to it every day as the summer progresses.*

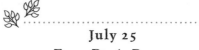

July 25
Easy Rock Runes

Rune stones are an ancient form of divination; the ones we use are usually based on the Norse runes, although there are others, such as the Ogham tree alphabet. Some people find them less complicated and intimidating than reading tarot cards.

There are plenty of premade rune sets, but it can be fun to make your own, which is not as hard as you might think. My first coven created sets of runes out of clay. But if you don't have the inclination to do that (or if you don't have access to a kiln), you can easily make a set of runes using plain old rocks. You'll need twenty-four stones that are all more or less the same size and shape. You can collect them from your yard, along a road, or on the seashore, or you can go to a garden center.

You will also need something to draw the rune signs. Permanent marker works well; to be more decorative, use one with gold ink. You can also use paint. Find a photo (online or in a book) of all the rune signs and draw one on each rock. The signs are simple, so don't worry about whether or not you have any particular artistic skill. Once you have your set completed, bless and consecrate the stones and put them into a decorative box or a drawstring pouch.

• • •

TRY THIS: *Make your own set of rune stones.*
If you don't have rocks, you can even use pieces
of cardboard or some other heavy paper.

July 26
Witchy Words of Wisdom:
Marion Weinstein

Another one of the books on my "highly recommended for all witches" list is *Positive Magic: Occult Self-Help* by Marion Weinstein. This book, originally published in 1978, is considered by many to be one of the classics on witchcraft.

My first high priestess had everyone in our group read the book, and we spent quite a bit of time working with the section on Words of Power. This approach to magic alone is one of the most useful I ever learned. In this chapter Weinstein writes about using words to create and trigger change:

> Words are symbols. They represent ideas, which are invisible; yet words themselves can be visible as written on a page, or otherwise perceived tangibly by our immediate senses... Anyone accustomed to working with his/her immediate senses can build a bridge to the Invisible Realm by way of words; they help us to span both worlds. Words are tools; they work in invisible ways to create visible results.

· · ·

> **TRY THIS:** *This book has one entire chapter—titled "The Ten-Foot Pole Department"—which talks about how to avoid the pitfalls of magic and negative people. If you haven't read this one yet, run—don't walk—to the store and get a copy!*

July 27
Oracle Cards

Some people collect tarot cards. I, on the other hand, only have one main tarot deck but an ever-increasing collection of oracle cards. Oracle cards are used for divination, general inspiration, and guidance. Sometimes they are specifically labeled as oracle cards, but I also like ones that simply have affirmations. They can be used as a kind of card-a-day or you can just pull one out when you need a boost, a push in the right direction, or to get a message from the universe.

I often use them with my group as a part of some of our rituals. We might, for instance, do some magical work to ask for guidance, then pass the deck around the circle, each pulling a card and then sharing it with the others. It can be remarkably effective.

A few of my favorite decks include the Goddess Inspiration Oracle Deck by Kris Waldherr (Llewellyn—the illustrations by Waldherr are amazing), the Conscious Spirit Oracle Deck by Kim Dreyer (U.S. Games Systems), the Goddess Knowledge Cards by Susan Seddon Boulet and Michael Babcock (Pomegranate), and The Gifts of the Goddess affirmation cards by Amy Zerner and Monte Farber (Chronicle Books). If you have oracle decks you particularly like, I'd love to hear about them!

• • •

TRY THIS: *Experiment with an oracle deck that appeals to you. Pull a card every day for a week and see if they give you guidance or clarity.*

July 28
Outdoor Festivals

If you like to gather with other Pagans, there are plenty of outdoor festivals for you to go to, many of which are held every year, so you can start planning ahead now. A couple of things to keep in mind as you consider picking a festival to attend: some of these can be quite large, so if you don't like crowds, look for a smaller one; many have rough sleeping arrangements (camping); and not all of them are handicap accessible. Figure out what you are comfortable with, and plan accordingly.

If you plan to make this a family affair, check to make sure that the festival you are considering is child friendly. Some outdoor festivals are clothing optional. On the other hand, plenty of festivals have activities for children. Lots of festivals have workshops and guest speakers, along with rituals. If there are Pagan notables you'd like to meet in person, check their schedules online; most of them post if they're going to be at a festival.

A few festivals have been in existence for a long time, including Rites of Spring (end of May, western Massachusetts), Pagan Spirit Gathering (Summer Solstice week in southern Illinois), Starwood (mid-July, Ohio), and the Pan Pagan Festival (August, Indiana).

• • •

TRY THIS: *Find out if there is a festival not too far from you. Consider attending at least once, just to see what it is like.*

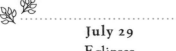

July 29
Eclipses

There are two main kinds of eclipses: the solar eclipse (when the sun vanishes behind the moon's shadow) and the lunar eclipse (when the moon moves into the earth's shadow). Partial eclipses are more common, whereas total eclipses are fairly rare. There are usually four to seven eclipses in any given year.

While these are cool natural phenomena, they also have specific uses in magical work. For obvious reasons, witches are primarily concerned with lunar eclipses since we are a fairly moon-centric bunch. Lunar eclipses only happen during the full moon, and since that is already a potent time for magical work, eclipses are believed to add an extra boost to whatever you are working on. Consider them a kind of supercharged battery that you can tap in to for the brief time they are available to you.

Lunar eclipses are a good time for work on healing, for dynamic goddess worship, or especially for growth and change, since the moon seems to go through an entire cycle of waxing and waning and waxing again all in one night.

• • •

TRY THIS: *Look up the date of the next eclipse and plan to do magical work on that day.*

July 30
Lugh

Lugh is the Celtic sun god from whom the holiday of Lughnasadh gets its name. One of the famed Tuatha Dé Danann, he is also the god of light, fire, and battle who carries a legendary sword and spear. In fact, he is sometimes known as Lugh of the Many Skills because he has so many different talents. One story says that when he presented himself at the entrance to Tara and told them of all the things he could do, he was first turned away because they already had someone who was adept at smithcraft, poetry, and the rest. To which he responded, "Yes, but do you have anyone who can do *all* these things?" They had to admit they did not and allowed him in.

In some traditions Lugh dies at Lughnasadh, sacrificing himself for the sake of the harvest. The sacrificial god or king is a classic tale told in many cultures. The ruler gives his life to ensure that the land will prosper, and although he is mourned, we know that he will be reborn again, just as the grain is cut down and then the seeds are sown in the year that follows.

The sun (Lugh) begins to fade away as the summer wanes, but we know it will always return as the wheel turns 'round again.

• • •

TRY THIS: *Do something crafty or write a poem or be creative in some other way to connect with Lugh today.*

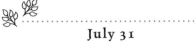

July 31
Harry Potter

Today is the birthday of author J. K. Rowling, who created the fabulous Harry Potter series. Everyone who loves those books, raise your hand. Yes, me too!

Most people will agree that the books are wonderful and entertaining, and there was much discussion about the fact that this series did an incredible job of getting kids interested in reading. But for us witchy types, there was a further benefit that I doubt was intended by the author. Suddenly, witches were cool again.

Everyone wanted to be a witch with a magical wand, a broom that flew, and a familiar—hopefully an owl and not a rat. Instead of the same old "wicked witch" image, the witch was seen as the hero of the story—someone you wanted to be friends with. Obviously, real-life witches are no Harry Potter, but in some ways the literary acceptance of Harry helped to ease the real-life acceptance of the rest of us. Not for everyone, of course, but in a general public sense, "witch" was no longer necessarily a bad thing.

So let's wish the lovely J. K. Rowling a very happy and magical birthday, and celebrate the increased popularity of witches everywhere.

• • •

TRY THIS: *If you somehow missed out on these books, now is a good time to start reading. If you've already read them, celebrate Rowling's birthday by rereading your favorite or watching the movies.*

August 1
Lammas

Lammas, also known as Lughnasadh, is the first of three harvest festivals in the Wiccan Wheel of the Year. Like the others, the holiday is a time for celebration and feasting, preferably on food that is, if not out of your own garden, at least seasonal and local.

Lammas falls at the time of the grain harvest, and so it celebrates grains of every kind. I like to bake fresh bread to serve as the "cakes" part of cakes and ale. The tradition of breaking bread goes back into the depths of human history, and passing bread from person to person in the circle connects us not only to each other, but to all of those who came before us who sat around a bonfire or a hearth and did the same thing. As we tear off a hunk and chew on it, the grainy sweetness reminds us to be grateful for the food on our tables and for the earth from which it comes.

If you aren't a baker, buy some fresh artisan bread. If you observe the holiday on your own, eat your piece of bread, knowing that all around the world there are others of like mind celebrating in much the same way. That's one of the reasons I like to use round bread instead of the usual rectangular loaf—to symbolize the unity of the gesture, going back into the past and out across the land.

• • •

TRY THIS: *When you celebrate Lammas this year, incorporate fresh bread of some kind into your ritual.*

August 2
Bread

This bread is so simple that anyone can make it. It requires no kneading, and you bake it in an oven-safe pot or casserole dish with a lid.

You will need:

> 3¼ cups all-purpose flour
>
> 1 cup whole wheat flour
>
> 2 teaspoons salt
>
> ½ teaspoon instant yeast
>
> 1¾ cups water
>
> 1 cup of anything you want to mix in, such as dried cranberries or raisins, nuts, or sunflower seeds. (For instance, ½ cup fruit and ½ cup chopped walnuts.)

Mix everything except the extras in a large bowl with your hands. Then add in any additional goodies until the dough forms a ball. Cover the bowl with a towel or plastic wrap and let it sit on the counter for eight hours or overnight. (This is a seriously lazy recipe—don't you love it?)

In the morning turn the dough out onto a floured surface and shape it to fit whatever covered pan you will be baking it in. I just use a large casserole with a lid. Let it sit in the pan with the lid on for about 2 hours; it should rise another little bit, but it won't get too much larger. Then put it in a cold oven and turn the heat to 450 degrees F. Bake for 45 minutes, then remove the lid and bake for another 5 to 10 minutes until the top is golden brown. Let it cool, then enjoy!

TRY THIS: *Give this recipe a chance and you may never get store-bought bread again!*

August 3
How Am I Doing So Far?

As we reach the harvest time of the year, it is time to start assessing our progress. If you set goals at the beginning of the year, how far have you come toward achieving them? If you planted seeds for new things you wanted in your life, are they growing well? Have you accomplished what you had hoped to by this time of the year?

• • •

TRY THIS: *Ask yourself, "How am I doing so far?"*
If you like the answer, celebrate your achievements.
If you don't, you still have time to make changes to
your plans, regroup, and push forward before the
year is over. Make a list of what you need to do next
in order to get where you want to be. Prioritize your
actions and start with the next thing that will move
you forward—and don't forget your magical tools!

August 4
Poseidon

If you happen to visit the ocean during the summer, be sure to make an offering at the water's edge to Poseidon, the god who rules the seas. Poseidon is one of the major Greek deities and is often pictured with a trident (a three-pronged fishing spear), riding a chariot pulled by horses that could walk on the waves. His palace beneath the ocean was said to be made of coral and precious stones.

As you can imagine, given the changeability of the element of water, Poseidon is seen as a benign god of calm seas, the creator of new islands, and as the "earth shaker" for the earthquakes he caused by striking the ground with his trident.

I have a great love of the ocean, changeable though it is, and I suppose that colors my view of Poseidon. In my mind I mostly see him cavorting amidst the waves with the dolphins and greeting me with warmth on the rare occasions I manage to make my way to the sea.

• • •

TRY THIS: *If you go to the ocean this summer, leave a small gift for Poseidon at the water's edge such as a cookie or a shiny bead. If you find a cool shell or stone, perhaps it is a gift from him in return.*

August 5
Witches in Books

I don't know about you, but one of my favorite parts of summer are "beach reads"—books that are light and fun and perfect for an afternoon sitting on the beach or in the hammock. Being of the witchy persuasion, I especially love books that feature witches as the main character. There are my Baba Yaga novels, of course, but once you've finished with those, check out a few of these:

- A *Girl's Guide to Witchcraft* (Book 1 in the Jane Madison series) by Mindy Klasky
- *Secondhand Spirits* (Book 1 in the Witchcraft series) by Juliet Blackwell
- *Charmed and Dangerous* (the Bronwyn series) by Candace Havens
- *50 Ways to Hex Your Lover* (Hex in High Heels series) by Linda Wisdom

Plus, if you read young adult books (which I do), there are always the wonderful Harry Potter books, and if you like them, check out Tamora Pierce (she writes about magic in her Circle of Magic quartet, although not specifically witches), Diana Wynne Jones, and there is an amazing and amusing historical trio of books by Patricia Wrede and Cynthia Stevermer that includes *Sorcery and Cecelia*, one of my favorite books.

Summers are busy times for all of us, but there is always time to read…especially if there is magic involved!

• • •

TRY THIS: *No matter how busy you are, steal away for an hour or two to read something just for fun. If it has witches in it, all the better!*

August 6
Spell for Energy and Focus

As we reach the peak of the summer, it is a perfect time to tap in to the energy of the season to give a little boost to our endeavors. If you are working toward a goal and things aren't going quite the way you wanted—especially if you feel you don't have enough time, energy, or focus to create the positive changes you desire—do this spell for energy and focus.

Go outside on any sunny day (noon is best, if you can manage it) or, if you have to be inside, be in a sunlit room. Light a yellow candle, if you like, or even a bonfire if you're outside.

Standing in the light, say:

> *Summer sunlight, bright and strong*
> *Send me energy all day long*
> *Give me focus, like your rays*
> *To keep my goals within my gaze*
> *Summer sunlight, long and slow*
> *Help me cause my dreams to grow*
> *Energize and focus me*
> *As I will, so mote it be!*

• • •

> **TRY THIS:** *Make sure you have something summery for cakes and ale afterward: fresh fruit such as watermelon, or tomatoes fresh out of the garden that taste like sunshine on a plate.*

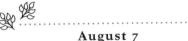

Carnelian

Many years ago (no, I'm not saying how many, but it was a lot) a friend of mine got me hooked on jewelry making. Much of those early days have vanished into the haze of time, but I still remember quite vividly the moment when she showed me a catalog filled with gemstones, and I pointed at a brownish-red stone and said, "Wow—what is that?"

That was carnelian, and not only was it the catalyst for my love of making gemstone jewelry, but it is still one of my favorite stones. Keep in mind, this day was long before my discovery of my identity as a witch or any knowledge of the power of stones, yet somehow I knew there was something special about this particular rock that seemed to me to be warm and comforting, bright and solid.

As it turns out, my instincts weren't far off. Magically, carnelian, a form of chalcedony, is used for peace and harmony, to increase courage and self-confidence (it is especially useful for public speaking), to fight negativity, and for healing. Some also consider it to be a boost to sexual energy, which makes sense if you look at all its other aspects.

• • •

TRY THIS: *At the time I first saw carnelian, I needed all of its qualities. If you are drawn to a particular stone, find out what it is used for magically and see if, in fact, it is just what you need.*

August 8
Dogs

Witches are most commonly pictured with cats, but the truth is, many magical folks are drawn to all kinds of animals, including dogs.

A number of gods and goddesses are particularly linked to dogs, including Hecate, who is often depicted with black dogs, and Diana, known as the Huntress, who is usually accompanied by her hounds. Anubis, the Egyptian jackal-headed god, is sometimes portrayed as taking the form of a dog instead. Numerous Celtic deities are also associated with dogs, including Cerridwen and Nuada.

Dogs are loyal, smart, and trainable, so they make good companions. But can they also be familiars, just as cats are? Of course they can. As with felines, canines often choose their "owners" and may or may not be magically inclined.

* * *

TRY THIS: *If you have a dog that shows an interest in your magical work, invite them into your circle and see if the dog's presence lends your work more power. Just be careful not to expose the animal to anything that might be hazardous, and make sure the dog participates because they are inclined to do so, not because you think it would be cool to have a dog as a familiar. After all, Hecate may be watching…and if she has to make the choice between the dog and you, she will probably pick the dog.*

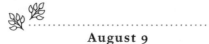

August 9
Gratitude No. 4:
Animal Companions

Of all the things I am grateful for in my life—and there are many—I am probably most grateful for my cats. They're at least in the top three, along with family and friends. My cats are more than just pets. They are my companions, my furry family, my comfort in times of trouble, and my inspiration to keep writing. (Somebody has to pay for the food, cat litter, and vet bills, after all.) When I am sad, there is always a furry face to cheer me up. They keep me company and make living alone much less lonely. Most of all, they give me unconditional love.

In truth, what they bring to my life is much greater than any expense or inconvenience they may cost me, and I thank the gods for them every day.

• • •

TRY THIS: *If you have an animal companion, take some time today to appreciate everything they add to your life, and maybe give them an extra treat or some special attention just to say thank you. If you don't have any animals of your own, do something to help animals in need. I'm sure the gods would approve.*

August 10
Witchy Words of Wisdom:
Raven Grimassi

Raven Grimassi is one of the foremost names in modern witchcraft and has been practicing and teaching the Craft for more than thirty years. He is the author of many books and has been initiated into a number of Wiccan traditions. In his book *Spirit of the Witch: Religion & Spirituality in Contemporary Witchcraft*, he said this:

> Participation in the seasonal rites places the witch in the direct flow of energy, which is drawn and accumulated in ritual circles. Here the witch is bathed in the condensed energy evoked within the magic circle, and the aura of the individual is charged with this power. Through continual immersion in the flow of seasonal energy, the witch becomes more aligned with both the energy and the source of that energy. Therefore the witch becomes more like Nature and the forces behind Nature.

• • •

TRY THIS: *Read this passage from Grimassi once more, and this time reflect on your witchy life and how you have become "more aligned with both the energy and the source of that energy." Can you feel that power in your own life?*

August 11
Lavender

Lavender is one of the most commonly used herbs. You can find it in all sorts of soaps and lotions, and it grows in almost every part of the world. It smells heavenly, which probably has something to do with its popularity.

Those beautiful purple flowers have many practical uses, from treating burns and bug bites to encouraging sleep and a calm mind. (It is also edible and can be used in cooking.) So it isn't surprising that it is used magically for healing, serenity, and sleep. It is also associated with love, protection, purity, and happiness.

I like to use lavender in sachets; I have a small silk one that I tuck under my pillow when I can't sleep. You can use the essential oil in a calming bath or add a few drops to a pink or red candle when doing love magic. Keep a bowl of the dried flowers on your altar or by the front door for protection. One of my favorite traditions is tossing a handful of lavender blossoms into the summer solstice bonfire as an offering to the Goddess. As the sharp, sweet smell drifts up to the heavens, I send my wishes for healing, love, and calm along with it.

• • •

TRY THIS: *Do something with lavender today and connect with its magical healing energy.*

August 12

Saying I'm Sorry

I think two of the hardest words to say in the English language are "I'm sorry." People think saying them will be an admission that they were wrong, and no one likes to be wrong. And I suspect some folks feel that saying "I'm sorry" makes them seem weak.

But I look at it the other way around. It takes a strong person to admit they screwed up (hell, I do it all the time, so by now I must be as tough as Hercules—or at least Xena the warrior princess). And it takes an open heart to give a genuine apology and try to make things better.

Think of all the times that someone has hurt you. Sometimes words can't fix a situation, but at the very least, a sincere apology shows that you acknowledge and own whatever it is you did.

As witches, we know that words have power. These two are among the most powerful, so don't be afraid to use them if they can help make a bad situation a little bit better. The Wiccan Rede says "an it harm none, do as ye will." I say if you *did* harm someone—no matter how accidentally—say you're sorry. You might be surprised to find out just how much power these two words have.

. . .

TRY THIS: *Have you wronged or hurt someone lately, even unintentionally? If so, say you're sorry and see how it makes you feel.*

August 13
Grounding

I first heard about grounding, also called "earthing," from a witchy friend who is a hypnotherapist with a PhD and years of experience dealing with various approaches to alternative healing. At its most basic, grounding is as simple as it sounds: getting into contact with the ground. This can mean walking barefoot or, as my friend recommended, lying full length on the grass or dirt. The theory is that human beings originally spent much more time in contact with the earth (walking barefoot, sleeping on the ground) and that our current existence has distanced us from that connection, thus depriving us of the natural energy put out by the earth itself. Touching the earth reestablishes that connection and helps to equalize our own energy.

Note that the grounding I'm writing about here is not the same thing as the "grounding and centering" technique we often use during ritual, although it has something of the same effect of connecting us to the earth. In fact, this type of grounding has nothing to do with witches at all, other than that it fits in well with many of our own beliefs and practices.

• • •

TRY THIS: *Ground yourself using this "new" technique, which is probably as old as the earth itself. Let me know if it works for you.*

August 14
Dragons

One of my favorite bumper stickers is the one that says "Meddle not in the affairs of dragons, for you are crunchy and taste good with ketchup." Heh. But it is certainly true that dragons should be approached with respect and caution, even when dealing with them on a purely magical level.

Dragons are normally depicted as great lizards with wings, often capable of breathing fire. The European version tended to be mostly maligned (especially post-Christianity), considered to be evil creatures that required a hero to vanquish them and who were hoarders of gold, precious jewels, and occasionally— although goodness knows why—virgins. The Chinese version, on the other hand, was more likely to be intelligent, magical, and revered. Although they are mythical creatures, I find it interesting that dragons in one form or another seem to show up in almost every culture across the globe.

Dragons are usually associated with the element of earth, although there are water dragons as well; because they fly, they could be seen as having an air element too. Plus, of course, they breathe fire. Magically, dragons can be used to symbolize strength, wisdom, and elemental powers, as well as protection. But if you call on them for help, remember to do so respectfully. And you might want to hide the ketchup.

• • •

TRY THIS: *Do some research on dragons and see which kind resonates with you.*

August 15

Vegetarianism and Mindful Eating

The spiritual practice of witchcraft does not require anyone to be a vegetarian. But I do think that being a Pagan should encourage a more mindful attitude about what we put into our bodies. We each have to make our own choices about how we go about doing that, of course.

My compromise is to eat a predominantly vegetarian diet, with some meat added in a few times a month. I try to buy meat that is humanely raised and organic if possible, and when I eat meat I send out gratitude to the animal for its sacrifice.

Some witches take the attitude that death is part of the cycle of life, and therefore eating meat is as natural for us as it was for our ancestors (very few of whom were vegetarians). Others believe that as spiritual beings we have the opportunity to rise above this, and since we can easily live without meat in this day and age, we should. There is no clear right or wrong answer, and each of us must make that choice for ourselves, along with all the other ethical and health choices we make every day. The best we can do is be grateful for the food on our tables since, whether animal or vegetable, there is always some kind of sacrifice involved.

* * *

TRY THIS: *If you eat meat, be mindful about it and grateful for the sacrifice involved. If you are so inclined, skip eating it a few days a week on purpose as part of your spiritual practice.*

"'Tis Moonlight, Summer Moonlight"

I think this is the perfect summer poem.

'Tis moonlight, summer moonlight,
All soft and still and fair;
The solemn hour of midnight
Breathes sweet thoughts everywhere,

But most where trees are sending
Their breezy boughs on high,
Or stooping low are lending
A shelter from the sky.

And there in those wild bowers
A lovely form is laid;
Green grass and dew-steeped flowers
Wave gently round her head.

(Emily Jane Brontë, 1840)

• • •

TRY THIS: *Step outside this evening and notice
the summer sights, sounds, and smells. Don't
worry, you don't have to do it at midnight.*

August 17
Diana

Back in earlier days in Rome, this day fell in the middle of a weeklong celebration of the goddess Diana. Diana is the goddess of the hunt, wild animals, and the woods, and she is also a moon goddess. A maiden goddess, she is the twin sister of the sun god Apollo, and her symbols are the bow, deer, and oak trees. Her Greek counterpart is Artemis.

Diana is considered to be the Queen of Witches by the Strega of Italy, and she is the inspiration for Dianic Wicca, one of the earlier forms of feminist, goddess-centered witchcraft.

• • •

TRY THIS: *Whether or not you follow this particular goddess, today is a good day to acknowledge the power of the feminine. Diana was strong and wise and bowed to no man, god or otherwise. If the moon is visible in the night sky, go outside and greet her. Or you can light a white or silver candle in her honor and say,* "Hail Diana, goddess of the hunt!"

August 18
Shooting Stars

Shooting stars are another name for meteors, the streaks of light in the sky that are bits of passing comets burning up in Earth's atmosphere. But that is a very prosaic explanation for a pretty magical phenomenon, isn't it?

If you have been lucky enough to see a shooting star, you know how beautiful and breathtaking it can be. There is something truly enchanting about watching this natural light show. While you may be able to see a shooting star on its own from time to time, you are much more likely to get a good showing if you go out and watch during one of the major meteor showers. (Look up the dates online since their peak dates and times for viewing change from year to year.) Meteor showers are named after the constellations they appear to originate from, such as the Perseids, which come from the direction of the constellation of Perseus, and the Leonid meteor shower, which comes from Leo.

It is much easier to see shooting stars in the country, away from the light pollution of the city that makes the night sky too bright to see much of anything. The best way to get a really good view is to go someplace where it is dark and lie on your back (feel free to bring a friend to keep you warm if it is a cool night).

. . .

TRY THIS: *If you see a shooting star, make a wish as you watch it winging across the sky.*

August 19
Foraging

Foraging is the acquisition of food by the gathering of plants. So what does foraging have to do with being a witch? Not much if you live in the city, unless you interpret it to mean finding the best local deli. But if you have access to fields and woods, then consider supplementing your diet with edibles straight from nature. You can't get more Pagan than that, and it will certainly give you a connection to our ancestors.

Mind you, I'm not suggesting you start walking around nibbling on weeds. Begin with something simple, like finding wild berry bushes or field strawberries. If you are interested in wildcrafting (another name for foraging), research what is edible in your area. If you go a'foraging, make sure you have correctly identified the plant, that it is the right time of year for it to be edible, that the environment it is growing in is suitable, and that you can prepare it using a safe method. Wild raspberries are a good example of a simple place to start, but there are plenty of plants considered weeds that are good to eat, including common ones such as dandelions and thistles.

• • •

TRY THIS: *Get in touch with nature and give foraging a try—just make sure you do your research first. And remember that you can use wild-grown plants in magic too!*

August 20
Go Fly a Kite

If someone tells you to go fly a kite, in theory that's an insult—but I think it is a great suggestion! After all, what better way to connect to the element of air than to take a piece of cloth or paper or what have you and send it flying out into the great blue yonder?

Kites can be simple and homemade or complicated and store-bought. Create one with the whole family as a project, dream up a work of art, or just find one you like and take it outside on a breezy day. People think of flying kites as an activity for children, but, in fact, competitions and festivals are held all over the world for people of every age. Besides, are you ever too old to go fly a kite? I don't think so.

All you need is a kite, a place to fly it, and some wind, and then you and the air can commune and play together. I've always wanted a kite in the shape of a dragon (did you know kites were invented in China?).

What about you? What kind of kite do you want to fly?

• • •

TRY THIS: *On the next windy day, create or buy a kite and go out and connect with the element of air.*

August 21
Simple Summer Pesto

As I write this book, it is the end of summer and, as always, I look around the garden and realize that I have gotten just a tiny bit carried away when I planted the basil—like "a dozen plants more than I needed" carried away. Did I mention I do this almost every year?

Thankfully, there is an easy solution to this tragic problem; when in doubt, make pesto.

Pesto is quite easy to make, and the ingredient list is short: basil, pine nuts (you can substitute walnuts), olive oil, garlic, Parmesan cheese, and salt. Look up a recipe if you want specific measurements; I never use them since I've been making it for years. Essentially, you use mostly basil, throw in a handful of nuts, some grated cheese, and a clove or six of garlic. Then blend it all together with as much olive oil as it takes to give you the consistency you like. Salt to taste, and voilà!

• • •

TRY THIS: *Look into pesto's magical qualities—it's a powerhouse. Basil has so many magical uses that one of its folk names is "the witches' herb." Prosperity and healing magic are just two of the things it is good for. Nuts are also great for prosperity magic, and garlic is known for healing, so if you need either of these things, making pesto with the intention of bringing out its magical qualities is an easy way to go.*

August 22
Virgo

Virgo is the sun sign for those born between August 22 and September 23. The folks who fall under this sign tend to be intelligent and precise, practical and capable, and yet unassuming. No matter how gifted they are, it is unlikely you will find them bragging about it. In fact, you might have to drag them out of the corner to take credit for their work. (I have a sister who is a Virgo, so I know of what I speak.)

On the downside, Virgos may be so particular that they come across as overcritical, both toward themselves and others, and they can be worriers and perfectionists in their attempts to get everything "just right."

• • •

> **TRY THIS:** *At this time of the year, whether*
> *or not you are a Virgo, cut yourself a little slack.*
> *Now is also a good time to work on any projects*
> *that require this kind of Virgo devotion to detail*
> *(particularly if you can get a Virgo to help).*

August 23
Poppets

A poppet is essentially a small doll used for doing magical work of one sort or another. The poppet stands in for the person it is meant to symbolize in a form of sympathetic magic.

It is easy to make a poppet, and you don't need to have great sewing skills to do it. Make it as detailed or as simple as you want, although as with all things magical, the more effort you put into it, the more of your energy it will hold. Start by picking out a piece of cloth, preferably something suitable for the magical work you have in mind, such as green for prosperity, or pink/red for love, or plain white is fine. Cut out a rough human figure (head, arms, legs) and sew it together. Use a thread whose color corresponds with the work as well. It is easiest to get most of the way done working inside out, then turn the fabric the other way so the messier sewing is on the inside.

Leave a space to add stuffing and any magical materials such as stones, herbs, or a little note, then finish sewing it up. Decorate the outside with yarn for hair (to match you or whomever the poppet is supposed to represent) and use thread or markers to make a face.

• • •

TRY THIS: *Make a poppet for some magical purpose. Remember to focus on your intention as you work since this will make the poppet even more powerful. If you're not comfortable with a needle and thread, make a poppet from clay or wax.*

August 24
The Fourth Chakra

The fourth chakra is the heart chakra, which is located about where you'd expect it to be! This chakra is associated with the emotions, especially the ability to give and receive love. If it is closed off, you will probably have a tough time with relationships of every kind, so it is a good idea to check in on this one from time to time.

The heart chakra is usually visualized as either green or pink in color. My favorite stone to use when working with this chakra is a little-known semi-precious gemstone called lapis Nevada. It is a beautiful swirl of pink, green, and white, which is perfect for the task. You can also use rose quartz, a soft green stone such as aventurine, or ruby-in-fuchsite, which is also green and pink.

• • •

TRY THIS: *If you feel as though your heart chakra might be stuck or out of balance, do a simple meditation. Focus on the area around your heart—you can even put your hands over it. Send love out into the world without reservation, then send more love inward, toward yourself. See your chakra open up like a flower blooming in the sunlight, as green as a growing plant or as pink as a baby's smiling face. The more love you send out, the more your heart chakra will open and allow you to take in love.*

August 25
Streams, Rivers, and Creeks

I love all forms of water. Oceans are magnificent and full of vibrant energy, but don't underestimate the power of streams, rivers, and creeks; they may be smaller and quieter, but they are still powerful in their own way and just as lovely.

To connect with the element of water, find a local river, stream, or creek, preferably one where you can stand next to it or even in it. These flowing waters carry life and energy too, and the larger ones are often sources of much-needed nutrients for the surrounding land. Sometimes they are filled with fish or they may only have moss and tiny tadpoles, but they are still vibrant, vital parts of nature.

・・・

TRY THIS: *Stand by the water and listen to it move; every river, stream, and creek has its own particular music, which changes depending on the time of year and the amount of rainfall. Does the water gurgle as it goes over rocks and underneath fallen trees? Does it grow wild as it crashes over a waterfall? Or is it quiet and peaceful, the perfect place for an afternoon's picnic? Does it speak to you? If so, what does it say?*

August 26

I Have Clarity; I Am Focused

It is hard to keep our minds clear and our focus strong in the midst of all the chaos and noise. Here is an affirmation that can help:

My mind is clear and focused. I am undistracted by the chaos of life.

• • •

TRY THIS: *Say this affirmation first thing in the morning, before all that chaos starts. Repeat as necessary throughout a busy day.*

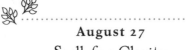

August 27
Spell for Clarity

Who among us couldn't use a little more clarity? If you feel muddled or need to make a tough decision, try this simple spell for clarity.

Focus on what it is you need to have more clarity about, then light a white or yellow candle, take a deep breath, and say this spell:

> God and Goddess, send to me
> The brilliant light of clarity
> Clear away mess and debris
> And help me now to clearly see

Close your eyes and listen to your inner wisdom. Maybe, if you're very quiet, the gods will speak back.

TRY THIS: *This is a nice spell to do under the full moon or at noon in the sunlight, both of which promote clarity. But if the timing isn't right for either of those, just light a candle instead. A sprig of rosemary is helpful, too, or some rosemary incense.*

August 28
Basil

If you read the pesto recipe earlier in the month, you are probably already excited about using basil. It is delicious and easy to grow and has a wonderful aroma, but as witches, we also know that it has a number of magical uses as well.

I like to use dried basil in my protection mixes, which I either sprinkle around the house or hang in sachets or charm bags. (I've got one over my front door right now.) It is also a wonderful herb for prosperity and has long been associated with love spells. It comes in many forms—the fresh plant, of course, as well as the dried leaves, essential oil, and incense. If you use it for magical work, be careful where you get it. For instance, the dried basil in the grocery store herb section has usually been mass-produced and irradiated, although the fresh herbs should be fine. I much prefer to get mine from the local health food store or dry it myself.

> **TRY THIS:** *Even if you don't have a place for a garden, grow a pot of basil on a sunny windowsill. Not only might you attract love and prosperity, you'll always have a couple of leaves to throw in a salad!*

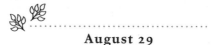

August 29
Know Thyself

It is said that if you went to the ancient Greek temple of Apollo at Delphi, you would have found written there these words: "know thyself." It is a common theme in Greek writings and that of many other cultures. Benjamin Franklin famously said in his book *Poor Richard's Almanack* that "there are three things extremely hard: steel, a diamond, and to know one's self."

And of course he was right. It is difficult to look clearly at the person you see in the mirror every day. Some of us have problems admitting to our flaws; others can't acknowledge their own positive traits. Either way, it is tough to be absolutely brutally honest about one's self.

It is also really important.

For one thing, you can't change what you can't see. None of us are perfect, but to me, part of a witchcraft practice is striving to become our own best selves. We can't do that if we don't know who we are, both the good and the bad. And magically speaking, we need to be honest with ourselves about what we are truly trying to achieve in order to make the magic work as we want it to.

• • •

> **TRY THIS:** *Do you know yourself? Maybe now is a good time to do a little self-exploration. Write down a list of all your good traits and those you think are bad. Are the "bad" ones as bad as you think? If so, work to change them. If not, maybe go a little easier on yourself.*

August 30
Walking and Hiking

One of the best ways to strengthen your bond with Mother Nature is also the simplest: go for a walk (or a hike, if you are more adventurous).

The difference between a witchy walk and just marching down the street to the store is a matter of mindfulness. Even in a city you can look for signs of nature: trees along the meridian, weeds growing in cracks in the sidewalks, birds, clouds…of course, if you go to a park, you can see even more.

If you can get away to the countryside (or happen to live there), nature is abundant. You will connect with it much more strongly if you look and listen and smell the passing scents as you walk instead of listening to an iPod and planning what you will make for dinner.

• • •

TRY THIS: *Make some time to take a walk or a hike on a regular basis. You might be surprised by what has been around you all along.*

August 31
Witchy Words of Wisdom:
Raymond Buckland

Today is the birthday of Raymond Buckland, arguably one of the most influential figures in the creation of modern witchcraft. Happy birthday, Ray, and many bright blessings!

A protégé of Gerald Gardner, the British-born Buckland brought Wicca to the United States in the 1960s, and nothing has ever been the same again. He has written many books on the subject, including one of my favorites, *Wicca for Life: The Way of the Craft from Birth to Summerland*. Here is just a taste of the wisdom he has to share:

> Everywhere in nature is both male and female, both in the animal kingdom and in the plant kingdom. It seems only natural, therefore, that the deities would be both male and female. The Christian concept of a lone all-male deity does not make sense. Many Wiccan traditions think in terms of a balance between the two energies, while others place more emphasis on one over the other…more emphasis on the Goddess during the summer months when it was possible to grow food, and more on the God in the winter months when hunting was important. This balance is still found today in most traditions.

. . .

TRY THIS: *Even if you follow a more eclectic form of witchcraft, as I do, there is a lot of good to be found in Buckland's more traditional writings. Find out more about him and his ideas online or buy a copy of one of his books.*

September 1
Gratitude No. 5

During the harvest season, it should be easy to find things to be grateful for. Hopefully you will celebrate some metaphorical harvests along with the more mundane but still yummy ones.

What have you harvested this year that you are grateful for? New friends and relationships? Improvements at work or in your home life? Prosperity? Health? A lot of zucchini? (Okay, maybe not that last one. I hate zucchini.)

· · ·

TRY THIS: *Nine is a magical number, and September is the ninth month. Make a list of nine things you are grateful for and add to it every night for the next nine days.*

September 2
Sapphire

September's birthstone is the sapphire, a beautiful deep blue precious stone whose association with magic goes back at least as far as the Greeks. It is, as most blue stones are, a healing stone, but it can also be used for increasing psychic ability, opening the third eye, peace, protection, and love magic.

While sapphires can be expensive, you don't need a large showy piece to do magical work; a simple ring or pendant will do, or a chunk of raw stone if you can find one.

If even that is beyond your reach, Scott Cunningham (in *Cunningham's Encyclopedia of Crystal, Gem & Metal Magic*) suggests using the following as substitutes: amethyst, blue tourmaline, or blue zircon. For most of those magical workings I also like to use lapis lazuli, a reasonably inexpensive tumbled stone that is also blue and very pretty.

* * *

TRY THIS: *Pick out your favorite blue stone (or a sapphire if you happen to have one) and do some magical work with it today.*

September 3
Dionysus

I'm a big fan of the Greek god Dionysus, also known as Bacchus to the Romans. After all, he is the god of wine, wine making, and the grape harvest, as well as theater, fertility, and ritual ecstasy, all of which kind of make sense when you consider the wine. In fact, his festivals are associated with the development of theater, so we owe him quite a lot.

Like wine itself, the worship of Dionysus could be taken too far, and he is often pictured as being followed by wild, uncontrollable women called maenads, along with packs of well-endowed satyrs. He is the god of all things chaotic and unexpected.

On the positive side, though, his worshippers use wine, ecstatic dance, and music to free themselves from fear and self-consciousness, and that is certainly a good thing.

• • •

TRY THIS: *If you enjoy a glass of wine, raise one today in thanks to Dionysus, and call on him to help you embrace your own wilder, less self-conscious self.*

September 4
Wine and Mead

Wine and mead, which is a sweet wine made from honey as opposed to grapes or other fruit, have long been used as part of ritual celebrations. Although the ending section of many rituals is called "cakes and ale," many witches are more likely to have wine in the chalice than beer.

Wine was considered a gift from the gods, especially around harvest time when the fruits used to make it were plentiful. Mead—especially magical because the efforts of many bees working together are required to produce the honey used to make it—is celebrated at Midsummer. When taking part in an outdoor ritual or even going out to greet the full moon, pour a small amount of wine onto the ground as a libation, or a religious offering in honor of deity.

Blue Moon Circle sometimes uses pomegranate juice instead of wine, especially if we meet early in the day, if children are present, or if someone new is in the circle and we aren't sure of their preferences. We also add just enough wine in the chalice for everyone to take a few sips because any more substantial consumption is much more suited for the feast to follow.

• • •

TRY THIS: *If you drink wine, try making it yourself or visit a local winery. If you haven't tried it yet, consider using mead during ritual.*

September 5
Labor Day

Around this day in the United States people observe Labor Day, a national holiday that celebrates the labor movement, specifically unions and other labor organizations, and all those who contribute to society with their hard work.

It was a hard-won battle for worker's rights—one that is still being fought today—but the holiday also has become the unofficial end of summer, falling as it does right before most kids go back to school.

. . .

TRY THIS: *Labor Day is a good occasion to have a picnic and get outside while it is still warm enough, but at some point during the day think about your own labors. What is it you work for? Do you labor for the love of what you do or to feed your family or to make a difference in the world? Do you feel as though your labor is valued? Do you value the labor of others? Think about what your work means to you and why you do it. Take the day to celebrate that, too, while you're at it.*

September 6
Education

This is the time of year when the kids go back to school. Whether it is kindergarten or college, they grab their books and supplies and head out to learn—and you know, that's not a bad idea, no matter your age.

One of the facets of witchcraft that I like the most is that it isn't just a matter of spiritual belief (in the gods or magic or the moon), it's also a path of personal growth. All the witches I respect the most, both famous and not, strive to become their best selves, growing and reaching out to be more, better, wiser.

This doesn't have to mean formal education, although it is never too late to go back to school and learn something new. But it does mean stretching your mind and your boundaries and never thinking, "This is good enough. I guess I'll stop here."

* * *

TRY THIS: *What do you want to learn more about? Is it some facet of the Craft or a form of art or some practical skill that will improve your life? Whatever interests you, study it. After all, you know what they say: knowledge is power—so go learn something!*

September 7
Learning and Growing

If we're going to talk about continuing to learn and grow (and yes, we *are* going to talk about that), then let's look specifically at the practice of witchcraft. There's a reason we call it a practice. Witchcraft isn't something that someone shows you how to do and voilà, you're all set. It is an ongoing journey during which, hopefully, you find new and interesting aspects that pique your interest. The idea is to always learn and grow as a witch and as a human being.

There's also a reason why it is called the Craft. Like any craft, such as pottery or cooking or writing, the more you study and practice, the better you will be at it. I might have started out with a gift for witchcraft, just as I started out with a gift for writing, but I didn't excel at either one the first day I started doing them. I practiced and honed my craft and read books that told me how to do both. And then I studied with people who knew more than I did or at least had mastered different aspects than I had, and I learned more from them.

There are lots of different ways to continue to learn and grow as a witch, and no one path is right for everyone. I can't tell you which way you should study or how you should practice your Craft. I can only tell you that it is worth the effort to do so.

• • •

TRY THIS: *What are you going to learn next?*
Pick some aspect of the Craft and learn more about it.

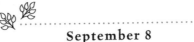

September 8
"Autumn Fires"

I love this poem, which perfectly captures the essence of fall.

> In the other gardens
> And all up the vale,
> From the autumn bonfires
> See the smoke trail!
>
> Pleasant summer over
> And all the summer flowers,
> The red fire blazes,
> The grey smoke towers.
>
> Sing a song of seasons!
> Something bright in all!
> Flowers in the summer,
> Fires in the fall!

(Robert Louis Stevenson, 1913)

TRY THIS: *Collect some things from nature or look for photos online that represent the fall season such as colorful leaves, fall flowers and plants. Display them or put them on your altar to celebrate this changing time of year.*

Witchy Words of Wisdom:
Dorothy Morrison

Dorothy Morrison has written some of the most popular and often-recommended books on witchcraft, but of all her books, I think *Everyday Moon Magic: Spells & Rituals for Abundant Living* is probably my favorite.

Here is a tidbit from her chapter on moon phases and their magic:

> Even though we usually associate the Full Moon with magic, it is not the only phase that tugs at our emotions. The waxing, waning, and dark phases also come into play. In fact, each phase exudes a particular and separate type of energy that feeds and energizes the emotional pool, and since pure, raw, and unadulterated emotion triggers successful magic, the Moon—in all Her phases—comprises one of the most powerful tools we can use in our efforts.

• • •

TRY THIS: *Read more of Morrison's writing. Her style in* Everyday Moon Magic *is practical, positive, and down to earth—an irony for a book on moon magic, perhaps—and I find her books very easy to read and follow.*

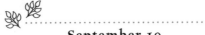

Thyme

Most people think of thyme as something you use to season a roasted chicken, but it is much more useful than that. I have a huge swath of thyme in my herb garden, since it tends to spread. I am particularly fond of lemon thyme, which has a sharp citrusy smell, but all the different types of thyme can be used interchangeably in magical work. Bees love the tiny flowers that blossom in the summer, so that brings an added bonus to your garden. It can even be used as a living path since most of it grows fairly low to the ground, like a carpet of magical herby goodness.

Traditionally, thyme has been used in healing spells—both those to attract good health and those to cure ill health. This makes sense since the herb has many medicinal qualities too. Use it in sleep sachets, healing baths, and most other forms of magic.

Thyme's other magical applications include purification (the Greeks burned it for purification in their temples, so burn it before beginning a ritual), love, increasing psychic abilities, and increasing courage.

Plus, of course, there is always that chicken…

* * *

TRY THIS: *Do something magical with thyme today, whether it is kitchen magic, herbal magic, or something else. One easy project is to roll a candle in the dried herb and then burn it, making sure that it is on a fire-safe plate in case of loose bits.*

September 11
What Does This Year's Harvest Look Like?

As we near the middle of the harvest season, it makes sense to take a good look at what we have harvested so far this year. When we planted our seeds—practical, spiritual, and anything in between—back in the spring, we had goals and aspirations for what we would accomplish in the year to come.

Take a good long honest look at where you are with these goals. Have you achieved what you had hoped to? If so, pat yourself on the back. If not, what can you change to improve things? Or have your goals themselves changed as you moved through the year?

· · ·

TRY THIS: *Ask yourself, what does this year's harvest look like? Am I happy with it? If you're not, write down three ways in which you can change your approach.*

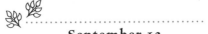

September 12
The Power of Words

One of the tenets of witchcraft is that words have power. That's why we usually speak our spells and wishes aloud. This concept can be taken a step further and applied to our everyday lives. After all, if words have enough power to create change through magic and ritual, it behooves us to think about how we use them the rest of the time.

Anyone who has ever been bullied knows how much pain simple words can cause, but words can also heal. Think about how an otherwise bad day can be improved by someone saying "I love you." Words have power.

In his classic *Magical Rites from the Crystal Well*, Ed Fitch included something he called "The Witches Rede of Chivalry." The language is somewhat flowery and archaic, but much of what he said still resonates. For instance, "A witch's word must have the validity of a signed and witnessed oath. Thus, give thy word sparingly, but adhere to it like iron." Or, put more simply: if you make a promise, keep it.

Another line says, "Refrain from speaking ill of others, for not all truths of the matter may be known." Gossip, like bullying, can be hurtful and negative. Would you want people saying bad things about you? Probably not.

• • •

TRY THIS: *There is no way to watch your words every minute of every day and never slip up. But being mindful of the power of words is a good place to start. For the next day or so, be extra careful of what you say and how your words affect others.*

September 13
The Fifth Chakra

The fifth chakra, also known as the throat chakra, is in the front of the neck, in the V of the collarbone. It rules speech, self-expression, communication, creativity, the arts, and speaking your own truth. Physically, it is associated with the thyroid, mouth, jaw, neck, and everything else in that general area.

The throat chakra is usually seen as blue in color, and when it is out of balance, you may feel powerless and unable to speak your mind. Many people store anger in this chakra, and letting it go can lead to positive change and transformation.

· · ·

TRY THIS: *Aquamarine is a good stone to use in working with the throat chakra. If you can find a piece of aquamarine or some other light blue stone, rest it gently on your throat and visualize it clearing away any anger or blockages with a softly glowing blue light of harmony and peace.*

September 14
I Will Speak My Truth

In our society we often feel it is risky to say what we really think and feel. Certainly there are times when it is inadvisable to speak your mind (if it would get you fired, for instance, or hurt someone else's feelings unnecessarily). But it is also important to be true to yourself, even in the face of negativity or rejection. Here is an affirmation to help you feel strong enough to stand up and be heard:

> I *speak my truth and am honest with myself and others.*
> I *embrace my own truth and speak it proudly.*

TRY THIS: *Say this affirmation as you stand in front of a mirror. Stand tall, with your head held high, and say it out loud in a firm, calm, decisive voice.*

September 15
The Moon

To many folks, the moon is simply an astronomical object in the sky, but if you are a Pagan, it is so much more than that. The moon is the symbol of our Goddess and a central part of our worship. For most witches, a magical practice includes the monthly celebration of the full moon, and often the new moon as well. The full moon is considered the most powerful time to do magic, recharge your spiritual batteries, and cleanse body and tools, as well as a night to connect with the Goddess.

We follow the waxing and waning of the moon and often approach our magical work differently depending on which stage the moon is at. (Waxing moons are good for increase, and the waning moon is more appropriate for decrease.) It is part of the ever-changing cycle of nature that is at the basis of a witchcraft practice.

She is also beautiful, our moon, as one would expect for an orb that symbolizes a goddess. Last night I glanced out my window and saw a bright crescent moon shining out from behind some clouds. As is traditional, I kissed the back of my hand and blew the kiss up to the Goddess. Then I continued on with what I was doing, my heart inexplicably lighter and filled with joy.

• • •

TRY THIS: *Do you go outside to greet the moon? If not, try it. Who knows—maybe she will answer you with a smile carried down on a moonbeam.*

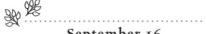

September 16
Shamanic Journeying

Shamans are in almost every culture across the globe, and shamanic journeying is a practice that has come to the modern Pagan experience through a long history. Shamans are usually healers, among other things, and shamanic journeying is used for healing, to increase self-knowledge, and to obtain information only accessible on a spiritual level.

To put it simply, the spirit of the person taking the journey travels outside the body to places often referred to as the upper, middle, and lower realms, or occasionally to actual places in the physical world. The traveler usually seeks something specific, whether it is healing or answers, and that search influences the journey. Drums or rattles are often used to shift the mind into a calm and receptive state and to facilitate the journeying. I have had several interesting and helpful experiences with shamanic journeying, most of them guided by a friend who is a shaman and hypnotherapist.

· · ·

TRY THIS: *You should be able to find a CD or a YouTube video that will guide you through a simple shamanic journey, although unless you have a natural gift for such things, you might be better off finding someone who can truly guide you into these mysterious realms and help you to return safely from your journeying.*

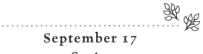

September 17
Snake

There is a certain primal aversion in many humans when it comes to snakes. This is probably a survival trait written into our DNA because so many of them can be poisonous. On the other hand, some folks love them. A friend of mine had a beautiful coral-colored milk snake named Sarah, who I got along with just fine, as long as she stayed in her space and I stayed in mine. And because I have a garden and an old farmhouse with a stone foundation, I have lots of garter snakes, which are perfectly harmless and quite helpful with small pests. (Although on the rare occasion one manages to make its way into the house, I must confess I help it back outside again as quickly as possible!)

Magically and spiritually, snakes are altogether positive. They symbolize healing (like the two snakes entwined around the caduceus, the staff of medicine), personal growth, the ability to move between two worlds (since they go below and above ground), metamorphosis, transitions, and spiritual renewal.

• • •

TRY THIS: *If a snake shows up as your totem animal, it is probably an indication that you are preparing for a time of change. Get ready to shed your old skin and transform yourself, inside and out. If this is something you need to do, see if you can connect with the snake spirit.*

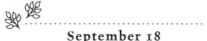

September 18
Transitions

Change is hard. Being in the midst of a transition—moving from one place or job or relationship or state of being—is even tougher. You've let go of the old and you haven't quite rooted yourself in the new yet. Maybe this transition was something you wanted and worked for willingly, or maybe it was thrust on you by life, by others, by circumstance; but however you've come to it, your world has been shaken up like a snow globe, and that can be tough to live through. You can't avoid transitions, but you can do some things to make them go a little more smoothly.

First: stop fighting. Most of us resist change and make transitions harder on ourselves than they need to be. Did you choose to make this transition? Then jump in and embrace the changes. Not fighting is harder if you didn't choose the changes—whether it is dealing with illness, the end of a relationship, job or money issues, or anything else—but if the change is inevitable and there is nothing you can do to stop it, then try to go with the flow of the transition.

The second tip can be even more difficult, but it is the key to making successful transitions: focus on the positive. If you're in transition because life threw you a curveball, try to look at the possibilities this change might open up for you. Sometimes tough transitions can be the beginning of something new and unexpected.

Remember that change and transition are opportunities for learning and growth. The lessons aren't always easy, but the paths you take may lead you to the place you were meant to be all along.

. . .

> **TRY THIS:** *Don't forget to lean on your spiritual beliefs either; it is always okay to ask the God and Goddess for the strength, wisdom, and guidance that will make your transition go as smoothly as possible.*

September 19
Demeter and Persephone

One of my favorite Greek myths is the bittersweet tale of Demeter and Persephone, which is used to explain why we have half a year of warmth and growth and half a year of winter. Demeter, the goddess of the earth, and her daughter, Persephone, were gathering plants in a meadow. Persephone wandered off and was snatched up by Hades, the god of the underworld, who was captivated by her youth and beauty. He carried her off to his kingdom. Demeter wandered the earth looking for her lost child, and in her grief she no longer tended to the growing things, which withered and died. Eventually, Hecate helped her to find Persephone, but by the time Demeter reclaimed her daughter, Persephone had eaten six pomegranate seeds and so had to stay in the underworld for half the year. And thus, half the year Demeter rejoices in the company of her daughter, and the world blooms. The other half she mourns, and the world is gray and the plants don't grow.

This seems like a sad ending to the story, but as Pagans, we know that it is just part of the cycle of life, death, and rebirth. The ground needs time to rest, as do those who work it. According to some of the tales, Persephone loved her dark husband, and her presence brought some light to the underworld.

* * *

TRY THIS: *Eat some pomegranate seeds at the*
fall equinox and think of what they symbolize
as you prepare for the cold months ahead.

September 20
Harvest Corn and Potato Salad

I love the harvest season because fresh produce makes it easy to whip up delicious dishes with very little effort. This is a twist on the usual boring potato salad, and I think you'll like it. Cook the corn ahead of time or make it when you toss the potatoes into the pot, and let them both cool off before you combine them.

Cook, cool, and chop into bite-sized pieces about two pounds of potatoes. I like to mix purple ones and fingerlings (both of which I grow) because the colors look so pretty with the other ingredients, but any kind of potato will do. Small red ones are nice too.

Add the kernels from one ear of corn, some chopped tomatoes (about a cup—I like the colorful cherry or grape tomatoes), a stalk or two of chopped celery, and some chopped fresh herbs (my favorites are parsley, basil, and chives). Toss with oil and vinegar or a summery vinaigrette, and you'll have a vibrant, bright looking and tasting harvest dish to serve for a feast or just for dinner.

· · ·

TRY THIS: *Vary the amounts of the ingredients depending on your own tastes, and substitute with ingredients you happen to have in the house, such as diced red onion, chopped hard-boiled eggs, or chopped walnuts.*

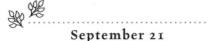

September 21
Fall Equinox

The fall equinox, also known as Mabon, is the second of the two harvest festivals on the witchy calendar. Its actual date varies, but one thing stays the same: it is the only other day of the year, besides its counterpart the spring equinox, on which the amount of daylight and night are exactly equal. But unlike in spring, when the light increases with every day that follows, after Mabon the light decreases as we enter the dark half of the year.

We celebrate what we have harvested—both physically and metaphorically—and we mourn those things we have failed to accomplish. We bid goodbye to the summer and turn our sights toward the colder, darker days to come.

But harvest festivals are mostly times to gather together and enjoy what we have—friends, family, and food on the table. I think this is one of those sabbats when the feast table should be filled with seasonal foods, and even if you don't happen to have a witchy group to share the day with, there's no reason you can't have an equinox party with your non-Pagan friends.

· · ·

TRY THIS: *Use this day to focus on your connection to all the witches who came before you, many of whom celebrated the same holiday in much the same way. As you sit down to your feast table, think about how important the harvest was to those who came before you, for whom a good harvest could mean the difference between life and death, and be grateful.*

September 22
Faith

The element of spirit is considerably more elusive than that of earth, air, fire, and water. Perhaps its most intangible aspect is faith. Faith manifests differently for all of us, but if you're reading this book, you probably have some kind of esoteric faith, a mystical belief in what cannot be seen, yet you still somehow believe exists.

I came late to faith. I never particularly believed in anything until I discovered witchcraft in my thirties. In the years since I found my way to my spiritual path, I have also come to have faith that, for the most part, things work out the way they are supposed to (which isn't, mind you, always the way I want them to work out)—not always, but mostly. That I can create positive changes in my life, and if I try hard enough, there will be help from outside me. And that no matter how many times I fall down, there will be a loving hand to help me get up, as long as I am willing to make the effort. That's what faith means to me and what the element of spirit means, at least in part.

• • •

TRY THIS: *Think about what faith means to you, and put it into words. Write it down in your journal or Book of Light or just sit quietly and feel it.*

September 23
Spell for Balance

One of my favorite aspects of the holiday of Mabon is that the fall equinox brings in the opportunity to work on energy for balance.

I don't know about you, but this is a challenge I have been working on for years, and I'm not making progress with this goal as well as I would like. Still, I plug away at it—striving for better balance between work and play, time alone and time spent with others, and everything else that contributes to leading a healthy, happy, productive life.

As you prepare to say this spell, light one black candle and one white candle or wind two ribbons of those colors together. Mostly, though, focus on the places in your life that are most out of balance, and open yourself up to shifting into a new equilibrium. Say:

> Black and white, white and black
> Help me get my balance back
> Balance work and balance play
> Balance all the night and day
> White and black, black and white
> Help me see with clearer sight
> How to balance want and need
> And for new balance plant the seed

TRY THIS: *Recite this spell on Mabon but also at any other time you feel the need for balance in your life.*

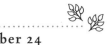

September 24
Libra

Those born between September 24 and October 23 have the sun sign of Libra, the scales. As you might expect from this symbol, Librans tend to prefer balance and harmony, and they will bend over backward to get along with others. Libra is an air sign, so creativity and intellect are often prominent traits. Of course, as with any other sign, there are downsides on occasion: because of their eagerness to please, they may be indecisive or easily influenced.

• • •

TRY THIS: *During this sun period, whether you are a Libra or not, work toward achieving balance in your life without giving up your own inner path. Creative and intellectual endeavors are also likely to shine.*

September 25
Fountains

I confess: I love fountains. There is something about the sound of trickling or splashing water that just seems to naturally soothe the human soul. The great thing about fountains is that they are an easy (and often pretty) way to connect with the element of water, with no more effort on your part than it takes to set one up.

I have a fountain in my small garden pond. It helps aerate the water to keep the pond and its inhabitants (goldfish, frogs, and newts) healthy, but it is also a lovely sound to listen to while I am out pulling weeds or harvesting tomatoes. I also have a standing solar fountain in my front yard, not too far from the window nearest to the couch. If I open the window, I can hear the water burbling away. (And because it is solar, it doesn't even use any energy.)

Of course, those fountains get put away at the end of the warm months, so I have a small tabletop fountain inside to give me my water fix during the winter.

Fountains require maintenance, and they can vary in price depending on their size and how fancy they are. But even a small, inexpensive indoor fountain can give you hours of pleasure, soothe your spirit, and help you connect to water.

* * *

TRY THIS: *Get a fountain of some kind, even if it is just a small one that sits on your counter.*

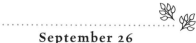

September 26
Orange

Orange may be the new black, but it is also the same old very useful orange, at least when it comes to magical work. Orange is the color of fall, of fire in its gentler form, and, like yellow, it also represents the sun and solar power. I use it primarily in spells for courage, increased energy, and increased confidence.

If you need a boost, carry an orange-colored stone such as light carnelian, amber, or dark citrine. These stones all come in a wide range of hues, so you can find the one that calls to you the most. One of my favorites is a piece of amber set into a silver sun symbol. Who wouldn't feel better while wearing that?

• • •

TRY THIS: *For increased energy, wear a necklace with one or all of these stones. Meditate on courage and self-confidence while holding a stone and staring at an orange candle. Orange clothing can give you a boost too!*

September 27
Witchy Words of Wisdom:
Edain McCoy

Edain McCoy has written many books on modern witchcraft, but the one I find most useful is the one on covens. There aren't as many books on "how to" for covens as you'd think. I wish I had found McCoy's book back when I was just starting out with my own coven.

This quote is from McCoy's *The Witch's Coven: Finding or Forming Your Own Circle*:

> Covens come in all sizes and structures, many of them good, some mediocre. A few could possibly be called dangerous. A coven may have only two members; I have known others containing as many as sixty. There are almost as many different types of covens as there are witches, and certainly there are as many different ways to run a coven as there are individual Craft traditions.

• • •

TRY THIS: *If you want to practice with others, I highly recommend reading McCoy's book. She has much witchy wisdom about why to work in a coven and how to find one.*

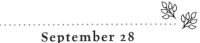

September 28
Covens

One of the ironies of my life is that in most aspects of my existence I tend to be solitary, and yet, when it comes to witchcraft, it turns out that I am a group kind of witch. This isn't to say that I don't practice on my own; even witches who belong to some sort of group do magical work by themselves too. But the core of my witchcraft experience began with a group run by the high priestess who introduced me to the Craft, and I spent years practicing with them before starting my own coven, Blue Moon Circle, in 2004.

Covens aren't for everyone. I have plenty of witchy friends who are happier being on their own. Some folks would like to be in a group but can't find one near them or can't find one that suits their own particular style or beliefs. And covens are much like any other relationship: it is better to be alone than it is to be with the wrong person or people. You don't want to do magic with people who make you stressed or unhappy. On the other hand, a truly good coven is a blessing. Practicing with others is like a relationship in other ways as well. It takes good communication, compromise, and a shared commitment to make it work—and when it does, it is magical indeed.

TRY THIS: *If you have a friend or two who have witchy inclinations, try doing some magic together. You don't have to form anything as formal as a coven to practice with others.*

September 29
The Speaking Stick

A speaking stick isn't a tool that a solitary witch will need, but if you practice with others, it can be extremely valuable.

Something that originated with Native Americans and tribes in other countries, the speaking stick (also called a talking stick) can be an ornate formal stick, carved and intricately decorated, or it can be as plain as a branch that was picked up off the ground. Blue Moon Circle has used driftwood, feathers, and other items, as well as actual sticks, for this purpose.

The speaking stick's role is simple: to give everyone in the circle a chance to speak and be heard. Toward the end of ritual, the stick is passed from person to person, and whoever holds it gets to say whatever is on their mind. Only the person holding the stick speaks. When that person is done speaking, they pass the stick to the next person.

This doesn't sound like much, but think about how rarely we get to speak without interruption, with the full attention of others focused on the words we say from the heart. In today's hectic world, where many feel isolated and disenfranchised, the speaking stick gives us a rare moment to speak freely and know that others are listening.

• • •

TRY THIS: *If you practice with others and don't already use a speaking stick, try it out at your next ritual.*

September 30
Worry Stones

No, worry stones are not rocks that fret about things. (I'm pretty sure that rocks don't fret, although I've never actually asked one.) A worry stone is simply a small, smooth oval stone that fits comfortably in the hand, usually with an indentation in the middle shaped so that the thumb can rub across it.

Worry stones have been used in many cultures, including Native American, Celtic, Greek, and Tibetan, and can be found these days in almost every Pagan or New Age shop. I have a couple of nice ones I've picked up in my travels. You can choose a specific type of gemstone—maybe a nice green one if you are always worrying about money, or rose quartz if you need something to keep you calm—or just find one that feels right when you hold it.

The idea is that instead of biting your nails or smoking a cigarette or just plain fretting, you stroke your thumb across the rock, and the motion and energy of the gemstone will soothe you instead. Don't worry, be happy—or at least get a worry stone.

● ● ●

TRY THIS: *Tuck a worry stone in your pocket or keep it on your altar until you need it.*

October 1
Ethics

Ethics in witchcraft are a tricky thing, and it means something a little bit different to everyone. Ethics, essentially, are a code of conduct—what is considered right and wrong in any given society. Witchcraft as a whole is primarily an ethical society, the problem being that not everyone agrees on what those ethics are.

For instance, the most commonly stated rule is the Wiccan Rede: An it harm none, do as ye will. But does that mean you can't harm someone in self-defense or the defense of someone else? Does it mean every witch has to be a vegetarian? What about things that harm yourself?

And what about hexing? Hexing is magic cast against a specific person with negative intent. Obviously that's against the rules, right? But there are those, like Z Budapest, who regularly hex rapists. Is this okay or not? That's a tricky one.

I can't answer those questions for you. Ethical decisions are very personal, and each of us must choose for ourselves what we believe to be right and what we believe to be wrong (and how much slack we cut ourselves and others when those lines are crossed). But it is a topic worthy of discussion if you have other Pagans in your social circles and one worth thinking about even if you don't.

• • •

TRY THIS: *Think about this topic. What do you think should be against the rules? Where do you draw the line when using your own power?*

October 2
Witches in Music

As a general rule, when we think about Pagan music, drumming, chanting, or meditative background CDs come to mind. But in fact, there are a number of truly impressive and talented witchy singers and bands out there, from folk to rock and everything in between. If you haven't listened to any of it yet, do some exploring online or at your nearest festival.

A few names are probably the most commonly associated with Pagan music, such as Wendy Rule, Sharon Knight, S. J. Tucker, Avalon Rising, Gaia Consort, Kellianna, Heather Dale, Blackmore's Night, Gabrielle Roth, and Heather Alexander. But you can find many more in whatever style you like just by going to YouTube and typing in "Pagan music." Or, of course, you could ask your friends what they like. One of my favorite CDs is *Rock the Goddess* by Daughters of Gaia, but I also love listening to everything from witchy folk, Celtic, and rock to chants.

* * *

TRY THIS: *If you want something to get you into the magical mood or just some fun witchy-themed music to work out to, start up your collection—assuming, that is, that you don't have one already. If you have one, add something new!*

October 3
Inclusion

One of the things I love most about being a witch is that it is a religion of inclusion, as opposed to exclusion. For the most part, we welcome everyone, regardless of the color of their skin, their sexual orientation, relationship preferences, or how they choose to worship. Funky piercings and a lot of tattoos? No one is going to look at you twice. A man wearing a dress? Mostly, I'm just jealous if they look better in it than I would.

Some might say that witchcraft attracts a lot of oddballs and unconventional types. Um, yes, we do. But those are my peeps you are talking about. (What—you thought I wasn't odd?) We welcome the people who don't feel welcome anywhere else, and I think that's wonderful. After all, everyone should feel welcome somewhere.

Mind you, being inclusive doesn't mean putting up with bad behavior or out-and-out craziness. Just because we accept most alternative lifestyles doesn't mean that everything goes. Almost everything, yes, but not *everything*.

Still, one of the things people say the most often about how they felt when they discovered witchcraft/Paganism is that it was like "coming home." And I love that we open the doors of our home to so many diverse types.

* * *

TRY THIS: *Are there witchy types you don't feel comfortable accepting? Do you feel as though you aren't accepted? Come up with ways to reach out to others with love and acceptance.*

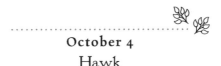

October 4
Hawk

I have a huge meadow out behind the tree line that marks the end of my yard. Hills surround the meadow and apparently provide the perfect conditions for large birds because almost every day I see hawks gliding effortlessly on the thermals. They are mostly red-tailed hawks, which are common in New York State, but for the last few years I have also had smaller kestrels nesting in a hole in the side of my barn.

Hawks represent clear sight, messages, swiftness, endurance, and the sun. In some mythology they were associated with war, although they also can be seen as protective. If the hawk appears as your spirit animal, it may mean you will receive an important message or that it is time for you to look clearly at your life. It may also be a protective totem.

To me, hawks represent freedom, wisdom, and the ability to rise above the baser aspects of existence to explore the spiritual level that is there if only we open our eyes to it.

• • •

TRY THIS: *See if you can find a place where you can watch hawks fly. If there isn't one near you, try a hawk cam online.*

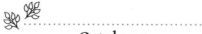

October 5
Skyclad

If someone invites you to a ritual and tells you that all those attending will be skyclad, you probably won't need to worry about wearing the same outfit as someone else or whether your shoes match your skirt—because you won't be needing either.

Skyclad is a term used in Pagan circles that means naked. In other words, you will be clad only in the sky around you. Needless to say, some folks are more comfortable with this than others. There are plenty of groups and festivals that are clothing-optional for those who prefer it.

Witches who perform rituals skyclad do so because they believe it is best not to have anything between them and the gods or because it makes them feel free. This practice mostly dates back to Gerald Gardner and to a section of the "Charge of the Goddess" poem, and it was common in some witchcraft traditions, especially those that stemmed from Gardnerian Wicca.

Being skyclad during ritual has nothing to do with sex. It is more a matter of being completely open and unrestricted in a safe place. But if it isn't for you, don't worry. There are plenty of other ways to worship and still keep your clothes on.

TRY THIS: *Even if you aren't comfortable going skyclad around others, try doing a ritual naked in the privacy of your own home.*

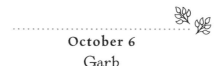

October 6
Garb

If you're not into going skyclad (or if you're going to a public event where doing so might get you arrested), another alternative is garb. Garb is basically special clothing—it may be reserved for ritual use or also worn to festivals, Renaissance Faires, or conventions.

I love garb. It can be as simple as a ritual robe that can either be worn over regular clothes, other garb, or nothing at all. It often is flowy and somewhat fanciful in style. I have a number of shirts that have long flowing sleeves and ribbon-tied bodices that would look equally at home at a ritual or at any faire. I also have a cloak I made in my early days of my witchcraft practice as part of my commitment to the Craft. (It helps that it is somewhat water-resistant and reasonably warm, especially on Samhain, when the weather can get very iffy.)

Garb is fun to wear, of course, but it also serves a purpose. When we put on garb, especially clothing reserved exclusively for ritual work, it reminds us that we are stepping out of our regular lives and into sacred space. Donning a hooded cloak or a pentacle necklace helps us to get into the right mind frame to perform magic. And it doesn't hurt if we look good doing it, does it?

• • •

TRY THIS: *Find a cool witchy piece of clothing or a cape and set it aside for magical work.*

October 7
Autumn Leaves

Where I live, fall is a beautiful season. The leaves turn vibrant colors, glowing in shades of yellow, orange, and red. The show doesn't last very long, but while it does you can gather up handfuls of leaves and do all sorts of crafty things with them.

One simple way to preserve leaves and keep them looking pretty is to dip them in wax. To imbue them with more witchy energy, collect the leftover ends of ritual candles and melt those down over a double boiler. Then hold the leaves by the stems, dip them in, and let the wax drip off a bit before laying them out on waxed paper to dry. Once your leaves are preserved, hang them from fishing line or thin ribbons to make decorative mobiles or a garland, turn them into wreaths using other seasonal elements such as acorns and tiny pinecones, or frame them and hang them on the wall.

Slightly less natural is the craft glue called Mod Podge, which is used for decoupage. Decorate your leaves with glitter or draw on them (inspirational words, spirals, goddess figures, stars), then seal them with Mod Podge. Or place the leaves onto tiles or stones and spread the Mod Podge over them. For a pretty fall candleholder, spread Mod Podge over leaves that you've arranged on the outside of a glass jar.

* * *

TRY THIS: *As with any other craft, the only limit is your imagination. Create something using leaves, perhaps with friends or your kids.*

October 8
Journaling

As we move into the dark time of the year, the energy shifts so that we are more internally focused than externally focused. (Unless you have kids, in which case you are always externally focused, but even so, you deserve a few minutes for you.) This is a good time to start journaling if you didn't do it with a Book of Light at the beginning of the calendar year.

The darker, quieter days of late fall and winter make it easier to turn your attention inward, and a journal is the perfect place to put those thoughts you don't necessarily feel like speaking aloud. You can also use it to keep track of any attempts you make at magic, psychic exercises, your dreams, and so on. A journal is a bit like talking to yourself, except that the idea is to be completely nonjudgmental. Let the words spill out on the paper and just be.

If you think a journal has to be like the diaries some of us had as kids, you haven't seen the new blank books out there. Find ones with pentacles or goddesses or moons or cats—or make your own. Either way, it should feel like a safe place to look inward and keep track of your thoughts, hopes, and dreams.

● ● ●

TRY THIS: *If you don't have one already, start a journal today.*

October 9
Witchy Words of Wisdom:
Christopher Penczak

One of the complaints I often hear is that most witchcraft books are what some call "Witchcraft 101"—that is to say, aimed at relative beginners. This isn't necessarily true (a couple of my books are definitely aimed at those who have been practicing for a while), nor is it a bad thing (since everyone needs to start somewhere), but if you want a deeper exploration of the Craft, you can't do any better than to turn to Christopher Penczak.

Penczak is the author of more than twenty books, the founder of the Temple of Witchcraft tradition, a witch, a teacher, and a healer. He's also a pretty cool guy. (We've hung out together at a few conventions.)

Here is what he had to say about the way we look at "positive" and "negative" (from his book *The Mystic Foundation: Understanding and Exploring the Magical Universe*):

> These days we use the term positive to denote all things "good" and negative to denote all things "bad," but this terminology is imprecise…What mystics mean when they say "banish all negative" is that they want to banish all energies that would cause harm or imbalance…
>
> So the next time you say a prayer, affirmation, or spell to be protected from "all negative forces," perhaps you should ask for protection from "all forces that bring me harm."

• • •

TRY THIS: *Do some research on Christopher Penczak. His books are definitely not light reading, but they are well worth the time if you want to deepen your approach to magic. His work really makes you think.*

October 10
Creating Sacred Space

Sacred space is just what it sounds like: a space set aside for rituals or spiritual work. It can be a permanent space: a church, sacred ground, the stone and grass circle out behind my barn where my group has been practicing magic for over a dozen years. Or it can be temporary, like when you cast a circle during ritual and then take it down as soon as you are done.

Anyone can create sacred space; all it takes is focus and intention. For rituals, we often light candles, call the quarters, and use incense or sage smudge sticks as we summon up sacred space. Those things aren't necessary, but they help us focus our energy on the task.

Sacred space should be treated as just that—sacred. That means no cell phones, no altered states unless it happens to be a part of your particular magical tradition, respect for anyone else who happens to be there with you, and a reasonably serious attitude. The best thing about sacred space is that it creates a place where it is easier to reach out and talk to deity. Not that we can't do that all the time, but sacred space is designed to facilitate that act, and for this alone, it is worth making.

• • •

TRY THIS: *Create some sacred space today.*

October 11
Am I the Witch I Want to Be?

As we go through life, it is always a good idea to periodically check in and see if we are living up to the goals and ideals we've set for ourselves. If, for instance, it is important for you to be a kind and honest person, occasionally look back over your recent interactions and make sure you are sticking to your intentions.

In that same way, most of us have a picture in our heads of the kind of witch we want to be. That picture probably won't be the same for any two of us. My idea of the "perfect witch" may not have much in common with yours. And let's face it, nobody lives up to "perfect." No, not even me. I don't practice as much as I'd like to (mostly because I am busy writing books telling other people how to practice...and yes, I see the irony there). But I do try to walk my talk the best I can in all the aspects of my day-to-day life.

• • •

TRY THIS: *Today and in some of the days that follow, ask yourself this: Am I the witch I want to be? And if the answer is no, what can you do to change that?*

October 12
Vervain

Vervain has long been associated with witches and witchcraft, and it is believed to have been sacred to the Druids as well. It is associated with the goddess Isis and was once said to have sprung from her tears. Priests in Roman temples used bundles of vervain to sweep the altars clean. In short, this herb is a magical powerhouse with a long history spread far and wide.

It was traditional to gather vervain on the summer solstice, but really you can harvest it any time the pretty purple flowers bloom. Use the dried herb in sachets, infusions, and incenses, among other things. Its magical uses include protection, healing, cleansing, love, peace, and sleep. No wonder one of its folk nicknames was "enchanter's plant."

I've been thinking of planting some outside my front door, both for its beauty and for its protective powers—an herbal double whammy, if you will. I'm pretty sure the Druids would approve.

• • •

TRY THIS: *Plant some seeds or use vervain in something magical today. If you can't do either, find a photo of vervain online or in a book and ponder its power and history.*

October 13
Opal and Labradorite

October's birthstone is opal, a beautiful stone that can vary from white with just the slightest shimmering hint of other colors to a flashy multicolored hue. This variation in colors, called opalescence, means that magically the opal can stand in for any other color or stone. Fire opals in particular can be used to draw in money, and black opals are supposed to be particularly magical. All opals can be used to increase psychic abilities and for beauty, prosperity, luck, and power.

Unfortunately, opals also can be quite expensive, so if you want a reasonably priced substitute, look for one of my personal favorite stones: labradorite. Labradorite is a grayish silver stone with that same subtle glimmering opalescence that shows hints of green, blue, and purple. It is a highly protective stone and is said to remove negative energies, thus paving the way for healing and better internal balance. It is also calming and aids in spiritual transformation.

Both stones are beautiful and unequivocally positive—plus, of course, they go with everything in your wardrobe, which is an extra bonus.

. . .

TRY THIS: *If you don't have an opal, look for a piece of labradorite to use instead.*

October 14
Spell for Courage

It can be hard to have courage in the face of life's challenges, but without it, it is difficult to keep moving forward in a positive way. As we edge slowly into the darker time of year, courage sometimes becomes even harder to find. Here is a spell to help, which can be used now or whenever you need it:

Strength of backbone, strength of heart
Arrive like sunrise at day's start
Grow throughout the passing day
Unimpressed by darkness's sway
Make me brave and make me strong
To face life's troubles all day long
Strength like trees that freely bend
Give me courage 'til day's end

• • •

TRY THIS: *If you want an extra boost, say this spell while holding one of the stones associated with courage (carnelian, amethyst, agate, lapis, tiger's-eye, or turquoise) and then tuck the stone into your pocket, under your pillow, or place it on your altar.*

October 15
The Horned God

The Horned God is perhaps the most widespread and iconic image of male deity, depicted back through the ages as a strong man with broad shoulders and the spreading antlers of a stag. Horned male figures have been found on cave walls; that's how much a part of human history he is.

The Horned God is a symbol of nature and fertility; as such, he is often depicted as the Goddess's consort. He may be called by the names Herne or Cernunnos, but for many of us, he is a different god in his own right. He may be as gentle as a faun or as playful as Pan, but make no mistake: he is nature personified and can be brutal and cruel as often as he is kind. The Horned God leads the Wild Hunt, is the protector of the animals, and is no one to be trifled with.

During the Middle Ages, the church tried to demonize this powerful deity by turning him into the devil—a frightening figure with horns, cloven hooves, and a tail. I suspect that the Horned God found this quite amusing. The church certainly didn't fool any of his followers, who exist to this day in the form of modern witches and Pagans, who still make his sign—pinky finger and thumb up (to look like horns), with the other three fingers folded down—in his honor.

• • •

TRY THIS: *Make an altar in honor of the Horned God in this, his season. Add whatever items or symbols you feel are appropriate.*

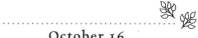

October 16
Beer

It is common for us to think of wine and mead as magical drinks, but most folks probably don't make that association for beer. But think about it…do they call it "cakes and wine"? No, they do not. In fact, the part of the ritual used to ground us at the end of magical work is called "cakes and ale," and ale, my friends, is beer.

Beer is as strongly rooted in the harvest season as wine. Unlike the grapes and fruit that make up its sweeter counterpart, beer is made from grains, perfect for this time of year. It can be made using wheat, barley, or other grains. The use of beer dates back to the oldest civilizations, including the Mesopotamians and the Sumerians. The Egyptians credited either Isis or Hathor for teaching humans how to make it. As with other forms of alcohol, it was used for celebration and health. (It is healthy too, as long as it is consumed in reasonable amounts and the person drinking it doesn't have any issues with alcohol.)

In Germany they have Oktoberfest, the world's largest celebration of beer, which dates back over two hundred years and has spawned many imitators across the globe.

• • •

TRY THIS: *Celebrate Oktoberfest at home. Sit in sacred space with a small glass of your favorite beer. Give thanks to the gods for the gift of fermentation, which provides us with both the bread and the beer for cakes and ale.*

October 17
Magic

There are many definitions of magic. Raymond Buckland prefers the definition that originated with occultist and ceremonial magician Aleister Crowley, who said, "Magic is the art or science of causing change to occur in conformity with will." Scott Cunningham, in his book *Wicca: A Guide for the Solitary Practitioner*, wrote, "Magic is the practice of moving natural (though little understood) energies to effect needed change." And in *The Spiral Dance*, Starhawk called magic "the art of sensing and shaping the subtle, unseen forces that flow through the world, of awakening deeper levels of consciousness beyond the rational."

All these definitions are good ones and express essentially the same notion in different ways. Magic is something we can't see or touch, but if we believe in it and hone our skills, we can manipulate this natural energy to create positive change in ourselves and in the world around us. To me, it is an aspect of the universe—like gravity or electrons or magnetic fields—that science as yet has been unable to quantify and therefore doesn't believe in. I view it as a tool, and like any other tool, it can be used for good or for harm and should be treated with respect and a certain healthy caution.

• • •

TRY THIS: *What does magic mean to you? Come up with your own definition based on your experiences.*

October 18

I Am the Magic and the Magic Is Me

Here is an affirmation to reinforce your connection to magic and reaffirm your own witchy powers:

> I *am the magic and the magic is me.*
> *There is no separation between us.*
> I *am the magic and the magic is me.*

* * *

TRY THIS: *Say this affirmation anytime you need to remind yourself that you, too, are magical.*

October 19
The Wild Hunt

The Wild Hunt is a legend found in many different countries, but its essence is always the same. The Wild Hunt is a supernatural processional, made up of riders, horses, and often dogs, racing through the dark and stormy night. In some cultures this took place at particular times, most especially at Samhain, Midsummer's Eve, or the twelve days of Yule. Some thought a god, such as Odin or Herne, or even a goddess, like Hulda, led the Wild Hunt. Others associated the Wild Hunt with the fairies.

The Wild Hunt is powerful and uncontrollable and therefore often perceived as frightening, but it was also sometimes depicted as a regal convoy that carried the souls of the dead to visit with their loved ones or led them off to their next plane of existence.

When I hear a truly tumultuous storm, I sometimes wonder if it is the Wild Hunt, led by some great god and filled with prancing red-eyed horses ridden by frightening yet starkly beautiful beings, their spectral hounds racing at their feet, on their way to someplace I can't even imagine. To me, the Wild Hunt is emblematic of nature itself: wild and beautiful and frightening and completely beyond our control.

* * *

TRY THIS: *Consider your vision of the Wild Hunt. Read a story about it and its participants if you're unsure of how you see it.*

October 20
Amber and Jet

Worn together, amber and jet are considered to be the traditional witch's gemstones, which is a little ironic, considering that neither of them is a stone.

They are both, in fact, the fossilized remains of ancient trees and resins; no wonder they have so much power. Amber is translucent, varying in color from very pale yellow to a deep, almost caramelized orange. Jet is black. They are both very light in weight, which is one way to tell if you have the genuine article.

Amber is a powerful stone, providing protection against negativity and considered especially helpful in protecting children and women during childbirth. It is also used for healing, love, prosperity, luck, and beauty spells. Jet has many of the same protective and healing properties and is also said to increase psychic powers. No wonder high priestesses wore necklaces that combined the two. I have one myself and have made them for the members of Blue Moon Circle.

* * *

TRY THIS: *Find yourself a piece of each stone. Hold them in your hand, one at a time, and connect with their energy. What do they feel like to you? Are they different from regular rocks? If you can't get amber and jet, find a photo of a necklace made from the two. Does it resonate with you? If so, put it on your witchy wish list.*

October 21
Hecate

Hecate is the goddess of witches and magic, of crossroads of all kinds (including between life and death), and a protector of women and children. Although most commonly known as a Greek deity, her roots stretch back through many countries in Europe, western Asia, and Egypt. She is often depicted as a mature woman or crone accompanied by black hounds, but she is actually a triple goddess of the moon—maiden, mother, and crone all at once. She is worshipped at night, often at the Dark Moon, and all the festivals in her name were traditionally held at night by the light of candles or torches. She is wise but fierce, as befits the goddess of witches. Blue Moon Circle invokes her every Samhain.

If you are at a crossroads in your life or need guidance on your path, Hecate is a good deity to call on for help. Despite her fearsome reputation, she is gentle with those who have been wronged, especially women and children, and can help with the birth of a child or ease the passing of someone making the transition from this world to the next. And she is the goddess of witches, so it is always appropriate for one of us to call her name.

• • •

TRY THIS: *Light a black candle on the night of the dark moon and call her name three times. You can also hold a traditional "Hecate's Supper" on Hecate's Night, which is November 16.*

October 22
Black

When people ask me what my favorite color is, they are always surprised when I say "black." The truth is, I find it soothing, and, of course, it is very witchy, although I liked it long before I was a witch. Black has gotten kind of a bad rap and was for many years associated with evil or negativity.

In fact, magically it is anything but, since the color is used for protection, banishing, balance, and to symbolize magical power. It is also the color of the Goddess as Crone, which may explain its use at Samhain, along with the orange of fire and fallen leaves.

I use a black candle when I need to get rid of something or protect myself from harmful energy. I use it when doing magic for any kind of balance, pairing a black candle and a white one. I also like to burn black candles around the Samhain bonfire.

Witches tend to wear a lot of black, so it's a good thing it is such a positive color!

• • •

TRY THIS: *Wear something black today or do some protective or banishing magic with a black candle.*

October 23
"Child Moon"

By now you have probably figured out that I love Carl Sandburg. He is one of the great American poets, with a way of capturing the simplest of moments with eloquence and imagery. Here is a lovely, magical, and evocative poem about a child's connection with the moon. How witchy is that?

> The child's wonder
> At the old moon
> Comes back nightly.
> She points her finger
> To the far silent yellow thing
> Shining through the branches
> Filtering on the leaves a golden sand,
> Crying with her little tongue, "See the moon!"
> And in her bed fading to sleep
> With babblings of the moon on her little mouth.

(Carl Sandburg, 1916)

* * *

TRY THIS: *Reflect for a moment on how you connect with the moon. How is that connection different now than from when you were a child?*

October 24
Scorpio

When you read about Scorpios, those born under the sun sign that falls between October 24 and November 22, you find words such as "intense," "focused," "forceful," and "determined." Clearly, these are not people to be taken lightly. They have a tendency to be intense, passionate, and loyal to those few they make commitments to.

Of course, as always, there is a downside to all this intensity; Scorpios may also be controlling, secretive, and ambitious. Like the scorpion that symbolizes the sign, if one turns against you, it will probably sting. Still, if you get a Scorpio on your side, you will have an ally you can always depend on.

• • •

TRY THIS: *During this time, work on projects you are passionate about and put all that Scorpio energy and focus to good use.*

October 25
Reincarnation

Many witches believe in reincarnation and the cycle of birth, growth, death, and rebirth. Reincarnation is the belief that when we die, we come back in another body to live another life. In many religions, especially those in India, it is thought that this continuing cycle allows us the chance to continue working on our flaws and become better human beings. In theory, we will eventually grow wise and pure enough that we will transmute into a form beyond that of the merely human and become something verging on the Divine.

The things I have learned about my own past lives have helped me to gain insight into issues I am dealing with in my current lifetime. There can be practical reasons for exploring your own earlier incarnations. One of the unexpected benefits I discovered about a belief in reincarnation was its effect on how I looked at death and loss. Don't get me wrong—losing someone you love still hurts, no matter what. When I lose someone, however, I take some consolation in the knowledge that they have simply moved on to their next turn on the wheel.

• • •

TRY THIS: *Enter a meditative state or just sit quietly. Ask to see who you were in a past life. What flashes into your head?*

October 26
Bonfires

The end of fall is the perfect time for a bonfire. The crackling sound of the flames, the acrid smell of the wood smoke, the heat that radiates outward, the flickering light…all these touch our senses and help us connect to the element of fire.

Blue Moon Circle almost always has a bonfire at our Samhain ritual. We try to be outside for this particular rite, no matter what the weather is like. We've gathered around the bonfire in the freezing cold, huddled in close under our cloaks, with long johns underneath our garb. We've watched the flames sputter in the rain but still burn in defiance. We've dodged the clouds of smoke on windy evenings and even rejoiced in the occasional perfect autumn night, when the fire seemed to hum in contentment, pulsing along with the beat of our drums.

Bonfires are highly evocative, making us think of all the fires that all the witches before us have gathered around, and connecting us not only with fire but also with those who have come before. Plus, of course, you can roast marshmallows over them once the ritual is over.

• • •

TRY THIS: *If a bonfire is not feasible, use our bad weather substitute: fill a plate or cauldron with sand and place a number of tealights on top.*

October 27
Black Cats

If cats are associated with witches and witchcraft, then that goes double for black cats. Unfortunately, this hasn't always been a good thing for the cats of that color. To this day, some people persist in believing that it is bad luck to have a black cat cross your path. My black cat, Magic, would have to disagree. (As would I.) And most witches are quite fond of black cats, whether they happen to have one or not.

Many myths and superstitions are associated with black cats, and not all of them are negative. In Scotland a strange black cat showing up on the doorstep is considered good luck. The Cat Sith, a giant black cat with a white spot on its chest from Celtic mythology, might bless your house if you leave a saucer of milk out for it. (You know that superstition had to have been started by a black cat, right?) Some say the Cat Sith is a fairy, and others say it is a witch who can change forms.

Apparently the old myths die hard, and black cats are the least likely to be adopted. In the UK, Cats Protection (formerly the Cat Protection League) has declared October 27 to be "Black Cat Day" to increase the adoption of black cats.

In my house, *every* day is black cat day, at least according to a certain feline.

. . .

TRY THIS: *The next time you are ready to get a new cat, consider adopting a black one.*

October 28
Scrying

Scrying is an ancient form of divination that involves looking into some kind of clear or reflective surface. The most traditional (or at least well-known) tool for scrying is the crystal ball, but practitioners may also use a black mirror or glass, a dark bowl filled with water, a natural source of still water such as a pond, dark stones like obsidian, or even the smoke from a fire.

Although it seems simple, scrying can be quite difficult if you don't have a natural gift for it. I am very psychic in general, and tools like tarot cards work well for me, as do rune stones, yet I have never successfully "seen" much of anything when I have attempted scrying, so don't be discouraged if you don't sense anything right away.

Scrying is done by entering a quiet or meditative state—a trance, if you can achieve such a thing. Then you gaze into the surface of whatever medium you are using and allow your eyes to unfocus a bit and let in any information that flows before them.

• • •

TRY THIS: *Using a black mirror or a dark bowl filled with water, try scrying today.*

October 29
Ancestor Altars

One way to celebrate Samhain is to set up an ancestor altar. This is an altar dedicated to those who have gone before—sometimes actual ancestors, sometimes our beloved dead, whether they were related to us or not. This can be done in a couple of different ways:

Set up an altar a few days before the sabbat. Decorate it with photos and mementos, items that symbolize those you've lost. For instance, the first year after my grandmother died, I set up an altar with her photo, some of the weaving she'd done for me, and the key to her old house, along with a candle to light in her honor. You can also put up a temporary altar just for the night of the holiday itself, and take it down the next day.

During our Samhain rituals, we sometimes have a table inside the circle set aside as an ancestor altar for the entire group, and everyone puts items on it that represent their ancestors and loved ones who have passed, including pets. We take turns going to the altar during the ritual, lighting a candle, and speaking to the dead. Because Samhain is one of two nights of the year when the veil between the worlds is at its thinnest, this is the perfect time to honor those who have gone before us and let them know they are still in our thoughts.

• • •

TRY THIS: *Create an ancestor altar this year at Samhain.*

Pumpkin Soup

What could be more fun to serve at your Samhain feast than a seasonal pumpkin soup, using a small hollowed-out pumpkin for a bowl? (Serve it with the top of the pumpkin as a lid, if you want to get fancy; if you don't feel like going to all that trouble, a plain old bowl will do.)

Here is a simple pumpkin soup recipe that takes hardly any time at all to make. All you have to do is sauté one chopped onion in a couple tablespoons of olive oil, add either a large (29 ounces or so) can of pumpkin or the equivalent amount of freshly cooked and pureed pumpkin (use pie pumpkins for this, not the kind you decorate—they have a different texture), about four cups of chicken broth, and half cup of cream or half and half. Season with salt and pepper and a pinch of pumpkin pie spice if you feel the urge. Top with toasted pumpkin seeds for a bit of extra fun.

• • •

TRY THIS: *If you don't want to make pumpkin soup from scratch, look for it at your local grocery store in the deli section.*

October 31
Samhain

Samhain is considered by many to be the most witchy holiday of all the sabbats in the Wheel of the Year; certainly it has that reputation with the general public! Samhain is more commonly known as Halloween, a name from the Christianized version of the holiday, All Hallows' Eve. The word "hallow" means holy, and this is certainly a holy time of year if you are a witch.

Some witches consider this night to be the witches' New Year, on which the old year ends and the new one begins. Blue Moon Circle often has a two-part ritual, the first half devoted to a solemn farewell to the year behind us and the second a joyous welcoming in of the year ahead, with all its potential, magical and otherwise. It is also a good night for divination and speaking to our beloved dead, although I always suggest using a little extra care with the cleansing and protection of your ritual space for either.

Some people celebrate the night with a dumb supper, a meal served and eaten in complete silence. It can be done on Samhain as a reverence to the beloved dead, and empty plates may be set for them. My first group held one of these on Samhain one year, and it was a surprisingly moving and powerful ritual: silence, candlelight, grief, joy, and communion, all mixed together.

TRY THIS: *Have a dumb supper this year for Samhain or at least eat part of the meal in silence.*

November 1
The Candle

One of the easiest to use and most affordable tools for today's witch is the candle. I like candles for their flexibility too, since they come in many different colors (suitable for various magical goals), sizes, and shapes. Plus, of course, you can make them yourself.

If you can't have a giant stash of candles in all different shapes, sizes, and colors, make do with simple white ones. To add color, tie a colored ribbon or thread around the base. To increase their magical focus, carve runes or other symbols into them. Beeswax is the most natural form of candle, if you can afford them, but many people use the regular store-bought type, which contain petroleum. We do the best we can.

Make your candles more powerful and specific to your spell work by carving runes or other symbols into them, anointing them with magical oils, or softening the wax a bit with heat and rolling them in dried herbs. Even when I am not doing a formal ritual, I often light a candle on my altar in the evening and say hello to the gods or ask for their help with whatever issue I'm dealing with that day.

• • •

TRY THIS: *To add a simple ritual to your day, light a candle.*

November 2
Shielding

Shielding is a specific form of protection work that is just what it sounds like: creating some form of magical or energetic shield around yourself, someone else (one of your children, for instance), your home, or even your car.

You can do complicated rituals for this—and if you are having a specific and ongoing issue, you may want to—but most of the time shielding is a simple matter of visualization and intent.

I often do a form of shielding when I am going into situations with a lot of people, such as conferences or conventions, where I know there will be a lot of free-floating energy, not all of it pleasant or beneficial. At the very least, shielding protects me from the intense energy such events tend to generate (and that tends to overwhelm me). It is also useful if you will be with people whose energy you know is unpleasant or aggressive but whose company you can't avoid (like your boss or a family member).

• • •

TRY THIS: *Think about situations where you may need some type of shielding. If you are in need of shielding, use the simple spell on the following page.*

Spell for Shielding

Shielding is quite simple, and as with all forms of magical work, it gets easier with practice. To create a shield for the first time, gather a black candle, a black ribbon or piece of yarn, and a mirror. Cast your circle and light the candle. Place the ribbon or yarn in a smaller circle around your feet, and visualize a wall of light coming up from it until it forms a protective bubble that covers you entirely. If you will be doing something or be with someone particularly unpleasant, hold the mirror in front of the candle's light and turn the mirror around so it is facing outward.

Slowly turn, holding the mirror, and visualize anything harmful bouncing off the mirror and back where it came from. Don't do this with anger or resentment; send it back with love. Hold that bubble of light around you until it seems steady and feel it become a part of you, like an invisible second skin. Put out the candle and open your circle. Wrap the ribbon or yarn around your waist, under your clothes, or around your wrist, as an extra reminder that you carry the shield with you.

• • •

TRY THIS: *When you are comfortable with shielding, simply visualize this ritual instead of physically doing it the next time you need this form of protection.*

November 4
Witches in Books for Kids

There was a time when there were very few books for kids and young adults that featured witches; most of the stories that existed were fairy tales or other accounts in which witches were evil, ugly hags. Of course, there were some early exceptions, such as the Wizard of Oz books, which had both good witches and bad ones, and the Narnia tales by C. S. Lewis, but for many modern children, Harry Potter was their first introduction to witches as the heroes of the story.

These days, thankfully, books with cool witches in them abound, and it is much easier to find books you can be happy to have your kids and teens read. Visit your local library or bookstore and explore the shelves; below are a few of my favorites to get you started.

British author Diana Wynne Jones created lots of great books for kids with witches in them, most notably the Chrestomanci series and *Howl's Moving Castle*. Madeleine L'Engle's classic *A Wrinkle in Time* series had witches of a sort, plus there is *Matilda* by Roald Dahl. This is just the tip of the broomstick—books I have read and loved. And don't be fooled by the fact that these books may be shelved in the juvenile section...I read most of them as an adult and loved them.

• • •

TRY THIS: *Search out one of these books today and read it with your kids. If you don't have kids, read it anyway!*

November 5
Cernunnos

Cernunnos is a Celtic god usually depicted with a man's body bearing the antlers of a stag atop his head (some consider Herne to be his British counterpart). He is the lord of the underworld and of the dead, as well as a god of healing, nature, animals, the hunt, sexuality, fertility, and abundance.

In short, he is in many ways the personification of nature itself: the beginning and the end of life, sometimes nurturing and other times brutal, and yet the source of much that is good. It would be a mistake to think of the gods we worship simply as benign and loving beings, although they certainly can take on that aspect and often do. But as I see them, our gods and goddesses are much more complex than that. Cernunnos may send you abundance if you ask him for it, but this hunter god knows that there is always a price to pay for the bounty you reap, and he is unlikely to give you the gift without expecting some sacrifice on your part.

* * *

TRY THIS: *As we enter the dark months of the year, set up an altar for Cernunnos and ask him to watch over you and yours in the coming months and help you keep food on the table and health in your home. In return, I suspect he would appreciate it if you made a small sacrifice of food to feed his wild creatures, as they, too, struggle to survive the long, cold winter.*

November 6
Topaz

Topaz is the birthstone for those born in November. It is most commonly found as a yellow stone, although it can vary in color (some of which, like blue, are almost always artificially enhanced by irradiation or the like).

Magically, topaz always has been considered a protective stone, and it can be helpful for work with any out-of-balance emotions, including depression, fear, jealousy, and anxiety. Tuck a topaz under your pillow—either by itself or in a charm bag filled with a soothing herb such as lavender—to prevent nightmares.

Topaz is also used for healing, pain relief, and (so they say) weight loss. It can be used in magic to draw love or prosperity too, so we can agree that it is a very handy stone to have around, whether you were born in November or not.

The only real drawback to topaz is its expense. As a precious stone, it can be quite pricy, although you can always look for a simple piece of jewelry set with a small topaz or perhaps a rough crystal. As a less expensive substitute, Scott Cunningham suggests using citrine, which looks nearly the same and has many of the same benefits as topaz.

• • •

TRY THIS: *Do some magical work with topaz or citrine, or look for a piece to add to your collection.*

November 7
Labyrinths

Labyrinths are an ancient type of maze found in many different countries and cultures. There often have been spiritual meanings attached to walking a labyrinth, which—unlike some types of mazes—usually only have one way in and one way out. So why walk it if you know you are going to get to the middle eventually? Labyrinths are usually used as a form of meditation, or even trance work. You walk through them slowly and methodically, clearing your mind of everything except following the path set before you.

My first group used a labyrinth as part of our Imbolc rite, which was done as a public ritual. We marked out the lines of the labyrinth with masking tape on the floor and set a small cauldron on a table at the center. Inside the cauldron were slips of paper, all bearing a word or phrase such as "patience," "embrace joy," or "healing." Participants sat in a circle around the labyrinth and drummed as people took turns walking slowly through the labyrinth. Other than the drumming, there was no sound at all, and it was a strangely powerful experience. The idea was to fix a question in your mind—for most, it was as simple as "what do I need to know in the year ahead?"—and then pull a slip of paper out of the cauldron when you arrived at the middle.

• • •

TRY THIS: *If you don't have a labyrinth near you or space to build one, draw one in a bowl full of sand using your finger or the tip of a wand or athame.*

November 8
Depression

Depression is like an invisible dark cloud that takes up residence over your head and blocks out the sun. Many people have had bouts of depression at least once in their lives, but for some people it is a never-ending battle. If you're dealing with depression, there may be aspects of your witchy life that can help lift the clouds. Try spell work, of course, and prayers to the God and Goddess to help you—to send you strength, ease the depression, and guide you to the people who can help you to heal. If your depression is situational rather than clinical, ask for the gods' help with the problem.

A spiritual practice can lift your mood and shift your focus from the dark to the light. Depression tells lies and tries to isolate you, so if you have people to practice magic with, by all means do. Depression makes everything seem dark, so try to focus on the light. Start with small things, like the beauty of nature. When you're having a bad day, make yourself look out the window or go for a walk and notice the birds, the flowers, the sun. The gods have gifted us with so much that is good, and the more you can connect with it, the less power depression will have.

• • •

TRY THIS: *If you are battling depression, seek out help—professional, friends, and magical. No matter what the depression tells you, you are worth it.*

November 9
Spell for Strength

We all have times when we need more strength, whether it is physical, emotional, or spiritual. It's a tough world we live in, and sometimes we need a little help to be strong enough to deal with everything life throws at us.

Here is a simple spell for strength.

> *God and Goddess, hear my plea*
> *Send your love to strengthen me*
> *Make me sturdy like the willow*
> *Bending with the storms that billow*
> *Strengthen body, spirit, and mind*
> *So my inner strength I'll find*
> *Give me all the strength I need*
> *So at my tasks I will succeed*
> *So mote it be!*

• • •

TRY THIS: *If you want, light a white or brown candle, but really, in this case, it is enough just to ask for help.*

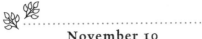

November 10
Cinnamon

You might not think of cinnamon as a magical herb, but in fact it has a long history of religious and spiritual use in cultures that include the ancient Hebrews, the Egyptians, and the Romans. If it was good enough for them, it is definitely good enough for me.

Cinnamon is actually tree bark that comes in a variety of different forms, powdered and sticks being the most common. Magically, it is used for love, lust, protection, healing, success, and prosperity, and to increase psychic power and magical power in general. Although I use it in essential oil form to make magical oils and sometimes add a stick or two to a sachet or charm bag, my favorite way to use cinnamon is in kitchen witchery because it goes so well in a multitude of magical recipes.

I put a sprinkling into my mocha every morning, as part of the kitchen alchemy with which I start my day, and I like to add it when I make homemade applesauce, since apples are also good for both love and healing. Plus, of course, it tastes yummy!

• • •

TRY THIS: *Do some magic with cinnamon today. Yes, apple pie counts.*

November 11
Decorative Cinnamon Brooms

To have cinnamon's abundant magical energy around all the time, make a simple cinnamon broom. The easiest way to do this, of course, is to buy a premade broom, as long as it uses natural material. Use either a small size, like the kind used to sweep hearths, or a full-sized one. You will need powdered cinnamon, some plain white glue and a brush, waxed paper and a plastic bag, and any other decorative items, including cinnamon sticks, ribbons, seasonal-themed decorations (such as pinecones and red and green ribbons if you are making one for Yule).

Lay your broom down on the waxed paper and brush the glue over one side of the broom, then sprinkle it with the cinnamon. If you are creating the broom for some particular magical use—such as protection or healing—focus on that intention as you sprinkle. Place the broom inside the plastic bag to dry overnight and absorb the scent. Repeat on the other side the next day. Once the broom is dry, add any decorations, then bless and consecrate it for magical use.

You can also say a simple spell such as:

Cinnamon, cinnamon, sacred and strong
Bless this home all year long

TRY THIS: *For more ideas and directions on making brooms from scratch, check out my book* The Witch's Broom: The Craft, Lore & Magick of Broomsticks.

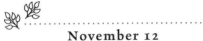

November 12
Acceptance of Self

When I use the word "acceptance" in speaking about my witch-craft practice, it means a couple of different things to me, both of them positive. The first is acceptance when dealing with others, but just as important is the acceptance of self. At some point, if you are a witch or a Pagan, you probably had to look in the mirror and accept that you were not going to be like every-one else. At least not in this particular way, and maybe not in other ways, like nontraditional sexual preferences or gender identity or (if you're like me) just plain general weirdness. It can be a struggle, and some of you may still be dealing with that struggle, but to me, a part of being a witch meant learning to accept myself just as I was, including all the bits and pieces that "regular" society might not have found acceptable.

One of the great benefits of an unconventional spiritual path is the freedom to accept that it is okay to be unconventional. That, just maybe, "normal" is overrated, or at least not a rea-sonable expectation for everyone. I truly believe that the gods accept us just as we are—which doesn't mean they don't expect us to learn more or work on any flaws we may have, but does mean that it is okay to be the you that you really are.

* * *

TRY THIS: *Look in the mirror today and say,*
"I accept myself just the way I am." Then go tell someone
else that you accept them just as they are, too.

November 13
Saying Grace

Some people grew up saying grace before their meals. I didn't because I was Jewish and that's not our thing (although we did give thanks every Friday night when we celebrated the Sabbath), but I remember sitting at friends' family tables while they said grace, especially at Thanksgiving.

I also have been at Thanksgiving meals where people went around the table and said what they were grateful for, which I have always thought was a particularly lovely thing to do. It is always nice to express gratitude.

As a part of my daily practice, a few years ago I started saying a brief thank you at the start of my meals, most of which are not nearly as fancy as a Thanksgiving dinner. It isn't anything complicated. I raise my glass (or my mug, at breakfast) and say, "Goddess, I thank you for the day and for the food and for the cats." If there is anything else major going on, I might add thanks for that too. As I said, simple.

Still, getting into the habit of saying a simple thank you before you eat is an easy way to add one more tiny spiritual component to your day. And as everyone knows, it never hurts to be polite.

• • •

TRY THIS: *Say grace or give thanks at your meals for a few days, and see how it feels.*

November 14
Random Acts of Kindness and Paying It Forward

You've probably heard the expression "random acts of kindness," which is actually short for "practice random acts of kindness and senseless acts of beauty," coined by Anne Herbert in 1982. Random acts of kindness is not a new idea, though. In the Jewish religion, such things are known as performing a mitzvah, which generally means a kind act with no expectation of anything in return.

I try to do random acts of kindness often, whether it is complimenting someone on a nice sweater or going out of my way to open a door for a mother struggling with a stroller. There are a million tiny ways in which you can make someone's day a little bit brighter. You don't have to be rich to make a difference in someone's life, and often the smallest gesture can make a large impact.

I'm also a big believer in paying it forward. Paying it forward simply means that if someone does something nice for you, eventually you go on to do something nice for someone else. This isn't done out of obligation but because if everyone did it, the world would be a much better place. It's a karma thing, to some extent, and a human thing too.

• • •

TRY THIS: *Over the next few days, go out of your way to practice random acts of kindness. I think you will find, as I have, that it is completely addictive.*

Purple

With the exception of black, purple is probably the witchiest color. It represents the power of spirit, which is why the third eye chakra is often seen as indigo, a bluish shade of purple, and the crown chakra is often pictured as violet. In earlier days purple dyes were expensive and difficult to procure, so the color became associated with royalty. If you need a little regal boost, wear purple to make you feel more powerful.

Purple comes in various shades, from the palest lavender to the darkest eggplant, almost black. The color is associated with magic, power, healing (especially of the spirit and emotions), peace, spirituality, and prosperity. Many of the stones and herbs that are purple, such as amethyst and lavender, have these same associations.

• • •

TRY THIS: *The color itself is mysterious and magical, so if you feel particularly witchy, why not wear purple?*

November 16
The Sixth Chakra

The sixth chakra, also known as the third eye chakra, is located in the center of the forehead and usually pictured as indigo, a bluish shade of purple.

The third eye chakra, as its name suggests, is associated with psychic vision, intuition, wisdom, the mind, perception, and visualization. If it is blocked, you may be unable to access those things, and your thinking in general might be muddled. If you have attempted divination and failed, it is a good idea to check in on your sixth chakra.

One way to clear and stimulate this chakra is to use a piece of amethyst or simply visualize the color purple permeating the center of your forehead. Let the color seep into your forehead and see it swirling clockwise slowly and then faster.

• • •

TRY THIS: *To test that the chakra is completely cleared, see if you can visualize the color purple swirling counterclockwise and then clockwise again in the center of your forehead.*

November 17
I Ching

If you want to try your hand at something different in divination, use the I Ching. The I Ching comes from ancient China and the name means Book of Changes. It is the oldest known Chinese text, which is pretty amazing all by itself.

The I Ching is made up of sixty-four possible answers or situations, as seen in various combinations of six broken and unbroken lines called hexagrams. Traditionally, these hexagrams were cast using sticks, but these days people often throw coins six times instead. Essentially, you ask a question and then throw your sticks or coins, then look up what the hexagram means in the book of the I Ching. As with most other forms of divination, you can find the I Ching online these days, and it can be interesting to enter your question and see what comes up.

I had a set for a while that had the book and some sticks, and I experimented with casting them every day. It was pretty fascinating, although it didn't work as well for me as the tarot and the runes do.

• • •

TRY THIS: *If tarot or rune stones don't
"talk" to you—and they don't for everyone—
it might be worth trying the I Ching.*

November 18

Listening to Your Inner Voice

One of the best ways to connect to the element of spirit is to connect to your own inner voice. Of course, in the hectic world we live in, this may be easier said than done. There are so many other voices—from others in our lives, from the television and social media—it can sometimes be difficult to figure out which voice is ours and which belongs to someone else.

Set aside some time to listen to your inner voice. It doesn't have to be a lot of time; five or ten minutes a few times a week can be enough to start. Sit comfortably in a quiet room. If you want, light a purple or white candle, or hold on to a piece of amethyst or quartz crystal.

Quiet your mind as much as possible. This isn't meditation, where you try not to think about things; it's merely an effort to turn down the noise from outside yourself so you can listen to the quiet voice inside.

• • •

TRY THIS: *As you sit quietly and comfortably, ask yourself, "What do you have to tell me?" or "What have you been trying to say that I haven't been hearing?" Then just sit and breathe and listen.*

November 19
Baba Yaga

You may be familiar with Baba Yaga from Russian fairy tales, where she is usually depicted as a frightening witch who lives in a wooden hut on chicken legs that moves around the forest, sometimes flying through the air in a mortar steered by a pestle. A few of you might even recognize her from my paranormal romance novels using a much-updated version of the characters from the old tales.

But what you may not realize—and what I didn't know until I started doing research for my novels—is that before she got downgraded to a scary "eat your peas or Baba Yaga will get you" kind of witch, Baba Yaga was actually a goddess. According to Judika Illes in *The Element Encyclopedia of Witchcraft*, Baba Yaga started out as an ancient Slavic goddess who controlled the forces of life and death. Like the witch she eventually came to be portrayed as, Baba Yaga was neither good nor evil but could both nurture or destroy, depending on how you approached her.

She was also the goddess of witches, which may have been how she eventually came to be called one herself, and was said to know all the secrets of healing with plants. If you have need of healing, call on Baba Yaga.

• • •

TRY THIS: *When you call on Baba Yaga, have an offering of food since she is known for her great appetite, and be sure to be polite.*

Guided Meditation

Guided meditation is exactly what it sounds like: a kind of meditation that is guided by someone other than the person actually doing the meditating. You can also buy CDs that lead you through guided meditation or listen to one online.

In witchcraft and Paganism, guided meditation is most likely to be used as part of a ritual or spiritual journey rather than as a healing technique or basic meditation. As a high priestess, I sometimes lead my group in a guided meditation during ritual. For instance, in an Imbolc ritual, I might lead a guided meditation to help everyone connect with the budding energies of the earth. For a spring equinox ritual, we might do a guided meditation that allows people to see themselves as seeds sprouting and growing into new life.

One of the advantages of guided meditation is that it can be easier for those who have a hard time focusing on their own. Guided meditation allows those participating to let go and simply follow the voice and words of the person leading the meditation. If you lead a group and want the full benefit, or you don't have anyone to act as a guide, record the guided meditation ahead of time and play it back for yourself.

• • •

TRY THIS: *Guided meditation during ritual can be surprisingly powerful. Experiment with it today.*

November 21

Asking for and Accepting Help

For most of us, the only thing worse than needing help is asking for it. I'm not sure why it is so difficult to ask for help. Perhaps it makes us feel as though we are admitting to weakness or failure because there is something we can't handle on our own. Maybe you are worried about being beholden, left owing a debt you aren't sure you can pay off. For some people, it is a feeling that they aren't worthy of being helped or the fear of seeming needy.

Obviously, you don't want to be constantly turning to others to do the things you can do for yourself. But what about when you can't do whatever it is because you are sick or it is outside your skill set or it just plain takes more than one person to accomplish? There is no shame in asking for help when you really need it, especially from people who like or love you, and especially if you are one of those people who does things for others. (You know who you are.) Don't get me wrong—I'm no better at asking for help than anyone else, but there are times when I have to say, "I can't do this on my own."

· · ·

TRY THIS: *If you need to ask for help, ask and accept with grace. Consider it an exercise in the element of spirit, since we are put here to help each other whenever we can. Pass it on when you get the chance.*

November 22
Obsidian

You might think that all stones are associated with the element of earth, but there is one that is also connected to fire, and that is obsidian. Obsidian is one of my favorite stones, both magical and otherwise, in part because it is just shiny and cool. Obsidian comes from volcanoes as a naturally occurring glass that is formed when lava cools very fast. It is black, with sheer planes that can be used for stone knives, spear tips, or arrowheads, much like flint. A shaman once told me that I should have an obsidian athame, and I have been looking for one I could afford ever since.

Because of its shiny surface, obsidian can be used for divination, much like a crystal ball or a scrying mirror. It is also protective, reflecting back any negative or malicious energy. Obsidian is grounding and can help you to center when you feel pulled in too many directions, and it can be used in spells for grounding, peace, and a quiet mind.

• • •

TRY THIS: *Because it is such a witchy stone, obsidian is also perfect for use in full moon rituals, perhaps paired with a piece of moonstone.*

November 23
Sagittarius

Those born between November 23 and December 22 fall under the sun sign of Sagittarius. Sagittarians tend to be optimistic and freedom-loving. They are honest and straightforward, so don't ask them a question if you don't really want the answer. Intellectual and energetic, they will throw themselves into any project or adventure with enthusiasm.

On the downside, all that optimism can sometimes blind the Sagittarian to pitfalls, and they may get carried way. They can be tactless, and they may have a rigid adherence to what they believe is right and wrong. On the whole, however, their good humor and positive outlook will usually carry them through.

• • •

TRY THIS: *At this time of year encourage your own optimism and enthusiasm, and find some project to take on that you believe in completely. But whether you are a Sagittarian or not, you will probably want to be careful not to be too blunt and step on any toes in the process.*

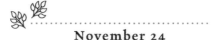

November 24
What Am I Thankful For?

In the United States, this is the time of year when we celebrate the national holiday of Thanksgiving. For most, it is an excuse to get together with friends and family and eat a huge meal of turkey and stuffing and pie. This isn't a bad thing, but I sometimes wonder if the "giving thanks" part of the holiday gets a little lost in the shuffle. So here's your question to ponder: what are you thankful for?

Take a pen and a piece of paper and start writing things down. Start with the obvious, like friends, family, animals, a job, a roof over your head, food on the table, the fact that your car is still running and you've had three whole days without a call from a telemarketer. When you think you've reached the end of your list, look around for the smaller things, like a bird singing outside your window and the evergreens that provide a bit of color when the rest of the world turns gray. In the end, I suspect that list might be longer than you would have expected. Post it someplace where you can see it, like the door of the refrigerator. On the days when life seems overwhelming or bleak, use it to remind yourself of how much you have to be grateful for.

· · ·

TRY THIS: *Every time you think of something else to be grateful for, add it to the list. If you actively look for things to be grateful for, you may just find them.*

[338]

November 25
Stuffed Spaghetti Squash

This simple, comforting yet elegant dish is something I make all winter long, but it also makes the perfect vegetarian Thanksgiving or harvest festival entrée or side.

Start by cooking a whole spaghetti squash. Poke a couple of holes into the skin, put it on a cookie sheet or a piece of aluminum foil, and cook it in a 400-degree Fahrenheit oven for about 45 minutes or until a fork slides easily into it. Let the squash cool enough to handle, then cut it in half and scoop out the seeds. Use a fork to rough up the inner fibers so they look like spaghetti (loosen them up all the way down and to the sides). Take the squash out and spread it into a casserole dish.

Layer the squash with any or all of these ingredients: pesto, ricotta cheese, chopped walnuts, sautéed onions and garlic, some form of tomato sauce or chopped fresh tomatoes, and shredded parmesan cheese.

Stick it in the oven at about 375 degrees, long enough to melt the cheese on top and warm the other ingredients, about 20 minutes. Voilà: harvest on a plate!

· · ·

TRY THIS: *Vary this dish any way you want,
leaving out or adding ingredients according to
taste or what you happen to have in the house.
For another variation, I like to serve it right in the
squash skin and not use a separate casserole dish.*

November 26
Witchy Words of Wisdom:
Raven Digitalis

One of today's wise witchcraft authors is Raven Digitalis. He sprang to fame with his first book, *Goth Craft*, and has continued to address the less commonly looked at aspects of the modern witchcraft practice.

I truly loved his book *Shadow Magick Compendium: Exploring Darker Aspects of Magickal Spirituality*, in which he explored the need to embrace what he called the five manifestations of darkness: the Internal Shadow, the External Shadow, the Astral Shadow, the Shadow of Nature, and the Shadow of Society. Here is an excerpt:

> The very essence of the concept of "shadow" is ambiguous. Throughout the ages and around the world, various cultures, religions, and individual philosophies have approached this idea in various ways, often discovering deep wells of meaning in the divine polarity of "light" and "dark." A number of shamanic religions, including those indigenous to Asia, Europe, and the Americas, have long recognized the portion of the self deemed "the shadow" for its role in human spiritual development and understanding. The view of the shadow as a spiritual force has also been carried into a number of modern religions. It is from the shadowed aspects of the psyche that our magickal reality is brought into vision.

> • • •

> **TRY THIS:** Shadow Magick *is fascinating stuff, and it completely changed the way I look at some of my preconceived notions—which is what the best books do. Look up Digitalis's book or find another that challenges some of your preconceived notions.*

November 27

"Hope Is the Thing with Feathers"

I love this poem about hope by Emily Dickinson, who captured emotion so well.

> Hope is the thing with feathers
> That perches in the soul,
> And sings the tune without the words,
> And never stops at all,
>
> And sweetest in the gale is heard;
> And sore must be the storm
> That could abash the little bird
> That kept so many warm.
>
> I've heard it in the chillest land
> And on the strangest sea;
> Yet, never, in extremity,
> It asked a crumb of me.

(Emily Dickinson, 1896)

• • •

TRY THIS: *What does the word "hope" mean to you? In these dark months of the year, take some time to embrace the feeling of hope..*

November 28
Bear

As we enter the colder months of the year, when it is tempting to stay indoors and hunker down against the dark and chill, it is fitting that we look at the noble bear. I don't know about you, but when the upstate New York winter howls around my ears, I often wish that I could hibernate until it is all over.

But while the bear in its spiritual form can symbolize the importance of solitude and rest, it is primarily known for its power, strength, and courage. When Bear appears as your totem animal, it may be there to support you during a time of difficulty or as you embark on a challenging new journey. Perhaps this is why stuffed bears are often given to new babies?

In many cultures bears have also been associated with shamans and healing, and a shaman would often wear a bear skin to symbolize their power. Obviously, I don't recommend this particular approach, but if you are drawn to Bear, find a necklace with a pendant in the shape of a bear or with the imprint of a bear's paw.

• • •

TRY THIS: *Ask Bear for help in healing, especially if you are at a point where retreating from the world for some solitary "me time" is the best medicine.*

November 29
Free Will

One of the most important tenets of modern witchcraft is the concept of free will. As with everything else in the witchy world, not everyone agrees on this, but I consider it to be intrinsic to my practice of the Craft. I hate to have anyone else impose their will on me, so why on earth would I impose mine on them?

How does the concept of free will affect how you practice witchcraft? Let's take the love spell as an example. Most witches who are new to the Craft are tempted to cast a spell to make a particular person fall in love or stay in love with them, but back away from the cauldron and put down the athame because trouble lies that way. If you cast a love spell on someone, you interfere with that person's free will, which is not only Not Cool but will also almost certainly backfire on you eventually. How would you feel if someone did that to you? Is that kind of love even real? Free will is an important rule because it keeps us from becoming so enamored with the use of power that we start to believe we know what is best for everyone. As witches, we have tools to create positive changes in our lives, but that doesn't give us the right to make choices for others.

• • •

TRY THIS: *If you want others to respect your free will to make your own decisions, respect theirs too. Double check any magic you do to make sure it doesn't cross the line.*

November 30
Energy Healing

Energy healing refers to a type of healing where the practitioner taps in to the energy of the universe (for lack of a better term) and moves it into the patient's body to promote healing. Some of the more commonly used types of energy healing are Reiki, therapeutic touch, and reflexology. Each healer has a different take on where the energy comes from and whether or not there are deities, guardian spirits, or any other guides involved.

One of energy healing's main benefits is that it can reach areas of the body that are difficult to access, and, if done correctly, it can also integrate emotional healing and past experiences. If you want to do energy healing on yourself, the basic techniques are relatively simple and easy to learn. As with anything else, some folks have a natural talent for it, but anyone can master the basics.

* * *

TRY THIS: *Rub your hands together briskly to get the energy flowing. Place your hands about two feet apart and move them slowly toward each other. At a certain point you will feel a slight resistance; that is the energy field from each hand meeting each other. Curve your hands together as if gathering the energy between them into a ball. Take that ball into one hand and run it lightly over the opposite arm, about an inch over the skin. Don't be surprised if you feel heat or tingling—that's the healing energy.*

December 1
Visualization

One of the most important tools in a witch's box of tricks won't be found on the altar or in any store. It resides, in fact, inside the witch's mind. I'm talking about visualization, the ability to "see" and often hear and smell what isn't there. We use visualization often in spell work. For instance, the spell instructions may tell you to visualize a pool of water for calmness. The better formed the image is in your mind, the more powerful its influence will be on your spell.

As with most things, some people find this easier to do than others. As a writer, visualization has always come very easily to me, but for those who find it difficult, it can be helpful to practice when not actually in the midst of ritual.

* * *

TRY THIS: *Close your eyes and form a picture of a beautiful meadow. (If you have problems visualizing, go online and find a photo to start with.) Picture yourself sitting in the meadow. Feel where your bottom meets the ground. Feel the air on your skin. Then add the warmth of the sun. Add some brightly colored flowers. Then visualize a bird and hear the sound it makes. Add as many more elements as you want until the meadow seems as real to you as you can make it.*

December 2

Incense

Many witches use incense as a part of their rituals, either for cleansing at the beginning or as an element of the ritual itself. It is an easy way to symbolize and connect to the element of air, which is perhaps the most difficult of the four elements to connect to otherwise since you can't see or touch it. Incense comes in many forms. There are the standard sticks and cones and also powdered or granular incense that are placed on a charcoal disk and burned that way. You can make your own incense at home by grinding dried herbs and adding them to resins or shredded wood, but you can also find some lovely premade magical incense if you don't want to go to the trouble.

My preference is to use only incense made from natural ingredients for my magical work (both because of allergies to artificial scents and because I want the power of the actual plants in my rituals). If you include other people in your rituals, check for sensitivities before using incense.

• • •

TRY THIS: *To use incense for a simple ritual to connect with the element of air, sit in sacred space (either inside or outside) and light your incense. Watch it spiral through the air in front of you, watching the shapes and patterns it makes. Cup it between your hands and then throw it up to the sky, thanking the air for all the gifts it gives you.*

December 3
The Seventh Chakra

The highest and final chakra is the crown chakra, which is located at the top of the head. This chakra opens us up to the universe, to the energy from above us, to intuition and spirit. Some people see it as violet in color and others see it as a bright, shining white. Either way, it is the chakra that represents enlightenment and the connection to deity.

Unfortunately, if you have ever suffered from any kind of psychic trauma, this chakra tends to shut down in an effort to protect you. And if the crown chakra isn't open, nothing flows completely through the chakra system.

To check in with the crown chakra, send energy up from the base chakra through the rest of the chakras until it reaches your head. If it feels like you've hit a brick wall, your crown chakra is probably blocked.

• • •

TRY THIS: *To open your crown chakra, send as strong a feeling of love and reassurance as you can, as if you were comforting a small child. Then visualize the top of your head opening like a flower in the sun, its petals spread to take in the light and energy of the universe, refreshing and reenergizing your entire system.*

December 4
Witchy Words of Wisdom:
Judika Illes

Judika Illes is one of my go-to authors for witchcraft info. She has written some of the most thorough and inclusive (and heaviest!) books on the Craft, including *The Element Encyclopedia of Witchcraft*, which is over 850 pages long and filled with amazing facts and tons of fun information. (My Baba Yaga novels were inspired in part by what Illes wrote about Baba Yaga in that book.)

But even without those 850 pages, the book is worth getting for the introduction alone. It is one of the most thorough and well-written explorations I have ever seen of what it means to be a witch. Here's a tiny taste to whet your appetite for the rest:

> Looking through the witch's eyes may offer a very different perspective than that which many modern people are accustomed. One sees a world of power and mystery, full of secrets, delights, and dangers to be uncovered. However, it is not a black-and-white world; it is not a world with rigidly distinct boundaries but a transformative world, a world filled with possibility, not what is but what could be, a blending, fluid, shifting but rhythmically consistent landscape.

• • •

TRY THIS: *Did that get your attention? Find a copy and read the rest of the introduction or look up one of Illes's other books, like* The Element Encyclopedia of 500 Spells.

December 5
Finding Beauty Everywhere

There is no denying that there are a lot of ugly things in this world we live in—but there is also an incredible amount of beauty. What you see when you look around you is, to some extent, under your control. I had an amazing experience years ago after a hypnotherapy session. I don't even remember what I was working on, but I remember clearly that for about an hour afterward, I somehow ended up with the ability to look at the world—and people in particular—completely differently. I'm not sure I can even describe it in a way that will communicate how it felt, but essentially, everyone was beautiful. It didn't matter what they looked like; I could see their beauty shining through.

After a bit, whatever had given me that unique vision wore off, but I have never forgotten that glimpse I saw of what I believe is the way we should see each other—perhaps even the way the gods see us. Since then, when I hear that voice in my head that automatically judges people by our society's arbitrary standards, I try to remember that beauty is in the eye of the beholder and see it anyway.

. . .

TRY THIS: As you walk through your day, find as many examples of beauty as you can, and see what happens when you stretch your definition of what is beautiful. You may find that the world is not quite as ugly as you thought.

December 6
Stars

As witches, we often focus on the moon when we look up at the night sky. She is the symbol of our goddess, after all. But while you're gazing up, don't forget to look at the stars.

If you live in a city, it may be difficult to see them because of all the light pollution, but if you can get to the countryside or someplace where the stars shine more brightly, you might be amazed at how many of them there are and how glorious they can be.

Of course, there are the constellations to pick out (if you can't get to the countryside, go to a planetarium), and the North Star is usually quite bright, but I love to walk outside my back door on a clear night and just look up. Do you remember being a child and lying in the grass, looking up at all those pinpricks of light in the summer sky? Recapture that sense of wonder if you can.

• • •

TRY THIS: *If you are outside just as the first
star appears, don't forget to recite that childhood spell:*
Star light, star bright
First star I see tonight
Wish I may, wish I might
Have the wish I wish tonight.
So mote it be!

December 7
I Am Star Stuff

Astronomer Carl Sagan famously said:

> The nitrogen in our DNA, the calcium in our teeth, the iron in our blood, the carbon in our apple pies were made in the interiors of collapsing stars. We are made of star stuff.

I love this idea that we are all made of the same elements as the stars—that everything, really, is made of the same stuff as stars are made. Think of it: somewhere inside of you is a tiny atom that once lived inside a star, galaxies away. How magical is that? You're a star (or at least a piece of one)!

For those days when you are feeling insignificant or unimportant, here is an affirmation to remind you that you are made of the same things that make up planets, stars, and even entire universes:

I am made of star stuff. I am as radiant and glorious as the stars.

· · ·

TRY THIS: *Go outside and look at the stars tonight or the next time the sky is clear. Feel the connection, no matter how small, between you and the rest of the universe.*

December 8

Maiden, Mother, and Crone

In the Wiccan religion we worship the Triple Goddess in her three forms of Maiden, Mother, and Crone. These three phases correspond to many elements of our practice—not just the stages of a woman's life, but also the seasons, the changing shape of the moon, and more.

The Maiden is young and full of energy. She is the spring, new beginnings, the moon as it waxes. The Mother is actual and spiritual motherhood, nurturing and fertile. She is the full moon, the Mother Goddess who brings the harvest to fruition in the summer, the middle of life.

And then there is the Crone—ah, the Crone. She is age and wisdom, the winter's darkness, the waning moon as it becomes the dark moon. To some, she is frightening. She represents mortality and is usually depicted as an old woman with gray hair and wrinkles. In today's society that is often a bad thing, but we witches know better. To be a Crone is to have lived and learned. We value the wisdom of our elders in the community and respect the knowledge they have to pass on to us.

Maiden, Mother, and Crone are all equally important. Each aspect of the Goddess is powerful and beautiful and has something different to offer to us.

• • •

TRY THIS: *In the month to come, as the moon shifts and changes her form, celebrate each phase of the Goddess by embracing your own youthful spirit, mature nurturing side, and thoughtful wisdom.*

December 9
Mindfulness and Awareness

How many times have you driven home from work and have no idea exactly how you got there? Or you've reached the end of the day and think, "What on earth did I do today?" For most of us, life is fast and hectic and over-full, even when things are going well. That's simply the reality of our existence, and it isn't likely to change anytime soon.

But a spiritual practice doesn't thrive in that environment, and, to be honest, neither do we. We miss a lot along the way simply because we're too busy to pay attention to the world around us. You might not think of it, but mindfulness and awareness are actually important components of a witchcraft practice. We're more likely to think of them as words associated with Buddhism or Taoism or other Eastern religions, but they are vital to witchcraft for exactly the same reasons.

How can you follow a nature-based spiritual path if you are not mindful and aware of the natural world around you? How can you worship a deity if you are not mindful and aware of his or her presence in your life? And how can you learn and improve yourself if you are not mindful and aware of who you are and how your actions affect you and those around you? Well, you can't, obviously.

• • •

TRY THIS: As you cook dinner, be mindful of the scents and textures of the food; think about where the ingredients came from and all the elements that go into preparing a meal.

December 10
Silence

One of the gifts that winter brings us is silence.

American author Ruth Stout said:

> There is a privacy about it which no other season gives you…In spring, summer and fall people sort of have an open season on each other; only in the winter, in the country, can you have longer, quiet stretches when you can savor belonging to yourself.

Winter is definitely the quietest of the seasons, especially if you live in an area of the country where the land lies covered with a blanket of snow, which muffles sound and makes you keep the windows closed against the cold. The birds don't sing as loudly, fewer people are outside, and the earth seems hushed as it rests up for the spring and new growth.

We don't hibernate in the winter, but we can go with the flow of the season and be a little more silent.

• • •

TRY THIS: *Talk a little less, turn off the television and read a book instead, go to bed early. In this quieter time of year, cultivate the silence inside yourself. Who knows what you will hear if you do?*

December 11

Dreams

Most of the time our dreams do little more than reflect back what is going on in our lives, something we saw during the day, or our hopes and fears. Sometimes we have much more vivid dreams than usual and they stick with us when we wake in the morning—those are worth paying attention to, and you might want to write them down in your journal.

It is also possible to deliberately get information from our dreams; this is called dream divination, and people have been doing it for centuries (shamans in particular). A technique called lucid dreaming, in which the sleeper is aware of being in a dream, can be used to help with this. Or you can simply go to sleep with the intention of dreaming about some particular question you need the answer to. Write the question on a piece of paper and tuck it under your pillow.

• • •

TRY THIS: *Put your journal or paper and pen by the bed. Focus on your question and turn out the light, then concentrate on what it is you want to know. In the morning write down any dreams you had.*

December 12
Psychic Development No. 3

Just as practice will hone your skills at a sport or art, exercising your psychic "muscles" will help them become stronger. There are lots of small things you can do on a daily basis that don't take much time or energy.

For instance, I like to practice with the tarot. Not doing readings, although that works too, but taking a few cards from the deck, turning them upside down, and guessing what they are before I turn them over. This also works with online tarot apps. You can also place a few questions into blank envelopes and then pull some cards to see if the answers you get match up at all.

Have fun practicing with equally interested friends too. Have someone hide an object somewhere in a room and see if you can sense where it is. Or your friend can clip pictures from magazines (or use photos), put them into envelopes, then have you concentrate on the image. See how many details you can pick up.

Experiment with seeing auras, the energy fields that surround the body. Some people perceive them as a color or even pick up on pain or illness from a person's aura. Animals and plants have auras too. Auras can sometimes be easier to see if, instead of staring, you unfocus your eyes a bit.

• • •

TRY THIS: *Practice some kind of psychic exercise every day for a few weeks or a month, and see if your abilities get stronger.*

Phoenix

The phoenix has always been one of my favorite mystical animals, second only to dragons…and cats, if you want to count them as mystical. A magical yellow, orange, and red bird with long, beautiful feathers, the phoenix bursts into flame each night (or, in some tales, once a year) and is reborn from its own ashes.

The phoenix is associated with fire and the sun (which also "dies" every night, only to be reborn in the morning). It symbolizes rebirth, hope, transformation, and renewal.

If you are in a period of despair and feel as though there are no answers, put up a picture of a phoenix to remind you that hope always returns in one form or another. If you are in a time of great transition, the phoenix might be a good totem animal to guide you through.

I find the phoenix both empowering and reassuring. To me, it is the spiritual manifestation of the turning wheel of birth, life, death, and rebirth, and a reminder that all things are constantly in a state of transformation, even when it seems like nothing is happening at all.

• • •

TRY THIS: *Find a picture, statue, or some kind of talisman that features a phoenix, and hang it up where you will see it often. Let it remind you that out of the flames can rise a new and better day.*

December 14
Spell for Rebirth

As we get ready to bid farewell to this year and enter another, it is the perfect time to perform a spell for rebirth. You will need a black candle and a red candle (although you can use white if that is all you have). If you have an egg-shaped stone, place it on a table or altar in front of you, along with the candles. A gemstone is nice, but even a plain old rock from the yard will work just fine if it is more or less oval. (Don't worry if you don't have one. You can either do without or use a picture of a phoenix.) You will also need a dark-colored sheet or cloak.

Cast a ritual circle, then light the black candle. Sit for a moment and think about the things you want to let go of or change, then say, "I am the phoenix; I cast my troubles to the flames of change and transformation." Pull the sheet or cloak over you and huddle underneath it for as long as feels right—take the rock under there with you if you're using one. When you're ready, throw off the sheet and light the red candle, placing the rock back on the altar. Say, "I am the phoenix; I am reborn into a new person, full of potential and unhindered by the past. I am reborn to be my own best self." Then blow out the black candle and focus on the red one until it is time to rejoin the world.

* * *

TRY THIS: *Use this spell anytime you feel
the need to re-create yourself or start anew.*

December 15

Charm Bag for Calm and Destressing

It is a little ironic that a time of year that should be filled with happiness and joy often ends up being more than a little stressful for most of us. Here is a simple charm bag that will help anytime you could use a little help being calmer and letting go of stress.

You can use either a small drawstring bag or make one yourself by sewing up three sides of a cloth and then using a piece of blue or white ribbon to seal it up once all the ingredients are inside. Good herbs to use for this are lavender, lemon balm, passion flower, and rosemary. I like to add a tumbled gemstone such as amethyst, carnelian, sodalite, or aventurine. Place everything you're using in the bag, then write on a piece of paper: "I let go of stress and embrace calm." Put that in, too, and close up the bag. (For good measure, you can add a peace sign or anything that represents peace to you.)

Bless and consecrate your charm bag before using it, or hold it up at your altar or under a full moon and repeat, "I let go of stress and embrace calm. So mote it be."

• • •

TRY THIS: *Tuck the charm bag into your purse or pocket, under your pillow, or place it on your altar.*

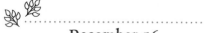

December 16
Family

Family can mean different things to different people. There is the family we are born to—our genetic family of mother, father, siblings, and so on. Sometimes we're lucky, and that family is pretty wonderful. Sometimes the family is toxic or nearly non-existent, and we have to do without. Most fall somewhere in between, and no matter how much we love them, being part of a family brings with it special challenges. Then there is the family we create. Sometimes that is a significant other or close friends. Unlike the family we are born to, we have control over who makes up our family of choice.

The holidays can be tricky times for those who don't get along with their families. But they can also be a chance to gather together with the ones you love and celebrate the fact that you are family. If you can, reach out to include others in that circle who may not have a place to be for the holidays. If you don't have family—or they're too far away to be with—visit a retirement or nursing home or help serve in a soup kitchen. After all, the human race is, in its own way, one big family, and no one should be alone at the holidays unless it is by choice.

· · ·

TRY THIS: *Whether it is the family you are born to or the family you chose, those connections are a gift to be treasured at the holidays and always. Make a little extra time for family today.*

December 17
Pines

Pine trees grow on all four sides of my house—maybe that's why it is so magical there. We tend to think about pine trees at this time of year when we bring them inside in the form of Christmas trees, Yule trees, or boughs to symbolize life in the midst of death.

But pines are pretty magical all year round. They are used for prosperity, abundance, and fertility magic, probably in part because of the way they reseed themselves from fallen pinecones. (On the rare occasions I dig up a small pine to use as a Yule tree, I always look for a volunteer seedling that is growing in some place it can't stay anyway.)

Pine nuts are a delicious and easy way to add the energy of the pine tree to your kitchen magic. Use pinecones or pine needles in spell work for prosperity, fertility, healing, and protection. Sweep your home with the end of a pine bough to bring in protection and cleansing.

• • •

TRY THIS: If you have a yard, plant a pine tree so you have access to its magic all the time, and provide a home for the birds as a bonus. If not, decorate a pinecone or eat some pine nuts to take in that pine tree energy.

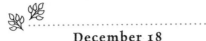

December 18
Nontraditional Gift Giving

It is traditional to give gifts at this time of year, but many of us don't need more stuff or don't have the money to buy extravagant presents. Here are a few suggestions for alternatives that might help keep down the spending, the craziness, and even help others at the same time.

The reverse advent basket: in some Christian traditions, advent calendars are used to count down the days to Christmas, starting on the first of December. These calendars usually have small gifts or treats hidden behind each day. Instead, why not put things into a basket every day—food, mittens, small gifts for children—and right before Christmas, take it to a local shelter or food pantry? Consider a pet-themed basket and donate it to your local animal shelter.

If you gather as a group, take the twenty or thirty dollars you would have each spent on a gift and pool it together for the charity of your choice. If money is an issue, exchange IOUs for helpful services (such as sharing a gift you have—cooking or sewing or plumbing—that others don't).

You don't have to spend a lot of money (or make people feel pressured to come up with the perfect gift) in order to celebrate the holiday.

• • •

> **TRY THIS:** *Perhaps it is time to look at gift giving in another way. Don't forget that love is the greatest gift of all, and it costs nothing while bringing great returns.*

December 19
Oak King and Holly King

One of the most fun rituals I ever attended had two of the participants acting out the battle of the Oak King and the Holly King. Since the ritual took place at Yule, the Oak King, who rules over the light half of the year, won the battle. At Midsummer his counterpart, the Holly King, takes over for the dark half of the year, as the light lessens every day. (In some traditions these roles are reversed.)

The Holly King is usually depicted as a jolly bearded man with a crown of holly and red attire. (Does this sound familiar?) The Oak King, on the other hand, is younger and virile, growing stronger with the growing light until it peaks at the summer solstice and the whole thing starts all over again.

Despite this yearly battle, these kings are not enemies but two halves of a whole, each as necessary as the other.

• • •

TRY THIS: *If you have a Yule celebration with children attending, ask a couple of them to act out this symbolic change of power, and then the Holly King can hand out candy and gifts to everyone under, say, ninety-seven.*

December 20
Wassail

If you have ever sung the Christmas carol "Here We Come A'wassailing," you may have wondered what the heck it actually meant. Wassailing was a Yule tradition that involved going in groups from house to house singing and being rewarded for their visit with a cup of wassail, a kind of spiked apple cider. I suspect the singing got quite a bit louder and quite a bit worse as the evening went along!

These days caroling is a much more sedate activity, but you can still make wassail for your Yule celebration. It is less a recipe than a general list of ingredients, which you can change according to your tastes. In a large pot on the stove or in a slow cooker, put a gallon of cider and one to two cups of either red wine, brandy, or whisky, or some combination of those. Make this as strong or as mild as you like or make a nonalcoholic version with just cider.

To this, add some form of sweetener. I like to use maple syrup, but you can use honey or sugar instead. Then toss in a small bag of mulling spices (a combination of cinnamon sticks, allspice, cloves, and ginger), which you take out before you serve. Some people like to float apple or orange slices in it too. Then you just let it heat up and enjoy it—with or without singing (your choice).

• • •

TRY THIS: *When you toast, shout*
"Wassail!" It means "to your health."

December 21
Yule

Yule is another name for the winter solstice, the day that marks the true start of winter. Like the other solstice and equinox holidays, the actual date can vary from the 20th to the 23rd.

The winter solstice celebrates the return of the sun since from this date forward there will be a little bit more light every day. So despite the fact that we observe the start of winter, we also take note of its eventual end. Yule is a time of joy that celebrates rebirth and hope. It is the perfect Pagan holiday to share with your non-Pagan friends since it has so much in common with Christmas.

To decorate your home in a way that touches on the roots of Yule, display a Yule tree adorned with ornaments made out of natural elements or strung with dried cranberries. If you have children, have them cut out silver moons and yellow suns, and hang those from the branches individually or in strands or over the mantle and doorways. Yule logs are another great tradition. In the old days, a family or village would have a Yule log that was burned almost all the way down. The tag end of that log would then be used to start the fire containing the new Yule log. Make your own by drilling holes into a piece of wood and inserting candles in each hole.

• • •

TRY THIS: *Light as many candles as is safe and give thanks for the returning sun.*

December 22
Green

Green might seem like a strange color to be talking about when outside it is more likely to be white or gray or brown, but green is associated with this season almost as much as it is with the new growth of spring. For instance, we bring in Yule trees because the evergreens celebrate life in the midst of death. And the Holly King's colors are dark green, while the Oak King's colors are light green. Green is also the color of the God, who is reborn at Yule.

Magically, green is used to represent the element of earth and for prosperity work, as well as good luck in general. When I do prosperity magic, I use a green candle. All green stones, including malachite, aventurine, and bloodstone (a dark green stone sometimes speckled with red that has healing associations as well), are good for prosperity and wealth too.

There is an old tradition that says it is good luck to burn a bayberry candle on Christmas Eve. There is even a saying that goes with it: a bayberry candle burnt to the socket brings food to the larder and gold to the pocket. It takes a lot of bayberries to make one candle, so most people don't make their own anymore.

• • •

TRY THIS: *Look for a bayberry candle and burn it to bring a little more luck into the new year. If you can't find bayberry, use any green candle and inscribe it with runes or magical symbols.*

December 23
Capricorn

"Practical," "patient," and "responsible" are words commonly associated with the sun sign Capricorn, those born between December 23 and January 20. These folks tend to be methodical and ambitious, and once they put their minds to a task, they are unlikely to stop until it is accomplished. On the downside, they can be so self-sufficient they end up taking on too much and shutting out those around them. They can also be critical and controlling if they aren't careful.

· · ·

TRY THIS: *During this period of the year, whether or not you are a Capricorn, think about if you play well with others; if not, figure out a way to improve on that. It is also a good time to take on any projects that require a practical approach and dedication, especially those that need patience and planning.*

December 24
Kindness

At this time of year, a lot of focus is put on the giving of gifts. But truly, the greatest gift we can give each other is kindness.

It probably doesn't seem like much; you can't put a bow on it, it doesn't cost any money, and anyone can give it. And yet, kindness can be one of the rarest gifts of all. Remember that lots of people have a tough time around the holidays. Depression worsens, some folks are alone when it seems as though everyone else has someone to be with, expectations aren't met, and then, of course, there are family dynamics…

So if you want to give a gift with meaning, just be kind. It is the true meaning behind the season, no matter what your religious or spiritual beliefs.

* * *

TRY THIS: *Be extra kind to people, especially those who seem crabby or unhappy. And don't forget to be kind to yourself.*

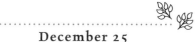

December 25
Christmas

I must confess, Christmas has never been my holiday. I grew up Jewish, so it isn't exactly my area of expertise. You can imagine my surprise when I began to study witchcraft and discovered that much of what most folks think of as Christmas was actually borrowed from the Pagan holiday of Yule. Half the carols even talk about "Yuletide merry."

The great thing about the fact that there is so much overlap between Christmas and Yule is that those people who grew up observing Christmas (or who have family or significant others who still do) can celebrate either or both without a problem. I know of non-Pagans, for instance, who have winter solstice parties every year, so there is no reason why you can't do that and invite anyone you want. Just leave out the formal ritual. Blue Moon Circle has a Yule dinner party for our members, their families, and some friends. For us, the celebration is of the season in general and the joy of being together.

If you are raising Pagan children, explain to them how the Christmas tree came from the practice of bringing greenery inside as a symbol of life in the midst of death, and tell them about the Holly King and the Oak King at the same time you tell them about Santa.

• • •

TRY THIS: *Throw a solstice party this year and invite witchy and non-witchy friends to celebrate together.*

"The Withering of the Boughs"

This poem is evocative and mystical, much like this time of year.

I cried when the moon was murmuring to the birds:
"Let peewit call and curlew cry where they will,
I long for your merry and tender and pitiful words,
For the roads are unending, and there is no place
    to my mind."
The honey-pale moon lay low on the sleepy hill,
And I fell asleep upon lonely Echtge of streams.
No boughs have withered because of the wintry wind;
The boughs have withered because I have told them
    my dreams.

I know of the leafy paths that the witches take
Who come with their crowns of pearl and their spindles
    of wool,
And their secret smile, out of the depths of the lake;
I know where a dim moon drifts, where the Danaan kind
Wind and unwind their dances when the light grows cool
On the island lawns, their feet where the pale foam
    gleams.
No boughs have withered because of the wintry wind;
The boughs have withered because I have told them
    my dreams.

I know of the sleepy country, where swans fly round
Coupled with golden chains, and sing as they fly.
A king and a queen are wandering there, and the sound
Has made them so happy and hopeless, so deaf and
    so blind
With wisdom, they wander till all the years have gone by;
I know, and the curlew and peewit on Echtge of streams.
No boughs have withered because of the wintry wind;
The boughs have withered because I have told them
    my dreams.

(William Butler Yeats, 1906)

• • •

TRY THIS: *The second stanza of this poem contains*
some of my favorite lines in poetry. Reread the poem
and enjoy these witchy lines in particular.

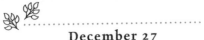

December 27
What Will Sustain Me
Through the Darkness?

We are moving into the period of the year that always seems the longest to me. Even though technically the winter solstice marked the point where there is a little bit more light every day, it takes quite a while before that becomes obvious. In the meanwhile, there are the dark, cold days of January and February to get through before March brings with it the first signs of spring.

I don't know about you, but these can be rough months for me. My energy levels are lower, and it can be tough to keep my spirits up. Thankfully, I have friends and cats and books to help me through the dark days. (There might also be chocolate. Lots and lots of chocolate.)

What will you use to help you get through the dark months? If you already have tools, make sure you take advantage of them. If you struggle during these days, as I do, give some thought to what you can do to keep yourself going. What things boost your energy and your spirits? If you hibernate, how can you make that hibernation productive? How can you help others get through if they struggle?

* * *

TRY THIS: *If nothing else, remember to look ahead to the warmer, lighter times to come. And feel free to have some chocolate.*

December 28
Rosemary

Rosemary is a great magical herb. I grow it in my garden every year, despite the fact that it rarely survives my zone 4 winters. In zones 5 and above, you can often keep rosemary going for years, and it will grow as large as a bush in some places. At the end of the season I clip off most of it and hang it up to dry, scenting the whole kitchen with its pungent aroma for weeks. Later I use it both for cooking and magical work.

You may have heard the phrase "rosemary for remembrance." And while it is true that it is sometimes used in funeral foliage or planted on graves, the remembrance has more to do with its medicinal and magical abilities to boost memory and all other mental abilities. If you do spell work to help you with a test, for instance, use rosemary.

Magically, rosemary is also used in spells for healing, love, and protection. I like the idea of planting rosemary by the entrance to your home as a form of magical protection. I also add the essential oil to a number of different magical oil mixtures, and the dried rosemary I have grown myself is an integral part of the protection mixture I sprinkle around the parameters of my home and property once a year.

• • •

TRY THIS: *Rosemary grows well in small pots on a windowsill, so add some to your everyday magical work and kitchen magic too.*

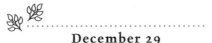

December 29
Gratitude No. 6

I hope by now you have gotten the hang of this gratitude thing and have integrated it into your everyday life. Cultivating an "attitude of gratitude," as they say, makes a huge difference in how you perceive the world. There will always be unpleasant realities to deal with, but, in my experience, if you focus on the positive, life is a lot more bearable.

If you keep a journal or a Book of Light, look back at all the gratitude exercises you have done and see if you still feel grateful for whatever you wrote down. Ask your friends what they are grateful for, especially if you all sit down for a feast or celebration together.

• • •

TRY THIS: As we reach the end of the year
(and this book), make a list of twelve things you
are grateful for from the year we leave behind us.
And yes, "I survived another one" counts.

December 30
Witchy Words of Wisdom:
Deborah Blake

Obviously, I don't need to quote from any of my other books (you've read them all, right?). And if I've done my job, this entire book has bits and pieces of wisdom from me in it, at least some of which you found inspiring, helpful, or at least entertaining. So I'm going to leave you with a few final thoughts on everyday witchcraft and what it means to me.

Being an everyday witch means that your spiritual beliefs are a part of how you live your life—not just on full moons and sabbats, but as you walk your path as a person, parent, significant other, child, sibling, friend, coworker, neighbor. It means inviting deity into your life in one form or another and co-existing with nature with love, appreciation, and care. It means being mindful of how your words and actions affect others, being kind to others and to yourself, and striving to continue to learn and grow both as a human being and as a witch.

Being an everyday witch is a gift and a blessing, and in one way or another, it connects you to all the other witches and Pagans who walk their own everyday paths in the past, present, and future. I am happy that you are a part of my witchy family and thank you for welcoming me into yours. Many bright blessings on the road that lies ahead.

• • •

TRY THIS: *In the year to come, find new ways to witchify your life every day.*

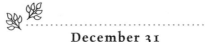

December 31
Year's End, Year's Beginning

Well, this is it: the end of another year. Was it a good one, filled with blessings, or one of the rough ones, filled with unexpected challenges? For most of us, the answer is probably a mixture of the two. Life rarely runs smoothly, even when you are a witch. (For some of us, especially when you are a witch.)

So really, the question is less "Was it a good year or a bad year?" than "What did you learn?" How did you meet the challenges of the 364 days that lie behind us, and did you learn anything in the process? What would you do differently if you had a chance? What blessings wouldn't you trade for anything in the world?

Some people like to celebrate New Year's Eve with a party and fireworks. Others, like me, tend to spend the evening alone, enjoying the quiet as we gather ourselves at the cusp of one year, ready to enter into whatever lies ahead in a new one. Whichever way you approach this night, take a few moments to appreciate everything that lies behind you (even if the biggest thing you celebrate is that it is behind you) and open yourself to all the potential that the new year may hold.

• • •

TRY THIS: *Send up a prayer to the gods that the year that lies ahead brings you everything you need and most of what you want. Light a white candle to signify hope for the future.*

January 1

Where Will You Go from Here?

So here we are, back where we began. It is the start of another new year, filled with potential. What will you do with it? What journey do you envision for yourself? What do you want to change and grow, and what do you want to continue to build upon? How will you nurture all that you learned in the past year and encourage a continuing spiritual practice?

Here is a simple ritual to get the new Year and a Day started off right, if you choose to use it. Otherwise, feel free to fill the lined pages following this with whatever you want!

Stand out under the night sky or find a quiet room and a few moments to yourself. Light a white candle. Put your arms up, held open to receive the gifts of the universe, and stand in silence for a moment. Feel the potential that awaits you and pull it inside. Then say these words or any variation that suits you better:

> I, (say your name), am a witch. I walk my path of my
> own free will. I choose this life and this path and will
> walk it with honor. I make this vow, to myself and to my
> gods, that I will do my best and strive to be my best self.
> That I will learn and grow and help others when I can.
> I will channel the love of the gods into the world because
> I know that they are with me, inside me, always. I am
> the light and the love and the magic. I am a witch.
> So mote it be.

. . .

TRY THIS: *Say these words and then stand in silence until you are ready to go out and begin your journey, whatever comes.*

Recommended Reading

Below is a list of the books I quoted from. I picked these particular books to share as "Witchy Words of Wisdom" because each of these authors has something important to say. If you want to expand your witchy library, these books are a good place to start.

Buckland, Raymond. *Wicca for Life: The Way of the Craft from Birth to Summerland*. New York: Citadel Press, 2001.

Cunningham, Scott. *Cunningham's Encyclopedia of Crystal, Gem & Metal Magic*. St. Paul: Llewellyn, 2002.

———. *Cunningham's Encyclopedia of Magical Herbs*. St. Paul: Llewellyn, 2003.

———. *Cunningham's Encyclopedia of Wicca in the Kitchen*. St. Paul: Llewellyn, 1990.

———. *Wicca: A Guide for the Solitary Practitioner*. St. Paul: Llewellyn, 1988.

Digitalis, Raven. *Shadow Magick Compendium: Exploring Darker Aspects of Magickal Spirituality*. Woodbury: Llewellyn, 2008.

Dugan, Ellen. *Garden Witchery: Magick from the Ground Up*. St. Paul: Llewellyn, 2003.

Dumars, Denise. *Be Blessed: Daily Devotions for Busy Wiccans and Pagans.* Franklin Lakes, NJ: New Page Books, 2006.

Fitch, Ed. *Magical Rites from the Crystal Well: The Classic Book for Witches and Pagans.* St. Paul: Llewellyn, 2000.

Grimassi, Raven. *Spirit of the Witch: Religion & Spirituality in Contemporary Witchcraft.* St. Paul: Llewellyn, 2003.

Illes, Judika. *The Element Encyclopedia of Witchcraft: The Complete A–Z for the Entire Magical World.* New York: Harper Element, 2005.

Marquis, Melanie. *The Witch's Bag of Tricks: Personalize Your Magick & Kickstart Your Craft.* Woodbury: Llewellyn, 2011.

McCoy, Edain. *The Witch's Coven: Finding or Forming Your Own Circle.* St. Paul: Llewellyn, 1997.

Morrison, Dorothy. *Everyday Moon Magic: Spells & Rituals for Abundant Living.* St. Paul: Llewellyn, 2003.

Moura, Ann. *Green Witchcraft: Folk Magic, Fairy Lore & Herb Craft.* St. Paul: Llewellyn, 1996.

Penczak, Christopher. *The Mystic Foundation: Understanding and Exploring the Magical Universe.* Woodbury: Llewellyn, 2006.

Starhawk. *The Spiral Dance: A Rebirth of the Ancient Religion of the Goddess: 20th Anniversary Edition.* New York: Harper, 1991.

Sylvan, Dianne. *The Circle Within: Creating a Wiccan Spiritual Tradition.* St. Paul: Llewellyn, 2003.

Telesco, Patricia. *365 Goddess: A Daily Guide to the Magic and Inspiration of the Goddess.* New York: HarperOne, 1998.

Weinstein, Marion. *Positive Magic: Occult Self-Help*. New York: Earth Magic Productions, 1994.

West, Kate. *The Real Witches' Year: Spells, Rituals and Meditations for Every Day of the Year*. London: Element, 2004.

Whitehurst, Tess. *Magical Housekeeping: Simple Charms and Practical Tips for Creating a Harmonious Home*. Woodbury: Llewellyn, 2010.

Index

Psychic Development:

Questions to Ponder:

Tools:

Witchy Activities:

[397]

Zodiac: